RUTH

VOLUME 7

THE ANCHOR BIBLE is a fresh approach to the world's greatest classic. Its object is to make the Bible accessible to the modern reader; its method is to arrive at the meaning of biblical literature through exact translation and extended exposition, and to reconstruct the ancient setting of the biblical story, as well as the circumstances of its transcription and the characteristics of its transcribers.

THE ANCHOR BIBLE is a project of international and interfaith scope: Protestant, Catholic, and Jewish scholars from many countries contribute individual volumes. The project is not sponsored by any ecclesiastical organization and is not intended to reflect any particular theological doctrine. Prepared under our joint supervision, THE ANCHOR BIBLE is an effort to make available all the significant historical and linguistic knowledge which bears on the interpretation of the biblical record.

THE ANCHOR BIBLE is aimed at the general reader with no special formal training in biblical studies; yet, it is written with the most exacting standards of scholarship, reflecting the highest technical accomplishment.

This project marks the beginning of a new era of co-operation among scholars in biblical research, thus forming a common body of knowledge to be shared by all.

William Foxwell Albright
David Noel Freedman
GENERAL EDITORS

THE ANCHOR BIBLE

RUTH

A New Translation
with Introduction, Notes, and Commentary
by

Edward F. Campbell, Jr.

The Anchor Bible
Doubleday
NEW YORK · LONDON · TORONTO · SYDNEY · AUCKLAND

The Anchor Bible
Published by Doubleday, a division of
Bantam Doubleday Dell Publishing Group, Inc.,
666 Fifth Avenue, New York, New York 10103

The **Anchor Bible, Doubleday** and the portrayal of an anchor
with the letters AB are trademarks of Doubleday, a division of
Bantam Doubleday Dell Publishing Group, Inc.

10   12   14   16   17   15   13   11

Library of Congress Cataloging in Publication Data
Bible. O.T. Ruth. English. Campbell. 1975
Ruth: a new translation with introduction, notes, and commentary.
(The Anchor Bible; vol. 7)
Bibliography: p. 42.
Includes index.
1. Bible. O.T. Ruth—Commentaries.   I. Campbell,
Edward Fay.   II. Title.   III. Series
BS192.2.A1 1964.G3 vol. 7 [BS1313] 220.6′6s [222′.35′077]
ISBN 0-385-05316-9
Library of Congress Catalog Card Number 74–18785

BG

To Two of God's Worthy People
My own Ruth, whose name is Phyllis
and
My mentor, the late G. Ernest Wright

PREFACE

The story of Ruth can be read with delight and edification by anyone. No part of this volume should be permitted to get in the way of that. On the other hand, there is a lot of very pertinent information about the story to be found even in the most technical of the explorations carried out in the NOTES in this volume. I have tried to avoid jargon and to speak plainly. I invite the reader to try it all, but never to get bogged down so as to miss enjoying the story. Since many of the things I have learned have come from observations by people with no greater credential than that they have their heads screwed on right, I hope the reader will find things here to turn his mind and heart loose to discover new things in the story.

When a book has been eight years in the making, there are too many colleagues, typists, students, teachers, and friends to thank. Besides, I have no intention of giving such people the usual exoneration from responsibility for errors which remain. They should have corrected me! And sometimes they are even responsible for ideas which may turn out in the long run to be wrong. Anyway, to such fellow explorers, my thanks.

Five I will name. Every writer should have editors like series editor D. Noel Freedman and Doubleday editor Susan Seuling. They know what to ask and how to persuade. Special thanks go to Francis I. Andersen for many ideas and aids. The same go to Robert G. Boling, colleague, gentleman, friend. And finally, never enough gratitude to one of the audience-to-be who found himself being asked to read things as I finished them and then told me whether they mattered, my father, E. Fay Campbell.

CONTENTS

CONTENTS

LIST OF ILLUSTRATIONS

following page 76

1. Woman holding a tambourine. Used by permission of the Taanach Expedition
2. David Roberts lithograph of Bethlehem
3. The Gezer Calendar
4. Captive Judean women in Sennacherib's siege of Lachish. Used by permission of the British Museum

following page 100

5. City gate of Gezer. Used by permission of the Tel Gezer Excavations of the Hebrew Union College Biblical and Archaeological School, Jerusalem
6. Chamber within the Gezer city gate. Used by permission of the Tel Gezer Excavations of the Hebrew Union College Biblical and Archaeological School, Jerusalem
7. Plan of the city gate at Dan. Used by courtesy of the Israel Department of Antiquities and Museums
8. Benches in the plaza of the Dan city gate. Used by courtesy of the Israel Department of Antiquities and Museums
9. Ceremonial judgment seat at Dan. Used by courtesy of the Israel Department of Antiquities and Museums

PRINCIPAL ABBREVIATIONS

1. PUBLICATIONS

AJSL   American Journal of Semitic Languages and Literatures
BA   The Biblical Archaeologist
BAR³   *The Biblical Archaeologist Reader 3,* eds. Edward F. Camp-
            bell, Jr., and David Noel Freedman. Garden City, N.Y.:
            Doubleday, 1970
BASOR   Bulletin of the American Schools of Oriental Research
BH³   *Biblia Hebraica,* ed. Rudolph Kittel et al. Stuttgart: Würt-
            tembergische Bibelanstalt, 3d ed., 1937 and since
GKC   *Gesenius' Hebrew Grammar,* by Emil Kautzsch, tr. A. E.
            Cowley. Oxford: Clarendon, 2d English ed., 1910 and since
JBL   Journal of Biblical Literature
MLLF   Jacob M. Myers, *The Linguistic and Literary Form of the
            Book of Ruth.* Leiden: Brill, 1955
UT   *Ugaritic Textbook,* by Cyrus H. Gordon. Rome: Pontificum
            Institutum Biblicum, 1965
VT   Vetus Testamentum
ZAW   Zeitschrift für die alttestamentliche Wissenschaft

The commentators whose works are listed in the Selected Bibliography,
pp. 42–45, are frequently cited by name and page number only.

2. ANCIENT VERSIONS

LXX   The Septuagint
LXXᴬ   Codex Alexandrinus
LXXᴮ   Codex Vaticanus
LXXᴸ   The major Lucianic manuscripts
LXXᴸ'   The complete Lucianic family of manuscripts
LXXᴹᴺ   Two codices belonging to Rahlfs' "unknown recension"
MT   Masoretic text
OL   Old Latin
OT   Old Testament

3. Modern Versions

AB	Anchor Bible
KJ	King James or Authorized Version
NEB	New English Bible
RSV	Revised Standard Version

4. Other Abbreviations

B.C.E.   Before the Common Era; corresponds to B.C.

C.E.   Common Era; corresponds to A.D.

E   The northern, or Ephraimite, version of Israel's national epic, preserved only in part in the books of Genesis through Numbers; also known as the Elohistic epic, because it uses the name "Elohim" for God prior to the call of Moses in Exodus 3

J   Ancient Israel's national epic, the main stratum in the books of Genesis through Numbers; also known as the Yahwistic epic, because it uses the name "Yahweh" for God throughout

P   Priestly lore and editorial activity culminating in the period of the Exile

Kennicott   B. Kennicott, *Vetus Testamentum Hebraicum cum variis lectionibus,* 2 vols. Oxford, 1776–80. (Kennicott collated over 600 Hebrew manuscripts and editions, and recorded their variant readings. Citations speak of the number of manuscripts attesting a certain variant.)

de Rossi   J. B. de Rossi, *Variae lectionis Veteris Testamenti,* 4 vols. Parma, 1784–88. (A similar enterprise to Kennicott's but fuller, and cited in similar fashion.)

TRANSCRIPTION EQUIVALENTS IN THE NOTES

The following signs indicate Hebrew letters about which confusion in sound value might exist; the remaining Hebrew letters have natural English equivalents.

'–aleph	k–kaph
ʻ–ayin	q–qoph
h–he	s–samekh
ḥ–heth	ṣ–tsade
ṭ–teth	ś–sin
t–taw	š–shin

No attempt has been made to indicate spirantization of the Hebrew sounds b, g, d, k, p, and t.

The names in Ruth are given their familiar English spellings, except that Kilyon is used for Chilion and Elimelek is used for Elimelech, thus avoiding any use of *ch* and *c* as transcription equivalents.

GLOSSARY OF TERMS

amphictyony, the term for Israel as the tribal league characteristic of the period of the "judges," from about 1225 to about 1000 B.C.E.; adj. amphictyonic.

assonance, similarity of sound, especially between words in a group.

chiasm, a stylistic technique in which the order of a pair of words or phrases is reversed on the second of two occurrences; in Ruth, frequently used as a special kind of *inclusio*.

dittography, the accidental repetition by a scribe, as he copies a manuscript, of a letter, word, or section of material.

enclitic mem, the retention of the Hebrew letter *mem*, equivalent to English *m*, at the end of a Hebrew word, the relic of an ending which had a significance the nature of which we can no longer be sure.

haplography, the accidental omission by a scribe, as he copies a manuscript, of a letter, word, or section of material.

hexaplaric, pertaining to the recension produced by Origen in the fifth column of his six-column presentation of the Hebrew and Greek texts of the Bible referred to as the Hexapla, in which he sought to conform the Septuagint tradition to the normative, "proto-Masoretic," Hebrew text.

Hiphil, one of the conjugations of the Hebrew verbal system, which imparts a causative meaning to the basic (*Qal*) meaning of the root.

Hithpael, one of the conjugations of the Hebrew verbal system, which imparts a reflexive meaning to the *Qal, Piel*, and/or *Hiphil* meanings.

Hophal, one of the conjugations of the Hebrew verbal system, serving as the passive of the *Hiphil*.

inclusio, a stylistic technique in which an author returns to a word, phrase, or motif he has already used in order to bracket what lies between the two uses and round it off.

jussive, a nuance of the Hebrew imperfect verb, often shown by a special form, which expresses an indirect imperative, "Let him do X."

levirate, levirate marriage, the ancient custom in which a brother-in-law (Latin, *levir*) takes the widow of his childless brother in order to produce an heir to his deceased brother.

minuscule, either as adjective or noun, pertaining to medieval manuscripts copied in cursive script derivative from earlier uncial scripts; see *uncial*.

Niphal, one of the conjugations of the Hebrew verbal system, usually expressing the passive or reflexive of the *Qal,* but frequently also with a nuance suggesting the result of an action.

onomasticon, the pool of proper names characteristic of an ethnic and/or linguistic group.

phratry, an anthropological term designating a kinship group larger than a family, smaller than a tribe; a kind of "brotherhood."

Piel, one of the conjugations of the Hebrew verbal system, serving to render transitive a basic meaning (e.g. *Qal,* "to be full," *Piel,* "to fill"), or in some cases to intensify the basic meaning.

Pual, one of the conjugations of the Hebrew verbal system, serving as the passive of the *Piel.*

Qal, the basic Hebrew verbal conjugation.

q^{e}re, an Aramaic word employed by the Masoretes to indicate that their vowel pointing is at variance with the consonants of the received consonantal text.

recension, a version brought about by the revision of a text based on a critical evaluation of other texts; here especially, the stages reached in a series of attempts to bring the Greek translation of the Old Testament into line with a Hebrew text prevailing at each stage and in a given location.

uncial, either as adjective or noun, pertaining to early medieval manuscripts (for our purposes, of the Septuagint) copied in large, capital letters; uncials are conventionally designated with upper case sigla, e.g. LXX[B].

INTRODUCTION

Ruth, "the gleaner-maid, meek ancestress" of David the psalmist for Dante, model for Christiana's youthful companion Mercy for Bunyan, chooser of the better part, and thus, like Mary, the paradigm for Milton's virtuous young lady—is a woman beloved by all who read her story. Some have found more in her than perhaps they ought; Keats had his nightingale singing to her homesickness as she "stood in tears amid the alien corn," and we will leave unsaid what Hollywood has made of her. But what a story! Work of a master story-teller, to Goethe it is the most beautiful "little whole" in the Old Testament. Reading it, studying it, never fails to yield something new and enchanting, robust and inspiring, sobering and compelling. Once a year the observant Jew hears the story anew, at Shabuot, by appointment. Judging from a sampling of Christian lectionaries and worship resources, the reading of Ruth may well be a matter of "never on Sunday" for many Christians. Perhaps that is just as well, for the story should be read in its entirety, as Goethe's evaluation demands.

And so another commentator sits down to dissect it and probe it. Some proposals will be a bit venturesome, for we do not know the answer to a multitude of interesting questions the book raises. One thing stands out as the dissection proceeds, however: this is an intricately woven, magnificently crafted tale, at base the work of one person, a person standing in the mid-stream of Israelite life and thought, a person wishing to communicate to his audiences things very close to the heart of the Old Testament. As well as being an artist, he is also a teacher, teaching with what in many instances is the most effective medium one can choose, a story.

WHAT IS THE BOOK OF RUTH?

Ruth is a Hebrew historical short story. The term *Novelle* is often used and can be defended. *Novelle* is a form-critical category which seems for most of those who use it to connote a combination of brevity with a plurality of episodes. It implies as well the evaluation that the style and structure are distinctive and well-wrought. There is, furthermore, the obvious implication that the content is at least primarily fictional, if not purely so. Then there is the matter of purpose; a *Novelle* should have one, according to most students, but what it will be is not particular to the form. It may be simply to entertain, but more often it is to edify or to advocate. It may even propagandize and polemicize. In fact, the term *Novelle* is so broad that if we adopt it as a formal category of Israelite literature and say that the Ruth story is a *Novelle,* we may find we have not said very much. And that is where we need to probe.

When one presses the authors of the various current introductions to the OT on the matter of the historical short story, he finds that it is not at all easy to set clear boundaries for each kind of prose composition found in Israelite literature. For one thing, form critics have not paid prose works anything like the attention they have devoted to poetry, and "there is an enormous job to be done" in classifying prose forms.[1] For another, there is real difficulty in drawing a distinction between stories with a legendary or heroic or fairy-tale dimension and those which are more historical or secular or oriented to the level of common human activity and experience.

If we lump the Ruth story with Esther, Tobit, and Judith, as Bentzen does,[2] we still have four different kinds of stories. In Tobit we see magical healing, demons, angels, and fairy-tale motifs. In Judith we find three other motifs: a heroine of legendary beauty, piety, and accomplishments, together with scrupulous attention to religious practice and the fabulous panic among the multitudinous enemy hordes. In Esther there are heroic persons, along with some legendary if not fairy-tale motifs, and a distinct concern to put forward the festival of Purim. Among these, one would want to use the adjective "historical" about the Esther novelette,[3] but, because of the legendary motifs, not in quite the same sense as he might like to use it about Ruth. If we turn to comparison with Jonah, another example of Hebrew short story, we have a legendary great fish to cope with, not to mention the fabulous picture of that great city Nineveh, entirely in repentance and clothed in sack, right down to the cattle. Recent analysis of stories has turned with greater frequency to comparing Ruth with the Joseph story in Genesis 37, 39–48, 50. This has proved more fruitful, but success here arises not so much from comparison to the old fairy-tale motif found in the scene between Joseph and Potiphar's wife in Genesis 39, proposed by Eissfeldt,[4] as from a range of other features, mainly stylistic, thematic, and theological ones.

[1] G. Fohrer, *Introduction to the Old Testament,* tr. D. E. Green (Nashville and New York: Abingdon, 1968), p. 41.

[2] A. Bentzen, *Introduction to the Old Testament,* 4th ed. (Copenhagen: Gad, 1958), pp. 240 f., 247. This entire section of Bentzen's work shows the difficulty involved in finding an acceptable covering term.

[3] C. A. Moore, *Esther,* AB, vol. 7B (1971), esp. pp. L–LIV.

[4] O. Eissfeldt, *The Old Testament: An Introduction,* tr. P. R. Ackroyd (New York and Evanston: Harper and Row, 1965), p. 38.

Stylistic Comparisons

An approach from a different direction is called for.[5] We begin with the assertion of J. M. Myers that "To one who has read the JE narratives of the Pentateuch, the narrative portions of the books of Joshua, Judges, Samuel, and Kings, the language of the book of Ruth sounds familiar" (MLLF, p. 4). This statement is valid even when one moves from language to literary structuring and quite frequently to theme. Especially good for comparison are the stories in Genesis 24, the Joseph cycle, Genesis 38 (a unit effectively redacted into the Joseph cycle), a number of the story units in the book of Judges (the Eglon-Ehud episode in 3:15–29 is an excellent example[6]), several scenes in the Court History of David (II Sam 9–20), and the prose frame of the book of Job.[7] At point after point in the NOTES, the value of comparing Ruth to such stories is demonstrated.

The Hebrew Short Story

Characteristics of this grouping of early stories begin to afford us a definition of the Hebrew short story. First, they were composed in a quite distinctive literary style, employing an artistic and elevated prose containing rhythmic elements which are poetic—a style which German scholars designate *Kunstprosa*. The rhythmic elements occur especially in speeches of the protagonists, but are not confined to them; indeed not all of these stories use speeches in the same proportion. Quite probably, this semipoetic quality was an aid in remembering the stories, for it is likely that they were carried for a time in oral tradition *in this elevated prose style*. When they were written down, their final composers wrote very much what had been carried orally.

A second characteristic has to do with content. In general, the stories combine an interest in rather typical people, even if they are important people, with an interest in mundane affairs, even when these affairs turn out to be significant on a national scale.

Third, these stories have a combination of purposes. They are by design both entertaining and instructive. Especially important: they look at ordinary events as being the scene of God's subtly providential activity.

---

[5] I have explored much of what follows in greater detail in "The Hebrew Short Story, Its Form, Style and Provenance," in the Festschrift for J. M. Myers, *A Light Unto My Path*, ed. by H. N. Bream, R. D. Heim, and C. A. Moore (Temple University Press, 1974), pp. 83–101.

[6] See Boling, pp. 29–38, and his treatment of 3:15–30. On this passage, see also L. Alonso-Schökel, "Erzählkunst im Buche der Richter," *Biblica* 42 (1961), 143–72.

[7] Cf. N. M. Sarna, "Epic Substratum in the Prose of Job," *JBL* 76 (1957), 13–25. The literary style of Job 1–2, 42:7–17 is strikingly comparable to that of Ruth in a great many respects. Sarna's judgment is that it depends directly upon an old epic, and clearly implies that the prose story is older than the poem which was placed in its midst, although he hazards no guess as to its date.

Fun and delight, pathos and violence, characterize the human portrayals; combined with the subtle divine dimension, the total effect is one of joy and seriousness together. The audience for such stories is "invited" again and again to participate in these moods and thus to learn from the experience of the stories' protagonists. The characters have a certain typicality and yet a certain individuality. Their examples can readily be emulated or avoided, and yet they are genuine human beings with distinctive personalities. This last point is important, for there is a tendency among scholars to claim that the actors in such stories as ours are painted two-dimensionally and without personality; I select only the portrayal of Naomi's complaint in 1:20–21 as one among several examples from Ruth which refutes such a claim. Sometimes, by the way, the moods and emotions are not very typical, and the audience must be led to identify with them.

That leads to a fourth characteristic of these stories. The hearer or reader, ancient or modern, finds himself delighting in the capacity of the creators of these stories to do what they are doing extremely well, appreciating not only the message of the story but also its artistry.

Literary Precursors

We will have more to say about these story-tellers later, but we must stop here on a question which frequently puts in an appearance when Israelite short stories are analyzed, the question of literary antecedents of a given story. Here we can turn particularly to the study of Ruth. The scholar whose work has been most influential in this regard, as in many others about Ruth, is Hermann Gunkel, who wrote a remarkable article in 1905 which then became a chapter of his *Reden und Aufsätze,* published in 1913. This article was the basis for his entries on Ruth in the encyclopedia *Die Religion in Geschichte und Gegenwart,* the first edition of which appeared in 1913 and the second in 1930.[8] No one appreciated the artistry of the Ruth story-teller more than did Gunkel, but he added to that in his 1913 work an analysis of the literary precursors to the story. He identified Genesis 38 as one of these; its rougher and coarser character, compared to Ruth, together with its simpler plot, were noted, and so it was dated earlier. Gunkel also noted motif resemblances to themes in the Egyptian Isis and Osiris myth (in which Isis magically contrives to conceive a son, Horus, by her husband, Osiris, after Osiris' death), and in even older fairy tales or fables (*Märchen*) from Egypt. He proposed that as a first step Israelite story-telling reclothed an ancient tale, in which magic and wizardry played a major part, by substituting good Israelite customary practice—namely redeemer responsibility and levirate mar-

---

[8] *Reden und Aufsätze,* pp. 65–92; RGG[1], vol. 5, cols. 106–8; RGG[2], vol. 4, cols. 2180–82.

riage (marriage of the widow of a deceased and childless man by a relative of that man)—to solve the major problem, that of acquiring a son
to carry on a family. In his 1930 update for RGG², he sketched out this
early stage as one in which Naomi, the only female actor, inveigled a
relative of her dead husband to sire the child through her. At that stage,
then, the story was much like the one in Genesis 38, in which Tamar,
whose circumstances call for levirate marriage, must use a ruse to trick Judah, her father-in-law, into fathering children through her. Later in its development, the story added Ruth; Naomi was transformed into the typical
crafty old woman who engineers things, while Ruth, the typical young
and obedient woman, became the child's mother. With development
came complexity of plot, and a steady cleansing of the pagan aspects of
the story.

In one way or another, a number of scholars have continued this search
for antecedent motifs. One striking example was proposed by W. E.
Staples,⁹ who found evidence for a Bethlehem cult-legend shot through
the story, especially in the names used in the story and in the scene in
chapter 3 at the threshing floor. This bizarre hypothesis is rarely considered in more recent study, but it does suggest one way in which antecedent stages have been reconstructed. Completely dissimilar, but based
on the search for antecedents, is a proposal of Margaret Crook, involving
two presumed stages of the story within the Israelite period.¹⁰

A far more interesting line of research into antecedents has focused
not on themes but on literary form. It is best represented by Jacob
Myers' *The Linguistic and Literary Form of the Book of Ruth* [cited as
MLLF]. Myers worked with the poetic language and the forms and spellings of the words in the text, as well as with those lines in the story which
could be metrically scanned as poetry. He was able to cast parts or all
of some thirty-three verses into poetry. He reasoned from this material
to an early poetic stage of the story, perhaps an old nursery tale, the relics
of which remained in the present form. The poetic tale, he proposed, persisted in oral tradition until it was finally written down as prose in the
postexilic period.

Taking his cue from Myers, but impressed by the fine prose quality of
the book as well—Myers had also noticed this—G. Glanzman added a
nuance to the theory by positing an intermediate stage of literary development, when the old poetic tale was turned into prose and brought up to
date with the law and custom of the time. The time, for Glanzman, was

⁹ Staples, pp. 145–57; Staples' lead was followed in a less extravagant way by H. G.
May, pp. 75–78. It has recently, but to me most unconvincingly, been resurrected by
J. F. X. Sheehan, pp. 35–46.
¹⁰ "The Book of Ruth: A New Solution," *Journal of Bible and Religion* 16 (1948),
155–60.

the ninth or eighth century.[11] Even more explicitly than had Myers, Glanzman then brought this theory of literary stages into conjunction with the theory of thematic stages. Stage one for him was an entertaining tale of human devotion between a daughter-in-law and her mother-in-law, devotion which received its reward in the form of a loving husband. Incidentally, Glanzman speculated that this stage of the tale ended with marriage consummation at the threshing floor. The second (ninth to sixth centuries) and third (postexilic) stages then saw prosifying and smoothing together, one gathers, with the addition of the final scenes and a general upgrading of the morality in the story.

In my judgment, the attempt to find and trace the themes of various stages of the story's development has proved to be rather a blind alley in Ruth research. It should not be maintained that Old Testament stories have no sources, but it can be maintained that speculation about their content leads practically nowhere. And it has to be reckoned that there just may not have been any precursor stages. More important, even when we can with some confidence identify a precursor (as for example has been done with the Egyptian folk tale about Anubis and his righteous younger brother Bata who spurns Anubis' wife's advances and is falsely accused by her of attempted adultery which must relate somehow to Joseph and Potiphar's wife in Genesis 39), the literary product which results is a totally new phenomenon and there is little to gain from knowing its predecessors. This is especially true when the literary form changes. One literary critic who has articulated this claim with cogency is Ben Edwin Perry, a student of the lusty Greek romances of the period 100 B.C.E. to the middle of the third century C.E.[12] What Perry claims as he introduces his subject is applicable generally in literary criticism. It is not evolutionary processes which produce new literary forms, but rather the creative efforts of persons who see a new need and fill it. When a new form comes into being, it does so as a fresh creation.

A New Form

Was the Hebrew historical short story a new form? I think it was. For one thing, a presumed transition from poetry to prose is a major transition, not simply a degrading of a high literary form to a lower one. For another thing, the stories with which we are concerned came into being under changing circumstances, in that they were involved with interpreting what has happily been called the Yahwist revolution, and were designed to portray the radical effect of a new and great commitment upon the part of a new people who were once not a people. The purpose of these stories was not simple entertainment but edification, indeed instruc-

---

[11] Glanzman, pp. 201–7.
[12] *The Ancient Romances* (University of California Press, 1967), esp. pp. 8–17.

tion, in the meaning of the new faith-commitment. The literary form was new, the people were new, the purpose was new. In fact, there is nothing quite like these stories known in the ancient Near East. Magic and fairy-tale motifs are not present in anything like recognizable form. It cannot be maintained that their creators were simple literary editors. A new occasion called for new creativity, and the Hebrew short story was one of the results.

As for the question of the poetic substratum of the Ruth story, just this much here and then more on the subject later. In a cogent analysis of Myers' proposal, Stanislav Segert has raised some fundamental objections to the approach used.[13] For one thing, Segert observed how often Myers had to depend upon slight emendations in order to get his poetic lines to scan metrically, in some cases violating grammatical needs. He noticed also the great variety of meters which Myers needed. And he was struck by the same problem we have noticed, namely on what grounds a later editor changed the literary vehicle from poetry to prose. Indeed, Myers himself admitted (MLLF, p. 46) that some of his poetic lines could be construed instead as rhythmic prose.

In short, then, it is defensible that the Ruth short story is a new literary creation, as are others belonging to this class. These short stories came into being relatively early in Israel's history, beginning in the period of the judges and continuing into the time of the united and divided monarchy. We shall return to the question of a more precise date for Ruth later, but one signal in that regard is the proposal that it was in the late examples of this form, really at a time of what we might call degeneration, that the fabulous and the fairy-tale elements reappeared. The stories of Esther, Tobit, Judith, and so on belong to this later period; they are not the best key to understanding the Ruth story, but perhaps the Ruth story is one of the keys to understanding them.

Historicity

Let us turn briefly to the question of the historical value of stories like Ruth. By classifying together such stories as the episodes in Judges, the Court History of David in II Sam 9–20, and the *J* and *E* strands of Genesis, we must conclude that there is no boundary to be found which clearly divides fiction from historical narrative. This is as it should be. The story form itself does not depend upon historicity. In the case of Ruth, the better question to ask, it seems to me, is one of plausibility, for these stories are characterized by attention to human beings often active only in very mundane events. The NOTES and COMMENTS at a number of places explore the question of the value of the Ruth story as an indicator of what early Israelite life was like.

---

[13] Segert, pp. 190–200.

What the reader will find is that Ruth is an eminently plausible story. The story-teller reflected accurately and knowingly such circumstances as those which would drive a family to leave Judah for Moab in the face of famine; such customs as levirate marriage and the responsibility of the redeemer, and their interrelationship, as well as an Israelite burial custom which elucidates 1:17; such features of a Judean town plan as the threshing floor and the city gate, the latter as the appropriate location for a sitting of the town council; such factors in common life as the growing seasons and harvest times of staple crops; such matters as the values in weights and measures which appear from time to time. In this sense, this historical novelette is historically plausible. I concur with most recent commentators in observing that there is quite likely a historical datum involved in tracing David's line back to Ruth and Boaz, as 4:17b maintains. Furthermore, it becomes increasingly clear that the names of the people in this story are not contrived so as to make them especially pertinent to the plot of the story; rather, they appear to be good representatives of the Hebrew (and Moabite?) pool of proper names (onomasticon) of the end of the Canaanite period and the beginning of the Israelite period. This in no way diminishes the judgment that the Ruth book contains a fictional story; it is simply a plausible one, and its information is a good guide to life and custom, and to realistic expectations about human living under the rule of God.

One more obvious conclusion, to which I have pointed regularly: I stand in awe of this author. He was a genius. Some of the ways in which he crafted his story will occupy us next.

THE ARTISTRY OF THE STORY-TELLER

We have spoken of an artistic, semipoetic style, and noted that a number of scholars have construed parts at least of the Ruth story as in every sense poetry.[14] Just at this time in history, we stand poised on the brink of a new breakthrough in the analysis of the meter and balance of Hebrew poetry. A particularly lucid account of the current position is given by D. Noel Freedman in his Prolegomenon to the reprint of George Buchanan Gray's classic *The Forms of Hebrew Poetry*, originally published in 1915.[15] In order to come to a judgment about poetic features in Ruth, a closer look at the poetry in Ruth is called for.

[14] See especially the commentary of Haller, listed in the Bibliography.

[15] Freedman's work fills pp. vii–lvi. On the topic under discussion here, see especially pp. xvi–xix and xxxii–xlii, as well as Freedman's contribution to the Myers Festschrift, eds. Bream et al., *A Light Unto My Path*, pp. 163–203. As an instructive comparison to the analysis which follows, see Boling on the Song of Deborah and Baraq (Judg 5:1–31).

Among other important observations, Freedman advocates counting both stressed and unstressed syllables in describing Hebrew poetic metrics. For some time now, scholars have focused their attention on the stressed, or accented, syllables only. What Freedman has shown, however, is that counting all the syllables of a poetic line quite frequently shows more clearly than stress counting does what the actual "weight" of a line is. On the stress-count method, a line may be, let us say, a bicolon of 3+3, and the next line of the poem a bicolon of 3+2. When one counts syllables, however, both lines may turn out to have sixteen. On the syllable-count method, the two bicola are balanced, while on the stress-count method one would have to speak of mixed meter. A considerable number of irregular poetic compositions turn out to be regular after all, when viewed from this perspective. We can ask ourselves whether the presumed poetry is at all regular in the Ruth text. As a rather typical example, I take the passage 1:16–17, the magnificent vow of Ruth, which almost everyone acknowledges to be poetic.

Myers, in MLLF, arranged this speech into six poetic bicola, which come out in transliteration as follows:

'al tipg^e'ī bī l^e'ozbēk	lāšūb mē'aḥ^{a}rayk ⟨habbēytāh⟩
kī 'el '^{a}šer tēl^{e}kī 'ēlēk	ubā'^{a}šer tālīnī 'ālīn
'ammēk 'ammī	wē'lōhayk '^{e}lōhāy
ba'^{a}šer tāmūtī 'āmūt	w^{e}šām 'eqqābēr
kōh ya'^{a}śeh Y(a)hw(e)h lī	w^{e}kōh yōsīp
kī ⟨raq⟩ hammāwet yaprīd	bēynī ubēynēk

Scanning this reconstruction by counting accented syllables yields a series of bicola with these meters: 3+3, 3+3, 2+2, 3+2, 3+2, 3+2. If instead we count all syllables, the count would run 8+9, 9+9, 4+6, 8+5, 7+4, and 6+5. (In fact, we should probably discount the occurrence of the conjunction "and"—w^e- or u—connecting the two halves of lines 2 through 5, and thereby reduce each of these lines by one syllable.) By either criterion, the meter is mixed, but it could be maintained for Myers' reconstruction that the first two lines are metrically of equivalent weight (same accent meter, 17 syllables), as are the last two (same accent meter, 10 or 11 syllables). But note that in order to achieve this balance Myers has made two additions to the text which are unsupported by any ancient manuscript or version.

In line 1, he proposes adding the final word habbēytāh, "homeward," for the reason that "another word is required by meter and context" (MLLF, p. 61, note 7). Without that word, the meter is probably 3+2 on the stress-count method (one can still argue for 3+3, if he gives a secondary accent to the first syllable of mē'aḥ^{a}rayk, "from after you,") but becomes 8+6 on the syllable-count method. The first two lines no longer have the same weight, especially on the syllable-count criterion.

In the final line, Myers adds the word *raq,* "only," claiming that "this addition improves meter and meaning" (ibid., note 8). Without that word, the meter is either 3+2 or 2+2 on the stress-count method, depending on wheither *kī* is reckoned as bearing independent stress or is subordinated to the word which follows it; the syllable count becomes 5+5. The NOTE on 1:17 will argue that *raq* added to this line actually violates the intended meaning. In any case, notice that it takes an emendation "for reasons of meter," *metri causa,* to get equal weight for the final three lines. Given where we are now in exploring Hebrew meter, it is singularly unwise to emend in order to suit meter; that smacks too much of arguing in a circle.

Poetic Qualities of the Prose Story

I would not want to argue that 1:16–17 is in no sense poetry. What I do argue against is the proposal of a poetic *substratum,* which presumes that the whole story was once set in poetry and that what we have now is a relic of the original poem. If that were so, we would have reason to expect much more metrical regularity. What poetic material we now have is an integral part of the composition. A better clue to its character comes from the work of Segert,[16] who identifies what are more or less poetic lines in many of the speeches in Ruth. These turn out to have mixed meter at best, and to bear direct relationship to the *forms* of the speeches themselves—whether they be blessings, or vows, or complaints, or whatever. Add to this a second consideration, which can be expressed with words Gunkel used in analyzing the prose narratives in Genesis:

> Meanwhile at least this may be said, that this prose is not the common colloquial language of every-day life, but is more artistic in its composition and has some sort of rhythmical construction . . . in reading Genesis aloud one feels an agreeable harmony of rhythmically balanced members.[17]

The translation offered in this book will look as though it had isolated poetry because many of the speeches are set in an indented format; rather, the purpose is to indicate the rhythmic, ceremonial literary style. In some cases, the reader will sense that other hallmark of Hebrew poetry, parallelism, but parallelism too can occur in elevated prose. The

---

[16] Segert, pp. 194–98.

[17] *The Legends of Genesis,* p. 38. This is a translation of the introduction to the first (1901) edition of Gunkel's Genesis commentary; in the 1910 edition, the sentence as such does not appear, since it yielded to a refutation of E. Sievers' attempt to set Genesis in poetry. Nevertheless, its general tenor is reflected in what Gunkel kept in the later edition, and it remains a valid judgment. Cf. William Foxwell Albright, *Archaeology and the Religion of Israel,* 5th ed. (Garden City, N.Y.: Doubleday, Anchor, 1969), pp. 21 f., and U. Cassuto, *A Commentary on the Book of Genesis,* 1 (Jerusalem: Magnes, 1961), p. 11, with special reference to the style of Genesis 1.

line of demarcation is so blurred that some of the speeches in chapters 3 and 4, which might have been given the indented format, have not been. If the reader inclines to read them as "poetic," he has caught the point precisely.

Word-play

The NOTES are full of indications of other stylistic characteristics of our story-teller's work. We cover a number of them by saying that he seems to have had an utter fascination with words. He clearly enjoyed assonance, for example. The cardinal instance occurs at 2:10. Another instance, rarely noticed before, yields some proposals about the meaning of certain passages. It relates to the fact that the words for "barley," for "gate," and for an unusual Hebrew unit of measure used in 3:17, all contain the combination *š/š'r*—and note that they would all have appeared in Hebrew consonantal manuscripts, before the Masoretes added diacritical marks, as precisely the same.

Assonance yields the potential of punning, and punning, along with other kinds of word-play, was a favorite device of the Ruth story-teller. One of his techniques is to establish a particular Hebrew vocable as a key word in a particular scene and to repeat it frequently throughout the scene, often picking it up once more in another scene to serve as a linking device. Another related technique is to plumb the assorted nuances of a particular vocable; this is done with particular effect in the scene at the threshing floor. Furthermore, sometimes it is a whole sentence (see 2: 5, 11) or a phrase (see 2:2, 10, 13) which provides the link.

Even more important is a series of words which occur only twice, or at least very infrequently; these serve to round out the themes of the story. This is such a striking characteristic of Ruth that it is worth our while to list the instances:

> "Lad(s)"—1:5, 4:16
> *ḥesed*—1:8, 2:20, 3:10
> "Security"—1:9, 3:1
> "Cling/attach/stay close"—1:14, 2:8, 21, 23
> "Lodge"—1:16, 3:13
> "Brought back/restorer"—1:21, 4:15
> "Empty"—1:21, 3:17
> "Covenant brother/covenant circle"—2:1, 3:2
> "Substance/worthy"—2:1, 3:11 (cf. 4:11)
> "Take special note/regard"—2:10, 2:19
> "Wing(s)"—2:12, 3:9[18]

---

[18] D. F. Rauber noticed a number of these, apparently without resort to Hebrew. See his article in JBL 89 (1970), 27–37.

The phenomenon is so prevalent that the translation ventures at 1:9 to restore a word, "recompense," to match its brother in 2:12.

Double occurrences of the same word are not simply a matter of repetition; they constitute brackets, as plot problems are transferred from one set of circumstances to another, from difficulty to be overcome to resolution of that difficulty. The first use of the word constitutes a foreshadowing of what is to come, perhaps not recognized as such until the term reappears. It takes an attentive audience to keep them in mind. Of the same order, but a great deal more complex, is the hint given of the way the plight of the two widows will be overcome, by the use of the word "sister" in 1:15 (see the pertinent NOTE) and the impossible musings of Naomi in 1:11–13. One can well imagine that the ancient audience would have experienced repeated delight, no matter how many times they heard the tale retold, at the discovery of these devices. Or perhaps we should venture instead the conclusion that the audience participated in crafting these delightful *inclusios* during the period of the oral transmission of the story aiding the story-teller in his craft!

These long-range word-plays are the most persistent examples of the story-teller's use of inclusio, the bracketing device in which a composer returns to a note he has already sounded in order to wrap it in an envelope. Another special kind of inclusio, usually bracketing short units, is signaled by the phenomenon of chiasm, a technique in which the order of a pair of words is reversed on the second occurrence. As examples, consider husband/boys in 1:3 with boys (lads)/husband in 1:5, go/return in 1:8 with return/go in 1:12, kiss/lament in 1:9 with lament/kiss in 1:14, Shadday/Yahweh in 1:20–21a with Yahweh/Shadday in 1:21b, elders/people in 4:9 with people/elders in 4:11, and Mahlon/Kilyon in 1:2, 5 with Kilyon/Mahlon in 4:9. The NOTES on these passages discuss nuances of chiasm and its impact.

There are other kinds of inclusio as well. It seems a strong possibility that his largest inclusio is a chronological one, which involves opening the story in the period when the judges judged in 1:1 and closing it with the signal word David in 4:17b. Here the inclusio relates to an historical problem, the transition from the amphictyonic period to the period of the monarchy; this pertains to the story's purpose, to which we will return below. Another thematic inclusio connects the observation that Elimelek's family was in Moab for ten years after the marriages of the sons (1:4) without any children being born, to the rapid-fire verse 4:13, where Ruth conceives at once. A host of other instances are to be found in the NOTES.

The Story's Design

These kinds of inclusios are to my mind the chief building blocks of the Ruth story. But there is more to say about its design than that. The

translation presents it in six units followed by an appendix, the genealogy of 4:18–22. There is general agreement that this appendix was
not a part of the original. It adds little to the story which is not already
indicated by 4:17b, with the exception that it draws a genealogical connection from Boaz, and hence David, back to Perez, the son of Judah and
Tamar, giving Boaz a patriarchal pedigree. It is probably correct to say,
with many others, that the hand which added the genealogy was at least
partially influenced by the mention of Perez in 4:12, and perhaps also by
the similarity of our story to the one in Genesis 38. From a story-telling
point of view, however, the genealogy seems a distinct anticlimax to a
story which is complete without it.

The first six units include the introductory "paragraph," which sets the
stage for the whole drama and is indispensable to it. As we have seen,
three of the inclusio openers are contained in the introduction (1:1–5),
the chronological one, the ten-year datum in 1:4, and the word "lads" in
1:5; all three openings will be closed in 4:1–17. After this introduction
come five episodes which we can legitimately call acts in the drama, the
first encompassing the journey home and the arrival in Bethlehem, the
second involving Ruth and Boaz at the barley harvest, the third comprising the encounter between Ruth and Boaz at the threshing floor, the
fourth portraying the civil process at the city gate, and the fifth celebrating the birth of the child.

In a perceptive article discussing the design of the story, Stephen Bertman[19] has pointed out a symmetry between acts 2 and 3, which contain
the entirety of chapters 2 and 3 respectively. In both, there is an opening
scene between Ruth and Naomi culminating in Ruth's setting out. In
both, as it happens, there is then an encounter between Ruth and Boaz
in which Boaz asks about the girl's identity (2:5 and 3:9—see the pertinent NOTES). In act 2, Boaz bids Ruth to stay and then pronounces a
blessing upon her for a deed of ḥesed; in act 3 he does the same thing in
reverse order. In both acts he then gives her food. Both acts end with
Ruth returning to Naomi, presenting her with food, recounting what has
happened, and receiving advice on how to proceed. In both concluding
scenes, a part of Ruth's recapitulation of her conversations with Boaz involves an extremely important motif which was not in fact a part of the
conversation the audience heard in the central scenes themselves: in
act 2 that she is to continue at the harvesting until it is finished, in act 3
that the gift of grain is to relieve Naomi's emptiness.

This symmetry of design seems undeniable, but in no way hampers
the story-teller's freedom. In filling up the design, he has Ruth act on her
own initiative in the opening scene of act 2, at Naomi's instruction in the
opening scene of act 3. He supplies necessary information about Boaz'

19 Bertman, pp. 165–68.

relationship to the family of Elimelek in 2:1 himself, but puts the recognition of the importance of this information in Naomi's mouth in 3:2. Especially interesting is the way the food which Ruth brings home is handled. There is an obvious correspondence between the barley which Ruth beats out in 2:17 and the grain Boaz gives her to take home in 3:15; both are measurable, and in both cases she hefts them just as the central scenes come to an end. The units of measure both have names which fit into their contexts because of the assonance of their designations with words in the vicinity (see the pertinent NOTES). But the emphasis in the two concluding scenes differs on the matter of the food; in 2:18 it is more on the leftovers of Ruth's satisfying meal, a mark of the concern Ruth has for her mother-in-law before she even has any inkling of what a fine supply of barley she will be taking home, while in 3:17 it is on the gift from Boaz. The first instance underscores Ruth's character, the second that of Boaz. Careful reading of these two acts will yield more indications of the story-teller's freedom to any reader. Design there is, and flexibility there is.

Bertman would also have us see symmetry between acts 1 and 4. In both, the major focus is upon responsibility inherent in ties of kinship (in 1:8–18 and 4:1–12). In each, there is person involved over against the main character who functions as a foil. In each case, the foil comes a long way toward fulfilling the dictates of responsible caring, and is not to be seen as unrighteous but only less righteous, when compared to Ruth and to Boaz. For Bertman, both acts conclude with a scene between Naomi and the neighbor women. Here, however, I disagree. To my mind, verse 4:13 is so important that it must be seen as inaugurating a final act with correspondences back to the introduction, closing out the inclusios set up by the word "lads," by the time designation "when the judges judged," and by the ten-year period of barrenness. What I see as act 5 corresponds both to 1:1–5 and to the scene at Bethlehem in 1:19–22. Symmetrical design has not hampered the story-teller from concluding climactically in 4:13–17 all the problems left over from chapter 1.[20]

We cannot leave the question of the story's design without attention to four further features. First, we should consider the sentences which serve as transitions from one act to the next. The final sentence of chapter 1 is a gem, summarizing what the first act has been about and reaching forward with its seemingly off-hand reference to the barley harvest. The final sentences of chapter 2, in verse 23, successfully bring us to the end of harvest, and thus to the time of threshing, and poise Ruth at home with her mother-in-law, who, it develops, has a plan. Naomi's words at the end of chapter 3 instruct Ruth to "sit tight" until she "knows"

---

[20] Bertman proposes instead to see the genealogical appendix as the correlative of the introduction, both being family histories.

what will happen, because Boaz will not let any time pass until he resolves things. The verb "sit" prepares us for 4:1–12, where everyone must be properly seated for the civil process to start. The verb "know" serves to recall that Boaz is part of that "knowing" circle mentioned in 2:1 and 3:2. And the note suggesting Boaz' determination to act is the perfect introduction to his steady steerage unerringly through the city gate scene. The rapid-fire verse 4:13 carries us at once from the solemn civil proceeding to the birth of a son. These transitions are masterful!

Second, careful reading of the story-teller's art reveals the way in which he manages the pace. The scenes of encounter are protracted, with a certain amount of repetition and long and rather solemn speeches. But even here there can be variation. The scene at the city gate is prolonged, but not too much, because the pace is both attentive to the solemnity of the occasion and observant of Boaz' determined progress toward the goal. When things need to move fast, they do; consider 2:18, 3:15, 4:13 and even the explanation in 4:7 in this connection. The pace is right, and every time it slows down, it is a signal for the audience to look more carefully and watch especially for those key words which signal progress. There is no wasted time in the story; it is even quite sparing in indicating speakers by name, a factor that frequently troubled the early Greek and Latin translators. The story-teller tends to let the content of the speeches identify the speakers.

Third is that the speeches fit the characters who speak them. The NOTES will spell this out, so we shall not linger on the matter here. Suffice it to say that Boaz and Naomi talk like older people. Their speeches contain archaic morphology and syntax. Perhaps the most delightful indication of this is the one instance when an archaic form is put into Ruth's mouth, at 2:21—where she is quoting Boaz! This is but one of the ways in which the story-teller gets across the personality of his characters. All of them are scrupulous in their behavior, but there is conveyed a greater buoyancy in Ruth. She marvels. For Naomi, there is marveling as well, but always under the shadow of the mood established for her in the first chapter, the mood of complaint. Ruth is pleased by every good thing done for her; Naomi moves as though she were gradually realizing that things are not as bitter as she had thought. As for Boaz, he moves through the story like the patriarch he is, warmly greeting his workers in the field, ceremoniously blessing Ruth in the name of Yahweh, recovering his aplomb quickly at the threshing floor so as again to bless Ruth, conducting the hearing at the gate methodically, but with alacrity. For him, Yahweh is no enemy, as Naomi has considered him to be. The story-teller's words about all three bring out the differences in their personalities.

Fourth is a feature so obvious that it easily eludes the reader's attention—as it did mine until D. N. Freedman pointed it out to me. The implausible aspect of this plausible story is the fact that Naomi and Boaz never meet! No scene has them talk together; never are they shown planning together ways to handle the difficulties which confront the widows. They know a great deal about one another—see 2:6 and 11, together with 2:20 and 3:2; why do they make no direct contact? Surely the story-teller could have brought them together in the scene of celebration over the child in 4:14–16, but instead he has given each a celebrative scene, his prospective and hers retrospective. This pattern simply cannot be a matter of accident. The story-teller has *contrived* to keep these two from meeting. And so, if we speculate that it was Boaz who gave the widows a house to live in, or that he and Naomi must have had to plan the sale of the field-plot which suddenly appears in 4:3, we may have plausibility on our side, but we are not letting the story-teller have his own way.

One of his reasons for constructing the story in this fashion must have been to give Ruth her full part in the drama. Through chapters 2 and 3, she functions virtually as an emissary between the two older people, who are managing the action. This keeps Ruth in the forefront—until that crucial moment when she takes matters into her own hands at 3:9.

There are likely to be other good reasons for this interesting piece of artistry. I invite the modern audience to participate in, and improve upon, my own sense of the story-teller's craft. To do that is to accept his own implied invitation, and to find new dimensions of appreciation for his art.

THE HEBREW SINGER OF TALES

If our story-teller is as clever as we have suggested, we must try to say something about who it was that told stories of this kind and under what circumstances. Our lack of information is so great on these matters that we must tread very softly. It is Gunkel again who gives us a starting point, in writing about what he terms the legends in Genesis:

> Many of the legends . . . have such a marked artistic style that they can scarcely be regarded in this form as products of the collective people. On the contrary, we must assume that there was in Israel, as well as among the Arabs, a class of professional story-tellers. These popular story-tellers, familiar with old songs and legends, wandered about the country, and were probably to be found regularly at the popular festivals.[21]

Gunkel's presupposition in writing this is that the story-tellers' products were orally performed. I have already suggested above that the Hebrew

[21] *The Legends of Genesis*, p. 41.

short story was told orally in substantially the literary style which ultimately came to be written down, namely in the elevated prose with rhythmic elements which we have already described. Can such a style have
been remembered and passed on in oral tradition, among people presumably illiterate? Perhaps our most informative resource for envisioning the
art of the ancient story-teller is afforded by the field researches of Mil-
man Parry and A. B. Lord, reported in Lord's *The Singer of Tales*. One
can summarize the information these two garnered by saying that ancient
singers of epic tales, in the Balkans at least, maintained the continuity of
the stories they told, from performance to performance, with the aid of
four ingredients. It was a combination of formulas (stock lines or parts
of lines), a standard line length, performance to the accompaniment of
a simple musical instrument, and a basic plot skeleton which kept the
story the "same" even as new ornamentation was included. Formulaic
language made itself visible in frequent repetitions within a song, and
from song to song. Therefore while each performance was something new,
a new creation, it was the same story.

All of this can help in envisioning how ancient Hebrew "singers" may
have carried out their profession. If their product was not poetry, and did
not have a standard line length, it still did have memory helps. Repetition
of words at frequent intervals within an episode would have stabilized
the plot and helped in memory. Inclusios, delightful to the audience,
would also have served to facilitate memory not only of the plot but also
of the structure of the entire rendition. Stock phrases and formulas,
while not necessarily of even meter, were nevertheless very much present—in the greetings, the blessing forms, the vow expressions (such as
the one at the end of 1:17)—and were easy to remember. One other
helping factor, which the researches of Parry and Lord, incidentally, do
not seem to have probed, would have been audience response, even to
the point of prompting the story-teller or of making direct contributions
to the embellishments. As for the matter of singing, we simply cannot be
sure. It would have been quite possible to intone such stories, but we
might feel more comfortable to think in terms of recitation rather than
song; the poetic speeches might very well have been sung.

In short, a good if speculative case can be made that stories such as
Ruth, and many of the others to which we have compared it, were transmitted orally for a period of time, in the elevated prose style which we
have attested in the end product, and indeed were probably originally
composed in that style. Differences of style between one story and another would be due to the individual creativity of the story-tellers, each
of whom could probably recite a number of tales from memory. They
were told and retold, and were passed down from one generation to the
next within the guild. The end product is the finely polished outcome

of an integrated process, and reflects the story pretty much as it started
out.

Where Stories Were Told

Who, then, in the Israelite community would have told these stories,
under what circumstances, and for what purposes? Here again our information is lamentably skimpy. Gunkel proposes as the setting the pop-
ular festivals. That doubtless was one pertinent occasion, but I doubt if
it was the only one. I have already proposed that the stories had as a
primary purpose instruction, explanation, advocacy. What a story like
Ruth, or like the Tamar and Judah episode in Genesis 38, advocates is a
particular style of living, one which is applicable to the common and
everyday experiences and concerns of people. My suspicion is that they
belong primarily not to the political capitals and the cult centers but to
the countryside, to the villages and towns, to which such stories would
have a particular appeal. It may well be an aspect of this purpose to
interpret to the people of the countryside what was going on in high
places, even to the point of interpreting the fact that the great King
David had a Moabitess for an ancestress. Interpretation of law and custom stemming from the past, interpretation of institutions such as that of
the prophetic office or of the judges of old, interpretations of the life of
the patriarchs—all these were included.

If purposes such as these are at the heart of the short stories, then an
edifying and entertaining evening around the town spring, or in the
plaza at the city gate, would serve as a fitting occasion. Here, in towns
such as those from which David originated, or from which came the majority of the prophets, interpretation of the meaning of Israel's theological commitment and the workings of her institutions was needed. It is
far from inconceivable that it was in the towns and villages that the
story of Micaiah in I Kings 22, a distinctly separable and unified composition about the role of the true prophet, would have been a favorite. The
story of Jonah, at base "an epic paradigm of the prophetic nature and
task,"[22] would indeed have been instructive in such places.

There will seem to be something of a modern ring to proposing such a
communications network in ancient Israel. But we ought not to think that
the metropolitan centers and the cult centers had a monopoly on the
theological education of the people of Israel! There was a strong egal-
itarian impulse to ancient Israel's commitment, and, we have every
reason to believe, a strong impulse toward full participation of all the

[22] The description is Martin Buber's, who speaks of the old legend lying behind
the present book, but does so as though the old legend contained the basic thrust of
the end product; see *The Prophetic Faith,* tr. C. Witton-Davies (New York: Mac-
millan, 1949), p. 104.

people in comprehending that commitment. Recall from whence the prophets came: Tekoah, Moresheth, Anathoth, Tishbe in Gilead, Abel-Meholah—small places at some distance from the capitals. They did not grow up in a vacuum.

Who Told Stories

This instructional aspect of the stories may give us a hint as to who were story-tellers in the countryside of Israel and Judah. In the complete absence of firm evidence, I risk here proposing two possible groups, one the country Levites and the other the "wise women" who appear in a couple of old narratives.

G. Ernest Wright has noted what he calls a "persistent tradition in the O.T. that one of the chief functions of the Levites was the work of teaching and exposition."[23] This function is tied to Torah, that is, the entire structure of theology and ethics, and to both the administration and interpretation of law. Deut 33:10, a verse which is probably quite old and contains a significant ancient vocational description,[24] styles the Levites as teachers of Yahweh's judgments to Jacob, and his Torah to Israel, as well as officiators at the altar. II Chron 35:3 and Neh 8:7-9 also suggest their teaching or at least expository function. But perhaps the most interesting evidence comes from two passages in Chronicles which describe facets of the reforms of Jehoshaphat, in material which the Chronicler possessed and used but which the Deuteronomic historian did not use in Kings. There is good reason to accept the description of the reforms as based on sound tradition.[25] In II Chron 17:7-9, a group of four "captains," eight Levites, and two priests are sent out, taking with them the book of the Torah of Yahweh, to all the cities of Judah to teach the people. In II Chron 19:4-11, Levites participate in handling the administration of justice, apparently from a Jerusalem base, in both civil and cultic cases. Albright suggests that a similar combination of officials functioned in the local courts as well.[26]

[23] "The Levites in Deuteronomy," VT 4 (1954), 329. I do not believe that A. Cody, in *A History of Old Testament Priesthood* (Rome: Pontifical Biblical Institute, 1969), pp. 187-190, has made a conclusive case at all against a teaching function for the Levites. Among other things, his treatment of the texts in Chronicles is arbitrary, and fails to take into account considerations brought up by Albright in the article cited in fn. 25.

[24] See now F. M. Cross, *Canaanite Myth and Hebrew Epic* (Harvard University Press, 1973), pp. 187-200, in contrast to Cross and D. N. Freedman, JBL 67 (1948), 203-4. Dr. Freedman has expressed his own doubts about his 1948 position in a private communication.

[25] Myers, *II Chronicles*, AB, vol. 13, pp. xxvii, 96-109; Myers is strongly dependent here on W. F. Albright, "The Judicial Reform of Jehoshaphat," in *Alexander Marx Jubilee Volume,* ed. S. Lieberman, English section (New York: The Jewish Theological Seminary of America, 1950), pp. 61-82.

[26] Albright, ibid., p. 77.

In Deuteronomy, we encounter Levites distributed throughout the land, living as dependents, much as do the other unfortunates in Deuteronomy, upon the good will of the people (Deut 12:12, 18–19, 14:27, 29, 16:11, 14, 26:11–13),[27] "for he has no portion or inheritance with you" (RSV). If Josh 21: 1–42, the list of Levitical cities, is indeed tenth century in date,[28] we have a further indication of Levites distributed throughout the land; when Jeroboam passed over them as celebrants at the sanctuaries of Bethel and Dan (I Kings 12:31), some at least of the northern Levites came south to Judah (II Chron 11:13–17) and may have been distributed in the cities which Rehoboam fortified at the beginning of his reign (so Mazar), as well as in the original Levitical cities of the south.

We can claim with confidence this much: Levites were distributed broadly throughout the land, in fortified cities and towns, and probably in villages as well. This is as true of the north as of the south. This distribution persisted during the period of the united monarchy and after the division of the kingdom. We have what certainly appears to be a teaching function lodged with them, particularly related to law, but to law within Torah, which includes both theology and ethic. We have indications of their participation in the administration of justice and in the interpretation of law. The Chronicler gives an abundance of evidence that they were skilled at singing, especially, of course, in relation to the sanctuaries. This much is not conjecture; what follows obviously is. Could these people be the ones who developed a new genre for the teaching of Torah and of what right living involves, and had involved, in Israel? This is a guess, but it is a possibility to be reckoned with. It would have been an additional way for the priestly families to carry out their role of theological educators of Israel, an expansion which fills an otherwise unfilled gap in the panorama of the institutions of ancient Israel.

The other possibility, that the story-tellers were wise women, is not as easy to document. We start from the story in II Sam 14:1–20, in which Joab selects a wise woman from Tekoah as the one to weave a story for King David, which turns out to be allegorical, in order to persuade him to bring Absalom back to the court. As we have it, Joab puts into her mouth the words she is to say. That may be so, but the scene that unfolds involves a nicely wrought, if very short, story of an injustice being done in the name of the dictates of justice; this is followed by the wise woman's having to adjust to the king's response with responses of her own.

[27] Wright, VT 4 (1954), 328.
[28] W. F. Albright, "The List of Levitical Cities," in *Louis Ginzberg Jubilee Volume*, eds. A. Marx et al., English section (New York: American Academy for Jewish Research, 1945), pp. 49–73; B. Mazar, "The Cities of the Priests and the Levites," VT *Supplement* 7 (1960), 193–205.

One cannot help wondering, then, whether this woman was chosen precisely for her quick wits and for her adeptness at telling the story well. A story within a story, and a wise woman at the center of it!

Still within the Court History of David (II Sam 9–20) there appears another wise woman, the one who persuades the town of Abel-beth-maacah to turn over the rebel Sheba to Joab (20:14–22). No stories here, but the wise woman cites an old adage, which has become scrambled in the transmission of the text, along the lines of "Ask counsel in Abel; in Dan it shall be settled."[29] She goes on to speak of the traditional role of the town in settling disputes.

Finally, there are the words of the "wisest" of the women around Sisera's mother, in Judg 5:29–30, which contain a snippet of a victory song the women intend to sing upon the successful return of Sisera—which of course does not materialize. Women as singers in Israel are a well-documented phenomenon, especially in victory and mourning song (Miriam, in Exod 15:21; Deborah, in Judg 5:12 [see Boling, ad loc.]; Jephthah's daughter, in Judg 11:34, and cf. vs. 40; Jer 9:17–22[Hebrew, vss. 16–21]; Jer 31:13, etc.). It is reported in the annals of Senacherib that Hezekiah's tribute to the Assyrian court included singers, both male and female (*Ancient Near Eastern Texts Relating to the Old Testament,* ed. James B. Pritchard, 2d. ed. [Princeton University Press, 1955], p. 228). Figurines from Palestinian excavations, all dating from the eleventh to the eighth century, show a woman with what has been identified as a tambourine held over her left breast;[30] relics of a Canaanite background, in all likelihood, they suggest nonetheless the role of women as singers and dancers in Israel (see illustration 1). May these women, especially the "wise women," be a locus of the story-telling art in ancient Israel?[31]

THE DATE OF COMPOSITION

There are implications for determining the date of Ruth in much of what has already been said. We have maintained that it is the early stories, in Genesis, in the Court History, in Judges, in I Kings 22:1–36, and in the Job prose frame, which afford the most effective basis for comparison to our story. Along with these parallels in genre, we have

[29] See the perceptive comment of H. W. Hertzberg, *I & II Samuel: A Commentary,* tr. J. S. Bowden (Philadelphia: Westminster, 1964), pp. 370, 373.

[30] See conveniently the description, with catalogue of comparable specimens, in P. W. Lapp, BASOR 173 (February 1964), 39–40, together with Lapp's correcting observation in BA 30 (1967), 24–25.

[31] I am grateful to Eunice B. Poethig for a seminar paper written in February 1974 at McCormick Seminary on this subject, and for subsequent conversations.

implied that the theological perspective of the book fits well into the early
monarchic period. At the same time, however, we have acknowledged
that there probably was a period of oral transmission of the story. Taking
all of this together, and assuming that the reference to David in 4:17b is
integral to the story, we have date brackets which would run from about
950 to about 700 B.C.E. Before we attempt to be more precise, we must
turn to a range of objections to this early date which have flourished in
studies of the Ruth book and tend still to dominate the discussion.[32]

One group of indications for a late date is linguistic in nature. First of
all, there are alleged to be Aramaisms throughout the text, which point to
a time when the influence of the Aramaic language upon Hebrew became significant, and that persumably means after the Babylonian exile.
As scholars have studied Ruth, the number of alleged Aramaisms has
steadily declined, so that by the time of the fine philological *commentary* of Joüon (*Commentaire*), published in 1924, only four seemed compelling. These included the expression "to take wives" in 1:4, the difficult "would you wait" in 1:13, and two words in 4:7, the ones translated
"to confirm" and "would draw off." Many would still point in addition
to the odd "for them" which occurs twice in 1:13 and "would you restrain yourselves" in the same verse. The fact is, as the NOTES on each
of these explains in detail, that there is nothing compelling about any of
these, either as Aramaisms or as necessarily late vocabulary. When Wagner published his catalogue of Aramaisms in Old Testament Hebrew,[33]
he listed only the two verbs in 1:13 as vocabulary examples and could
find no Aramaic grammatical constructions.

Another linguistic characteristic often claimed to indicate lateness is an
alleged confusion of grammatical forms indicating gender. There are
seven places in the Ruth text where what appears to be a masculine
plural suffix is used with a feminine plural antecedent. The third NOTE
to 1:8 has tackled this question by observing that on every occasion of this
phenomenon in Ruth the antecedent is *two* women. There are comparable instances in other narrative texts, most of them early, and I have
proposed (following the lead of F. I. Andersen) that we have instead
evidence of a feminine dual suffix which is probably archaic and dialectal.
Apart from this group, the only apparent instance of gender confusion
is in 1:22, where what looks like the masculine plural pronoun is used
to refer to Naomi and Ruth; the last NOTE on that verse suggests a valid

---

[32] For the most recent defense of a late date, see R. Gordis, pp. 243–46; cf. J.-L.
Vesco, O.P., pp. 235–47, and J. Gray, pp. 398–400.

[33] M. Wagner, *Die lexikalischen und grammatikalischen Aramaismen in alttestamentlichen Hebräisch* (Berlin: Töpelmann, 1966); for a set of cogent principles which
should govern drawing chronological conclusions based on the occurrence of Aramaisms, see A. Hurvitz, "The Chronological Significance of 'Aramaisms' in Biblical
Hebrew," *Israel Exploration Journal* 18 (1968), 234–40.

alternative there as well. One other possible place is at 1:13 (but see the NOTE there), and there is contention over whether the final verb in 3:15 should read "and she went" instead of "and he went" (again see the pertinent NOTE). In short, confusion of grammatical gender indicators is not a characteristic of the text of Ruth.

The reader will find a few places where grammatical and syntactic constructions occurring elsewhere only in one or several late passages are used to help understand something in Ruth. For example, in 1:12 there is a use of the word *gam,* usually "also," as a conjunction, a usage paralleled only in Ps 119:23. The NOTE on this construction gives the reasons why this may well have been a syntactic usage available in Hebrew but not much used, perhaps because it belonged to a regional dialect. In no case does Ruth employ vocabulary, morphology, or syntax which is inescapably late, and for which the comparative material is all in clearly late passages, with the one possible exception of the idiom "to take wives" in 1:4, where the verb is *nś'* instead of the usual *lqḥ.* This idiom does appear in Judg 21:23, which may stem from the Deuteronomistic editor but almost certainly contains old traditionary material. All other uses of the idiom belong to the language of the Chronicler.

We have, then, strikingly few indications of late linguistic characteristics in Ruth. On the other hand, we find many instances of early usage, and the problem here becomes one of determining whether these are archaic, archaistic, or conceivably dialectal. All of these have been listed by Myers in MLLF. Included are six examples of what the grammars call the paragogic letter *nun,* probably the relic of an originally longer spelling and generally characteristic of older texts. Four of the six in Ruth occur on second person feminine singular imperfect verbs, at 2:8, 2:21, 3:4, and 3:18. The occurrence of this form of the verb is quite rare; three other instances appear in I Sam 1:14; Jer 31:22; and Isa 45:10. The other two examples in Ruth are third person plurals, both in 2:9. Two other probably archaic verb forms in Ruth are second person feminine singular perfects in 3:3 and 4 (see the first NOTE on 3:3). Then there is an odd spelling of a verb in 2:8—see textual note [h] to the translation—which Myers (MLLF, pp. 10, 17) thinks may be archaic. These nine verb forms constitute a group to be reckoned with. But it is important to note that all of them occur in the speeches of Boaz and Naomi. It seems a much more likely explanation that our story-teller employs them to indicate the senior status of the two. In addition, the ones in 3:3 and 4 are used in an artistically balanced way to round off two series of verbs. These forms were carefully chosen and properly used by the story-teller; they are in one sense archaistic, but they appear to belong to the living language of the story-teller's time and place.

Other old usages include the term "sister" in 1:15 (see the NOTE), the name Shadday for God in 1:20–21, and the possible occurrence of an archaic divine epithet *mā'ēd* in 1:13 (see the fourth NOTE on that verse). All three are ambiguous; they may represent conscious archaizing on the part of the story-teller, but all seem to be just the right terms to get across a point and thus are used with full knowledge of their impact in the larger dimensions of the story—and their impact on the audience.

Finally there is the unusual orthography of the word translated "plateau" of Moab, occurring at 1:1, 2, 6, and 22, while the usual spelling occurs at 1:6, 2:6, and 4:3. This is not an accident, since the same word when it is applied to the fields around Bethlehem is always spelled in the usual way. This may be an archaic term with the specific meaning of "plateau," but is more likely a by-form (Myers) or dialect variant. Its chronological significance is nil.

What about this matter of dialect variation? The NOTES venture the following as belonging to peculiar dialect, even if that means only the argot of the countryside as opposed to the more fully attested cosmopolitan language of the political and religious centers: "plateau" (seven times, beginning in 1:1), the feminine dual suffix (seven times, beginning at 1:8), the syntax with *gam* in 1:12, possibly *lāhēn* in 1:13, possibly "sister" in 1:15, and *'ānāh* for "Where?" in 2:19. This list could probably be augmented by several of the terms belonging to the social structure of the towns, to which we shall return later.

In sum, no linguistic datum points unerringly toward a late date. Indeed, the impact is just the opposite. While a number of features may be conscious archaisms, they are not used randomly or unknowingly; there is nothing artificial about them. The language of Ruth is language of the monarchic period, tinged with the archaic. The archaic features may be due to a "cultural lag" in the countryside, but the overall impression is one of close relationship to stories stemming from the tenth and ninth centuries, the time of *J* and *E* and the Court History. On language alone, one would be justified in leaning toward the earlier part of our spread 950–700 B.C.E.

Three other chronological arguments are frequently met with. The first is that the appropriate occasion for the composition of a story like Ruth would be the time of the Jewish community under Ezra and Nehemiah, when two presumed streams were flowing, one of narrow nationalism which would put away foreign wives and purify the community from foreign contamination (Ezra 9–10; Neh 13:23–29) and the other of a new universalistic theological perspective presumed to find its classic expression in the exilic prophecy of Deutero-Isaiah. According to this argument, Ruth was a protest paper by the universalists against the stringency of Ezra-Nehemiah nationalism, based on the subtle reminder that David's great-grandmother was a Moabitess.

The contrast presumed by those who argue in this fashion, between narrow nationalism and wide universalism, is to my mind vastly over-drawn and is at the same time seen as pertinent to a much too confined period of time. In any case, Ruth is anything but a polemical piece, and it is highly debatable that such an approach to polemic is to be found in any Old Testament writing—including, by the way, Jonah, which many commentators think of as late and polemical. The entire proposal has far too modern a ring, as the majority of recent commentators agree. Indeed, if the author of Ruth really meant to oppose nationalism, Deut 7:3 and I Kings 11:1-2 suggest that such opposition would have been just as badly needed at the time of the Deuteronomic historian, and probably considerably earlier! Streams of thought making for openness to foreigners and to the nations around Israel were in full flow from early in Israel's life as a nation—as the marriages of David and Solomon attest, even without considering such prophetic materials as the first two chapters of Amos. Without other cogent reason to look to the exilic period as the date of Ruth, this argument carries little if any weight.

Another argument for late date is constructed around the relation between legal prescriptions concerning gleaning, inheritance rights for women, levirate marriage, and redemption responsibility on the one hand, and the portrayal of "law-in-action" in Ruth on the other. Stated most baldly, this argument works on the assumption that the date assigned to the various law-codes, for example Deuteronomy 12-26 in the late seventh century, the Holiness Code of Leviticus 17-26 in the early sixth century and the P code in the exilic period, is the date when the various laws they contain first came into effect. In subtle ways, this assumption continues to operate.[34] The result is the claim that stories which show the laws being applied must date later than the codes. Much of the COMMENT on Section IV is devoted to stating a different understanding of the so-called law codes, and we will touch on the matter again below, but it is now all but universally agreed that such an approach to Israelite law misses the mark widely. Indeed, this commentary will contend that arguments which run in the opposite direction, tracing a unilinear development within our scattered resources, are also of relatively little value for deciding date. Thus, a development in levirate practice running down a single track from Genesis 38 to Ruth to Deut 25:5-10 is very unlikely. The argument from comparative law should be removed from the discussion of the date of Ruth completely.

Finally, there is the matter of the explanatory sentences in 4:7. Rudolph (pp. 27 f.) has asserted, and I support him, that this verse is not a gloss, but rather forms an integral part of the context in which it appears (unlike a passage to which it is often compared, I Sam 9:9). The ques-

---

[34] As an example of its subtle operation, see M. David, *Het huwelijk van Ruth* (1941), and "The Date of the Book of Ruth," *Oudtestamentische Studiën* 1 (1942), 55-63.

tion is how long a period of time is needed for a custom to become sufficiently obscure to require explanation of this sort. Need there be a major disruption, such as the Babylonian exile, between the "now" and the "formerly"? Rudolph answers the second question in the negative, but his section on the date of Ruth, which proposes a similar set of chronological brackets to what we have proposed here, finally comes to its decision on the basis of a need for at least something of a gap in time between Solomon's reign and the telling of the story. Some time is needed for 4:7 to have any meaning and also for the term "judges," as a designation of the amphictyonic office, to have settled down as a fixed term to describe a by-gone era. Result for Rudolph: rather later in the period between the tenth and the seventh centuries than earlier.

This is a cogent judgment. We ought not to forget, however, that the transitions from the amphictyonic period to the early monarchy, and then from the united monarchy to the division of the kingdom, were times of considerable disruption and also times for alteration of older ways of thinking to accommodate the idea of monarchy. Taking everything we have looked at here together, my own suspicion is that the Ruth book belongs earlier in the spread 950–700 than later. I can imagine its origins to lie in the Solomonic period, and its fixing in writing to have taken place in the ninth century. If the reader will take it for what it is, why not hazard a guess: Could the story have become fixed, with embellishments of its strong interest in right judgment and care for the unfortunates, in some relationship to the Jehoshaphat reform, in the second quarter of the ninth century B.C.E. (II Chron 17, 19:4–11)?

THE THEOLOGY

The larger part of each of the COMMENT portions in this volume is given over to probing the theological insights of the Ruth story. The reader will want to come at theological questions in the way the story-teller sought to present them; all that should be done here, then, is to summarize briefly the highlights of the story's impact theologically. I do so under four headings.

The Activity of God[35]

It is correct to observe that God's activity in the Ruth book is very much that of the one in the shadows, the one whose manifestation is not

[35] The excellent monograph of R. M. Hals, *The Theology of the Book of Ruth*, could have been noted at a number of points previously in the Introduction. Its decision about the date of Ruth is very close to the one defended here, as is its understanding of the literary style and the architecture of the book. Especially useful is its analysis of the comparisons to be found between Ruth and the story literature of the "Solomonic Enlightenment."

by intervention but by a lightly exercised providential control. It is equally correct to say as well that God is the primary actor in the drama. His presence is signaled not only by the direct assertion of the story-teller at 1:6 and 4:13, but also by a constant stream of blessings and invocations, together with Naomi's complaint, which are spoken in his name. Of special note among these occurrences in speeches is that crucial occasion in 1:17 when for the one and only time in the book the name "Yahweh" falls from Ruth's lips—at the climax of her "return" to join the people of God. More subtly, his presence is indicated by four delightful touches of the story-teller: he is obviously, but of course not explicitly, behind the "luck" which brings Ruth to Boaz' field in 2:3; twice, his activity lies behind the emphasizing particle which introduces just the right person to the scene at just the right time (Boaz in 2:4, and the near redeemer in 4:1); finally, he hovers behind the words of Naomi at 3:18, when she advises Ruth to "sit tight" until she sees "how the matter will fall out."

The single most characteristic way in which the story-teller makes God manifest, however, is by working out a correspondence between the way God acts and the way the people in the story act. Blessing, invocation, even complaint, all express ways in which God is expected to work out his will for the people who are involved in this openly human story—and in each case it is the people, living as they are to live under God's sovereignty, who proceed to work it out. Boaz describes God as the one under whose wings Ruth has come to seek refuge, but it is the wing of Boaz under which Ruth finds the resolution of her needs and the needs of the mother-in-law for whom she has taken responsibility (1:12 with 3:9). Naomi in her bitterness complains that Yahweh has brought her back "empty," implying that it is he who ought to get at rectifying the situation, but it is Boaz who will not send Ruth home to her mother-in-law "empty" (1:21 with 3:17). Naomi invokes Yahweh as the one to grant the girls to find security, but it is she who plans the way to gain security for Ruth (1:9 with 3:1). It is Yahweh who is implored to do *hesed* with the two girls and is blessed for not having forsaken his *hesed* (1:8 and 2:20), but it is first the two girls, and then Ruth even more so, who carry out that *hesed* (1:8 and 3:10). God is present and active in the Ruth story especially in the way in which the people behave toward one another. God it is who brings about *shalom* in the context of this town, among these people, through the caring responsibility of human beings for one another.

The Prospect of ḥesed-*living*

The Ruth story does not represent the style of life which exercises caring responsibility as a foregone conclusion for God's people. It is portrayed as attainable, but elusive. Two particular motifs indicate the difficulties involved. The first is the way in which Orpah and the near redeemer behave. It can be said of Orpah that she like Ruth has exercised *ḥesed* in her life with her mother-in-law after the death of all the men of the family in Moab. If the story-teller means this, he has thereby heightened the remarkable character of Ruth, who will be praised by Boaz for *two* acts of *ḥesed* at 3:10. The near redeemer is a foil for Boaz in somewhat the same way. There are, then, people who do not do all that ought to be done to bring about needed relief in the very mundane matter of caring for widows and keeping alive one of the families of the town.

The second motif which points up the difficulty is the subject of the mysterious scene at the threshing floor. With intricate artistry, the story-teller gets across that the outcome is by no means predictable. It is hard to avoid the conclusion that temptation is a distinct ingredient here, temptation combined with risk. We cannot be sure that things would have been substantially altered had Boaz had intercourse with Ruth there and the act been discovered. But the point seems to be that under very compromising circumstances these two proceeded to carry forward the story's almost burdensome determination that things will be done in the proper manner.

The impact is that living out a righteous and responsible life is a matter of determination to do so. The story-teller, not by being preachy but by portraying people living so, commends for his audience one of several available choices. Combined with this is a particular way of looking at the matter of reward. In a sense it can be said that such living is rewarded, but it must also be said that such reward lies with the God who first himself "rewards" his people with his presence as their God. Before one concludes that Ruth is mechanically rewarded for her faithfulness to her mother-in-law and for her sense of responsibility, one wants to recall that there has been an inexplicable famine which set this story in motion, and there has been an inexplicable series of calamities which complicated the situation severely. Furthermore, there has been an amelioration of the famine in Judah, which sets the stage for the return of Naomi and Ruth. And there is that undercurrent of complaint, to which we shall return below. There is no mechanical doctrine of reward and punishment here; there is instead the commendation of a style of living which can be blessed by the God who would have it so among his people.

Covenant and Law

Much of what has been said can be arranged under the theological structure of the covenant between God and his people, a covenant which during the past twenty years has become so much a matter of discussion and elucidation. The COMMENT to 1:6–22 and to chapter 2 gives some idea of its dynamic and commends Delbert Hillers' fine book on the subject. Is that frame of reference operative in Ruth? I venture that it is. Certain key words which are central to covenant language put in their appearance in Ruth, such as "clung" in 1:14, "seen to the needs" (Hebrew *pqd*) in 1:6, and the very word *ḥesed*. In Ruth, they especially refer to relationship on the horizontal level; if what we have just said about the correspondence of human and divine will is valid, however, this is what we should expect in Ruth.

One of the corollaries of the covenant model is that law in ancient Israel is to be thought of on two levels, the level of overarching policy and the level of actual cases when policy is applied. The sovereign God commands from his people obedience to stipulations of policy, policy which is effectively summed up in the combination of loving God wholeheartedly and single-mindedly and of loving neighbor as oneself. Case law consists of examples of how to do this. In the Ruth story, opportunity for obeying basic stipulation with specific action and application of pertinent custom is repeatedly the subject. Custom is clearly adapted and given new application so as to meet the basic need. All of the decisions to be made and acts to be taken are governed by the overarching commitments of honoring God by caring for neighbor.

The Ruth story portrays covenant life within a particular social situation. The NOTES and COMMENTS return to this theme again and again. In particular, it is suggested that there are signals throughout the story of a social structure which is aimed at enshrining social righteousness. I have ventured an interpretation of two obscure terms, translated "covenant-brother" in 2:1 and "covenant circle" in 3:2, which suggest that there is more than simply a matter of family self-interest involved in this story. We can only guess at all the ties which bound people in a small town like Bethlehem and impelled them toward mutual responsibility. The suggestion put forward is that these ties were manifold, extending beyond family to wider circles of association and ultimately to the responsibilities of "the gate," the assembly, of the entire town. In all of these ties, the story-teller is asserting, there is a way in which life is meant to be lived. And under that commended style of living, all law, all decision-making in judicial situations, is simply the means to an end.

Complaint and Celebration

Beginning at 1:14 and continuing in verses 20–21, there rings forth a cry from Naomi which takes the form of complaint; couched in language containing strong juridical terms, and aimed at Shadday as the name of God as well as at Yahweh, it is in effect an indictment of God. To put the matter in covenant terms, it is a charge of unfaithfulness directed at the God whose relationship to his people is squarely based upon the presupposition of his faithfulness and trustworthiness. It is one of *the* characteristic postures of God's people, who place their trust so completely in him that they cannot understand when events suggest that God has abandoned them. Such complaint occurs frequently in the Bible, a way, as it were, of bringing a lawsuit against God by those who have been led to trust him. Looked at from this perspective, it is in a very real sense a profound affirmation of faith!

One important undercurrent of the Ruth story is the complaint of Naomi and its steady resolution. We sense the progress of her mood as the story progresses. After her outcry, she next appears as passively giving approval to Ruth's plan to set forth to glean in 2:3. When Ruth returns from gleaning, it is as though a slim ray of light has penetrated her troubled soul, as she greets Ruth with a question and an immediate blessing upon whoever it was who showed regard for Ruth. When she learns that it was Boaz, the ray becomes a beam, and her passivity gives way to activity, both in terms of a dawning of a plan and, perhaps more important, of a blessing expressed in the name of Yahweh, who has seemed her enemy. By the end of chapter 3, she can counsel Ruth to bide her time, in the confidence that things are now manifestly on their way to a conclusion and a resolution. Her part in the scene at the city gate is purely as a part of the background—it seems quite possible that she was not even aware of the piece of property which Boaz makes the pivotal factor in the juridical proceeding. Once that scene is over, however, she returns to center stage, along with the women who had heard her outcry in 1:20–21, in a scene of pure joy and celebration. All of this our story-teller handles with a deftness which is as effective as anything he does with his words. The final spoken words in the book come from the women celebrating Naomi's joy as she holds the lad who replaces her own sons to her bosom: "A son is born to Naomi!"

We have already suggested the important role this undercurrent motif plays in the overall story. A casual reading of the book might suggest that life is indeed idyllic in this lovely town in the countryside of Judah. But life is not like that, and our story-teller is as cognizant of this as he is of the validity of what Boaz and Ruth do for Naomi. In his story, he has made Naomi the profound recipient. Appropriately, then, it is around her that the scene is built which concludes the story in an outpouring of celebration.

CANONICAL STATUS AND CANONICAL PLACE

The canonical status of the book of Ruth seems all but assured, if by that one means the recognition of its authority by the late first-century C.E.

councils within Judaism. The one indication otherwise is a single sentence in Tractate *Megillah* of the Babylonian Talmud (folio 7a; see p. 36 of the 1938 Soncino edition). Here there is the barest hint of polemic in the assurance that Ruth, Song of Songs, and Esther "make the hands unclean," i.e., are authoritative. As the context shows, the rabbis were debating the canonicity of Esther at great length, but they make no other mention of Ruth. There seems to be nothing polemical about the assertion that Ruth was written by Samuel, which appears in *Baba Bathra,* folio 14b (p. 71 of the 1935 Soncino edition). Nor does any evidence to the contrary appear from Qumran, which has yielded fragments of four manuscripts of Ruth—the same number as are attested of Samuel, Jeremiah, Song of Songs, and Lamentations. The far more complicated problem is where in the canon the book was placed.

With the Prophets or the Writings?

There are fundamentally two traditions pertaining to its placement, one of which has its own set of complications. According to one tradition, Ruth seems to have been included in the second part of the canon, the Prophets, and all the indications are that it was located immediately after Judges, in the position it occupies according to the Septuagint, the Vulgate, and in Christian tradition ever since. Josephus seems to have thought of this as its place. In *Against Apion* 1.8, he speaks of twenty-two books which pass canonical muster; the only way to make that come out correctly, short of assuming that he denied canonicity to such books as Esther and Song of Songs,[36] is to assume that Ruth was counted with Judges, and Lamentations with Jeremiah. Jerome, in his Prologue to Samuel and Kings, gives the same twenty-two datum as the position held by the majority of Jews, and says explicitly that one way this was achieved was to attach Ruth to Judges; he also notes, however, that "not a few" put Ruth and Lamentations in the third part of the canon, the Writings. Apparently this was his own view, since in his Prologue to Daniel he mentions that the Writings contained eleven books, a figure which calls for numbering Ruth and Lamentations among them. In short, then, there is a tradition, probably held in hellenized Jewish circles, that Ruth belongs after Judges, but it is difficult to push back to the origins of this tradition.

The problem is that little more can be said about the pedigree of the contrary position, namely that Ruth was originally among the Writings. 4 Ezra 14:44–46 (II Esdras 14:44–46; see Myers, *I & II Esdras,* AB, vol. 42, ad loc.), approximately contemporary with Josephus in the late first century C.E., almost certainly transmits a figure of twenty-four for the authoritative books, which would admit Ruth and Lamentations to

---

[36] L. B. Wolfenson, Hebrew Union College Annual 1 (1924), 151–78. Wolfenson's useful catalogue will be referred to again below simply by using his name.

the Writings and give them each a separate status. This accords with *Baba Bathra* 14b, which states the order of the Writings and places Ruth first, ahead of Psalms and the other nine. The tractate then goes on to make it clear that the criterion is chronological, Ruth coming first because Samuel wrote it, followed by Psalms written by David, Proverbs written by Solomon, and so on. Almost all students of the subject agree now that this position for Ruth antedates its being moved to a position with the other four "little scrolls," the Megillot, namely Song of Songs, Ecclesiastes, Lamentations, and Esther.

With Ruth in the Megillot, the question then becomes one of what order these little five will take. One arrangement, which seems to have arisen sometime between the sixth and the ninth centuries C.E., has them in the order of the Jewish festivals at which they were read: Song of Songs (Passover), Ruth (Weeks, or Shabuoth, because of the harvest setting and because of the story's pertinence to law and law-giving), Ecclesiastes (Tabernacles, or Sukkoth), Lamentations (ninth of Ab) and Esther (Purim). This is the order they take in most printed editions of the Hebrew Bible published before 1937. That was the year when the third edition of *Biblia Hebraica* (BH³) appeared, its text based on a superb manuscript from Leningrad which represented the work of the ben Asher family of Masoretes. This manuscript antedated by several centuries the one taken as normative up to that time, from the ben Ḥayyim family. In BH³ the order is: Ruth, Song of Songs, Ecclesiastes, Lamentations, and Esther. This order may represent a chronological arrangement within the Megillot: Ruth pertaining to David, Song of Songs from Solomon's younger years, Ecclesiastes from his wise old age, Lamentations from the time of the exile, and Esther from the Persian period. This makes sense, but still another factor must also be taken into account. In the Leningrad text, and in a few other canonical arrangements charted by Wolfenson, Ruth as the first of the Megillot follows immediately upon Proverbs; the order of the large books, Psalms, Proverbs, and Job, is instead Psalms, Job, Proverbs. I submit we must consider the possibility that Ruth follows Proverbs because of a link in their subject matter, specifically that Proverbs concludes with an acrostic poem celebrating a "worthy woman," in Hebrew *'ēšet ḥayl*, and Ruth then goes on to describe just such a woman, calling her an *'ēšet ḥayl* in 3:11. In short, chronological or calendrical considerations may provide criteria for arrangements, but so may considerations of subject matter.

Modern commentators agree that, whatever the internal order, the tradition which places Ruth among the Writings rather than after Judges must be original. All Jewish tradition treats the book as an entity and not as an appendage to Judges. And it is difficult to see why a book would be moved out of the Prophets portion of the canon into the Writings, while a "promotion" in the opposite direction would be more easily understood. Nevertheless I would caution that there is a great deal more to be learned in this regard, especially on the question of the canonical status of the Prophets section of the canon, from the intensive study of the Dead Sea scrolls.[37] Furthermore, I think we should not dismiss from consideration that one cause for the fluidity in the relative location of Ruth may have to do with matters of content.

That leads to one other consideration. In his analysis of the final, disheartening episode of the book of Judges, in chapters 19–21, R. G. Boling has proposed that this story was appended to the Judges book, as first constructed by the Deuteronomic historian, by a Deuteronomistic editor of the exilic period. He drew upon "previously neglected traditionary units" in doing this.[38] Boling also observes, in his NOTE on 19:24, that there are a number of correspondences in the story here to the book of Ruth. Some of the same sort of careful crafting is present (see Boling's COMMENT on chapter 19). There is a series of verbal correspondences which, when taken together, may suggest a relationship between the two stories. Thus, Judg 19:23 and Ruth 1:13 both use Hebrew 'al as an independent negative, two of only six occurrences in the OT. Judg 19:24 uses a suffix which must be analyzed as the archaic or dialectal feminine dual, comparable to the seven instances of this phenomenon in Ruth. Judg 20:40 uses hinnēh as an expression of surprise, "lo and behold," in a manner recalling its usage in Ruth 2:4 and 4:1. In Judg 19:6 and 22, the Levite and each of his hosts eat and drink until their hearts became "good" (merry); at least in the second instance the outcome is unexpectedly dire. This recalls the same idiom in the ambiguous circumstances of Ruth 3:7. Then, of course, there is the fact that the Levite's concubine comes from Bethlehem in Judah. Finally, in Judg 21:23 there occurs the only other preexilic use of the idiom "to take wives" using the verb nś', besides the use in Ruth 1:4.

On a broader scale, the two stories are completely contrastive. In Judges 19–21, everything is done wrongly. Old institutions are thoroughly misapplied. A Levite dismembers his dead concubine in order to call the amphictyonic muster, becoming, as Boling points out, a self-appointed judge. The muster produces a civil war and nearly wipes out one of its own tribes, the Benjaminites. In order to keep the letter of their own sworn oath not to supply wives for the remnant of the Benjaminites— whose idea was that?—they put Jabesh-Gilead to the sword and round up their virgin daughters; that proving insufficient, they allow the Benjaminites to thoroughly disrupt the annual festival of Yahweh at Shiloh. In

[37] See J. A. Sanders, "The Dead Sea Scrolls—A Quarter Century of Study," BA 36 (1973), esp. 140–42.
[38] Boling, p. 276.

the whole miserable performance, they have obviously lost track of Yahweh completely! Striking in this connection, perhaps, is the designation
given to the Benjaminites who have fallen in 20:44 and 46; after all
sorts of military designations throughout the narrative, here they are
'anšē ḥayl, "prosperous men" (Boling) but also perhaps "substantial
men," recalling the description of Boaz in 2:1 and Ruth in 3:11. It is
ironic that the victims of all this chaotic action are given the only acco-
lades. And one more thing: in the Israel of which Judges 19–21 tells, the
only person who will give the Levite and his concubine hospitality in
Gibeah is a sojourner (19:16).

The contrast with the Ruth story is striking. Older commentators often
observed that the placement of the Ruth story after the book of Judges
was not due simply to their chronological connection, but also to the contrast between the two portrayals. That contrast, however, really pertains
to Judges 19–21 only. Here are convenant, custom, institutions gone awry,
contrasted with a scene in which things go as they should, in which people
make the right decisions, in which Yahweh is anything but lost. It is
enough to suggest that there may have been an original connection between Judges 19–21 (as redacted by the Deuteronomistic editor in the exilic
period) and the Ruth story. If so, we may have evidence that the position
of Ruth after the Judges book has antiquity and goes back six centuries
earlier than is attested in the divided tradition preserved in Jewish and
Christian resources of the early centuries C.E.

The Text

In 1922, after years of research, Alfred Rahlfs published a remarkably
thorough analysis of the Greek text of Ruth, that is, of all the great
variety of textual tradition which is lumped under the general term
Septuagint (LXX).[39] Rahlfs' study was a pilot project toward an attempt
to study the entire Old Testament in this fashion, but Ruth was the only
book to be given such an exhaustive treatment. What Rahlfs did was to
analyze the fifty Greek manuscripts collated by Alan E. Brooke and
Norman McLean in the "Cambridge Septuagint"[40] and arrange them
in families which represented recensions, that is, a series of attempts to
bring the Greek translation into line with the Hebrew text prevailing at
each stage when such an enterprise was undertaken.

Rahlfs' Four Manuscript Families

Rahlfs found four such families. The first is designated hexaplaric, because it relates closely to the Septuagint text worked out by Origen, the

---

[39] See in Bibliography, Rahlfs.
[40] *The Old Testament in Greek,* pp. 887–97.

third-century C.E. textual scholar, in the fifth column of his Hexapla. Origen conformed this column to the Hebrew text fixed by the rabbis at the end of the first century C.E. as normative. Our fullest testimony to the Hexapla is the Syriac translation of it known as the Syro-Hexapla; it retains the marks—asterisks and obeli—by which Origen indicated where the Septuagint he had prepared showed plusses and minuses over against the Hebrew text.

Rahlfs' second family is the Lucianic (LXX$^{L'}$), named after Lucian of Antioch who lived until about 311 C.E. The third he designated K, from Latin *catena,* "chain," because it contained readings characteristic of an exegetical enterprise of certain Christian fathers who arranged their comments in chain-like compendia. The fourth represented an unknown recension, and Rahlfs styled it R. When the cataloguing was complete, two great uncial manuscripts, the Alexandrinus (LXX^A) of the fifth century C.E. and the Vaticanus (LXX^B) of the fourth, were unclassified; they showed the greatest divergence from the hexaplaric recension of Origen, and Rahlfs concluded that they belonged back at the beginning of the whole process. LXX^B, he was confident, represented the Old Greek, as close a representative as was available of the original translation of the Hebrew into Greek in Egypt, which for Ruth probably took place in the second century B.C.E. or just possibly in the third century. LXX^A was like LXX^B in many ways, but it did not seem to be as pure a representative. If we turn all of this around into chronological order, LXX^B would represent the oldest stage, and the others would follow thereafter, as various scholars brought the Greek tradition into greater and greater conformity to the Hebrew text, the final step being the hexaplaric one.

I have left out a great deal of detail in this description, notably about the manuscripts which belong to the margins of one or another of the families but cross the boundaries at points, and about a few manuscripts which defy classification. But enough has been said to suggest the position in 1922, and Rahlfs' portrayal as here outlined has dominated the discussion of the Septuagint in Ruth ever since. Using LXX^B as the standard, he went on to evaluate also the Old Latin, Vulgate, Syriac, Ethiopic, and Armenian versions in relation to it, and the guidelines were set for the text criticism of Ruth, at least until very recently.

Another Recension

The first breach in the wall was hardly noticeable. In 1921, Henry St. John Thackeray[41] pointed out that a substantial portion of the text of LXX^B in the books of Samuel and Kings differed noticeably in style from the characteristics of the Old Greek translation attested elsewhere in these books. Apparently a substitution had been made, in II Sam 11:2 through

---

[41] *The Septuagint and Jewish Worship,* Oxford University Press, 1921.

I Kings 2:11 and in I Kings 22:1 through the end of II Kings, of another Greek recension. The next step could not be taken until the Dead Sea scrolls came to light, and since then considerable definition has been given to this newly discovered recension. Dominique Barthélemy in 1963, and subsequently James D. Shenkel, Michael Smith, and John M. Grindel[42] are the chief contributors to discovering its features.

Barthélemy gave the recension its name, Kaige, after the Greek word with which it regularly translated Hebrew *gam*, "also." In all, some twenty-six criteria, most of them involving the way in which Kaige always translates a particular Hebrew word, are now identified, so it is possible to search out the presence of this recension in other Old Testament books besides Samuel and Kings where it was first found.

Is Ruth included in the Kaige recension? Twenty-two of the criteria are not applicable, because the words involved simply do not occur. Three, however, do apply clearly to the LXX[B] of Ruth. Out of nine occurrences of Hebrew *gam*, LXX[B] translates with *kaige* six times; in five out of seven occurrences of the pronoun *'ānōkī*, "I," it uses the typical Kaige translation *egō eimi;* at one point where Hebrew *'īš*, usually "man," has the meaning "each" (3:14), it uses *anēr* instead of the more fluent *hekastos*. On one other criterion, it goes the way Kaige does, but the statistics are not conclusive: when the expression "in the eyes of," Hebrew *bᵉʿēyn*-plus suffix, occurs with someone other than God as the object, Kaige always translates with *en ophthalmois*, while the Old Greek uses other expressions one-third of the time and *en ophthalmois* two-thirds of the time. Ruth's three instances, in 2:2, 10, 13, all use *en ophthalmois*. At the least, this last statistic does not overturn the rather strong indications that the LXX[B] of Ruth is not the Old Greek representative Rahlfs thought it was, but represents the Kaige recension.

Hebrew Text Traditions

It is Frank M. Cross[43] who has brought some sensible order into this mass of data, by proposing a theory to account for the complex recensional development within the Greek translation tradition. He posits three

---

[42] Barthélemy, *Les devanciers d'Aquila*, VT *Supplement* 10 (1963); Shenkel, *Chronology and Recensional Development in the Greek Text of Kings*, Harvard University Press, 1968; Smith, "Another Criterion for the Kaige Recension," *Biblica* 48 (1967), 443–45; Grindel, "Another Characteristic of the Kaige Recension," *Catholic Biblical Quarterly* 31 (1969), 449–513. The Introduction and chapter 1 of Shenkel's book give a very clear overview of the present state of research for those who wish to pursue this matter further.

[43] "The Contribution of the Qumran Discoveries to the Study of the Biblical Text," *Israel Exploration Journal* 16 (1966), 81–95, and "The History of the Biblical Text in the Light of the Discoveries in the Judean Desert," *Harvard Theological Review* 57 (1964), 281–99.

basic steps in the Greek development and, most important, three different Hebrew text types to which each of the three steps was related. In Egypt, one Hebrew text tradition which had developed a least for a century in isolation from other text traditions, was used as the basis for the Old Greek translation. In Palestine meanwhile, another text tradition was developing in its own way, also in isolation from the others. At a point in the second or early first century B.C.E., the Palestinian tradition served as the basis upon which the Old Greek was revised, and the witness to this Greek recension is the Lucianic family of manuscripts. Cross calls this recension "proto-Lucianic," since it predates the time of Lucian by some four hundred years. Hebrew texts in this tradition are turning up in great profusion among the Dead Sea scrolls. In Babylonia, Cross posits, still another Hebrew text tradition was developing, again in isolation, and it is this one which in the first century C.E. was the basis for another Greek revision, the Kaige. By and large, it is this last one which is closest to the Masoretic text which has come down to us.

Notice what this means: there seem to have been three different places where Hebrew texts were developing, undergoing all the changes which isolated text traditions will undergo, maintaining some good old readings which the others will not maintain, experiencing the normal scribal errors of loss by haplography and gain by dittography, each showing a degree of expansion and conflation—with the proto-Lucianic being by far the most expansionist. For Ruth, access to this full panorama of Hebrew development is still gained primarily from the Greek recensions augmented by what little can be learned from the scraps from Qumran. Insofar as the three traditions can be recovered, they all need to be examined for good text readings.

Implications for Ruth

What does all this mean for Ruth? These observations seem to be warranted:

1. LXX^B of Ruth is no longer to be taken as the touchstone for judging all the others, or for evaluating the versions. We apparently have no sure attestation of the Old Greek of Ruth, not even in LXX^A, which remains a close ally of LXX^B and is apparently itself more or less a Kaige exemplar.

2. Proto-Lucianic readings should be considered all the more carefully as containing valuable variants. The reader will find such variants indicated with the siglum LXX^L when they are found in the main exemplars of this tradition but not in the ones that are at the margins of the family, and by $LXX^{L'}$ when the whole group contains them. Once in a while mention will be made of the minor Lucianic witnesses, the ones at

the margin only. One other witness of the Lucianic recension is Theodoret, a Christian exegete of the fifth century, who wrote a running comment on the book and quoted certain passages from it.

3. The Old Latin (OL), preserved only in a few quotes in early Church fathers and in a manuscript from the ninth century now in Madrid (which seems to have suffered a tear near its conclusion and was augmented in its last few verses from the Vulgate), becomes an independent witness.[44] When it joins forces with the Lucianic witnesses, it becomes a force to be reckoned with.

4. The Syriac, although partly dependent upon the LXX, has a rather unusual character. Gerleman has taken it quite seriously in his commentary, and studies it carefully on pp. 3–4 of his introduction. It adds explanations from time to time, which the NOTES will examine. Some of them are rather sensitive to the meaning; on the other hand, the Syriac seems not to have recognized some of the story-teller's more subtle techniques, and sometimes vitiates their impact by paraphrasing.

5. Four Hebrew manuscripts of Ruth are attested from Qumran, two from Cave 2 which have been published,[45] and two from Cave 4.[46] The eight fragments of 2QRuth^a, probably datable to the first century C.E., contain a considerable portion of the text from the middle of chapter 2 to the early verses of chapter 4, and attest a Masoretic text type with no important variants. Similarly, 4QRuth^a, which represents fourteen lines of the first chapter, is Masoretic in type, and affords only the one interesting variant, *qōlăm* for *qōlān*, discussed in the second NOTE on 1:9. A slightly earlier (first-century B.C.E.) manuscript is represented by the two small fragments of 2QRuth^b; one fragment is too small even to be properly placed in the book, but the other contains parts of 3:13–18 and has some striking variants. At the end of verse 14, it omits the word "the woman" and reads simply "that she came to the threshing floor." The versions show some divergence here, but none are as frugal as this. At the end of verse 15, this text adds the word *šam*, presumably "there," in the clause "and measured *there* six *šā'ār*-measures." Again this is anomalous. Finally, in Naomi's question to Ruth in 3:16, it reads *māh*, "what," instead of *mī*, "who." The meaning of Naomi's question is already a problem, and the versions had their own set of difficulties with it (see the NOTE),

---

[44] A. Sperber, "Wiederherstellung einer griechischen Textgestalt des Buches Ruth," *Monatschrift für Geschichte und Wissenschaft des Judentums* 81 (1937), 55–65, opposed Rahlfs' linkage of the OL to LXX^B, seeing it instead as related to an otherwise unknown Greek translation, a judgment which now looks plausible.

[45] M. Baillet, J. T. Milik, and R. de Vaux, *Les "petites grottes" de Qumrân*, Discoveries in the Judaean Desert, III (Oxford: Clarendon, 1962), 71–75 and plates XIV and XV.

[46] My appreciation to Frank M. Cross, for permitting the use of the photographs of Ruth fragments from Cave 4.

but this new Hebrew reading does not untie the knot and is simply one more evidence of ancient wrestling with a difficult syntax.

Even more perplexing is the first fragment of the two tiny pieces making up 4QRuth[b]. It contains the first word of each of four lines from chapter 1. Just to the *left* of these a piece of fiber thread attaches at two points, which seems to mean that another parchment was sewn on here, in the midst of a column, an odd state of affairs! As if this oddity were not enough, there seems to be no way to reconstruct the four lines which would run between each pair of words so that the lines would have even approximately the same length. What the nature of this manuscript is completely eludes me at this point, and must await further study to see if any sense can be made of it.

6. The reader will find a great number of textual variants cited in this commentary, but relatively few are accepted unequivocally. In a number of instances, it is proposed that two or more variant readings are valid, and may have stood as alternatives within the tradition viewed as a whole. That is, one old text tradition may have had one, another may have had another, and we cannot be sure that one is "original" and the other "secondary." The text of Ruth probably tolerated such divergences. I deem it better to show the reader the alternatives in these instances, to let him participate in sensing the process of passing the tradition as the book came down in what probably was a somewhat fluid state from the exilic period onward.

SELECTED BIBLIOGRAPHY

Andersen, Francis I. "Israelite Kinship Terminology and Social Structure," *The Bible Translator* 20 (1969), 29–39.

Beattie, D. R. G. "The Book of Ruth as Evidence for Israelite Legal Practice," VT 24 (1974), 251–67.

Bertholet, Alfred. *Das Buch Ruth*, Kurzer Hand-Commentar zum Alten Testament, 17 (Leipzig and Tübingen: Mohr, 1898), 49–69.

Bertman, Stephen. "Symmetrical Design in the Book of Ruth," JBL 84 (1965), 165–68.

Bettan, Israel. *The Five Scrolls*, The Jewish Commentary for Bible Readers (Cincinnati: Union of American Hebrew Congregations, 1950), pp. 49–72.

Boling, Robert G. *Judges*, AB, vol. 6A, 1975.

Brooke, Alan E., and Norman McLean. *The Old Testament in Greek*, I (Cambridge University Press, 1917), part IV, 887–97.

Bruno, Arvid. *Die Bücher Josua-Richter-Ruth: Eine rhythmisch Untersuchung* (Stockholm: Almqvist and Wiksell, 1955), pp. 197–210, 244–45.

Bruppacher, Hans. "Die Bedeutung des Namens Ruth," *Theologische Zeitschrift* 22 (1966), 12–18.

Burrows, Millar. "The Marriage of Boaz and Ruth," JBL 59 (1940), 445–54.

Campbell, Edward F., Jr. "The Hebrew Short Story: Its Form, Style and Provenance," in *A Light Unto My Path: Old Testament Studies in Honor of Jacob M. Myers*, eds. H. N. Bream, R. D. Heim, and C. A. Moore (Temple University Press, 1974), pp. 83–101.

Dahood, Mitchell. *Psalms I, 1–50*, AB, vol. 16, 1966; *Psalms II, 51–100*, AB, vol. 17, 1968; *Psalms III, 101–150*, AB, vol. 17A, 1970.

David, Martin. *Het huwelijk van Ruth*, Uitgaven vanwege de Stichting voor Oud-semietische, Hellenistische en Joodsche Rechtsgeschiedenis gevestigd te Leiden, 2, 1941.

Dommershausen, Werner. "Leitwortstil in der Ruthrolle," in *Theologie im Wandel* (Munich and Freiburg: Wewel, 1967), pp. 394–407.

Ehrlich, Arnold B. *Randglossen zur hebräischen Bibel*, VII (Leipzig: Hinrichs, 1914), 19–24.

Eissfeldt, Otto. "Wahrheit und Dichtung in der Ruth-Erzählung," *Sitzungsbericht der Sächsischen Akademie der Wissenschaften zu Leipzig*, Phil.-hist. Kl., 110, 4 (1965), 23–28.

Freedman, D. Noel. See under Gray, George Buchanan.

Gerleman, Gillis. *Ruth*, Biblischer Kommentar, 18/1. Neukirchen Kreis Moers: Buchhandlung des Erziehungsvereins, 1960.

Glanzman, George S. "The Origin and Date of the Book of Ruth," *Catholic Biblical Quarterly* 21 (1959), 201–7.

Glueck, Nelson. *Ḥesed in the Bible*, tr. Alfred Gottschalk. Hebrew Union College Press, 1967.

Gordis, Robert. "Love, Marriage, and Business in the Book of Ruth," in *A Light Unto My Path: Old Testament Studies in Honor of Jacob M. Myers*, eds. H. N. Bream, R. D. Heim, and C. A. Moore (Temple University Press, 1974), pp. 241–64.

Gray, George Buchanan. *The Forms of Hebrew Poetry*. London: Hodder and Stoughton, 1915; repr. with "Prolegomenon" by D. Noel Freedman, New York: Ktav, 1972.

Gray, John. *Joshua, Judges and Ruth*, The Century Bible. London: Nelson, 1967.

Gunkel, Hermann. *The Legends of Genesis*, tr. W. H. Carruth, with an introduction by W. F. Albright. New York: Schocken, 1964.

———— "Ruth," in his *Reden and Aufsätze* (Göttingen: Vandenhoeck and Ruprecht, 1913), pp. 65–92.

Haller, Max. *Ruth*, Handbuch zum Alten Testament, 1/18. Tübingen: Mohr, 1940.

Hals, Ronald M. *The Theology of the Book of Ruth*, Biblical Series, 23, Philadelphia: Fortress, Facet, 1969.

Hertzberg, Hans Wilhelm. *Die Bücher Josua, Richter, Ruth*, Das Alte Testament Deutsch, 9, 2d ed. (Göttingen: Vandenhoeck and Ruprecht, 1959), 255–81.

Humbert, Paul. "Art et leçon de l'histoire de Ruth," *Révue de théologie et philosophie*, n.s. 26 (1938), 257–86.

Joüon, Paul. *Ruth: commentaire philologique et exégétique*. Rome: Institut Biblique Pontifical, 1953.

Knight, George A. F. *Ruth and Jonah*, 2d ed., London: SCM, 1966.

Köhler, Ludwig. *Hebrew Man*, tr. Peter R. Ackroyd. Nashville and New York: Abingdon, 1956.

Labuschagne, C. J. "The Crux in Ruth 4:11," ZAW 79 (1967), 364–67.

Lamparter, Helmut. *Das Buch der Sehnsucht*, Die Botschaft des Alten Testaments, 16/11 (Stuttgart: Calwer Verlag, 1962), 9–56.

Lattey, Cuthbert. *The Book of Ruth*. Westminster Version of the Sacred Scriptures. London: Longmans, Green, 1935.

Lord, Albert B. *The Singer of Tales*. New York: Atheneum, 1965.

Loretz, Oswald. "The Theme of the Ruth Story," *Catholic Biblical Quarterly* 22 (1960), 391–99.

Mace, David R. *Hebrew Marriage: A Sociological Study*. London: Epworth Press, 1953.

May, Herbert Gordon. "Ruth's Visit to the High Place at Bethlehem," *Journal of the Royal Asiatic Society* (1939), 75–78.

Mendenhall, George E. *The Tenth Generation*. Johns Hopkins University Press, 1973.

Midrash Rabbah: Ruth, tr. Louis I. Rabinowitz. London: Soncino, 1939.

Myers, Jacob M. *I Chronicles*, AB, vol. 12, 1965; *II Chronicles*, AB, vol. 13, 1965.

———— *The Linguistic and Literary Form of the Book of Ruth*. Leiden: Brill, 1955. *Cited as* MLLF.

Noth, Martin. *Die israelitischen Personennamen im Rahmen der gemein-semitischen Namengebung.* Stuttgart: Kohlhammer, 1928.

von Rad, Gerhard. "Predigt über Ruth 1," *Evangelische Theologie* 12 (1952–53), 1–6.

Rahlfs, Alfred. *Studie über den griechischen Text des Buches Ruth,* Nachrichten von der Gesellschaft der Wissenschaften zu Göttingen, Phil.-Hist. Kl. (1922), pp. 47–164.

Rauber, D. F. "Literary Values in the Bible: The Book of Ruth," JBL 89 (1970), 27–37.

Rowley, Harold H. "The Marriage of Ruth," in *The Servant of the Lord and Other Essays on the Old Testament* (London: Lutterworth, 1952), pp. 163–86.

Rudolph, Wilhelm. *Das Buch Ruth, Das Hohe Lied, Die Klagelieder,* Kommentar zum Alten Testament, XVII.1–3, 2d ed. (Gütersloh: Mohn, 1962), 23–72.

Saarisalo, Aapeli. "The Targum of the Book of Ruth," *Studia Orientalia* 2 (1928), 88–104.

Scott, R. B. Y. "Weights and Measures of the Bible," BAR³, pp. 345–65.

Segert, Stanislav. "Vorarbeiten zur hebräischen Metrik, III: Zum Problem der metrischen Elemente im Buche Ruth," *Archiv Orientální* 25 (1957), 190–200.

Sheehan, J. F. X. "The Word of God as Myth: The Book of Ruth," in *The Word in the World: Essays in Honor of Frederick L. Moriarty,* eds. R. J. Clifford and George W. MacRae (Weston College Press, 1973), pp. 35–46.

Sievers, Eduard. *Metrischen Studien,* I (Leipzig: Teubner, 1901), 390–93.

Slotki, Judah J. "Ruth," in *The Five Megilloth,* ed. A. Cohen (Hindhead, Surrey: Soncino, 1946), pp. 35–65.

Speiser, Ephraim A. " 'Coming' and 'Going' at the 'City' Gate," BASOR 144 (December 1956), 20–23.

——— *Genesis,* AB, vol. 1, 1964.

——— "Of Shoes and Shekels," BASOR 77 (February 1940), 15–20.

Staples, W. E. "The Book of Ruth," AJSL 53(1937), 145–57.

Thompson, Thomas and Dorothy. "Some Legal Problems in the Book of Ruth," VT 18 (1968), 79–99.

Thornhill, Raymond. "The Greek Text of the Book of Ruth: A Grouping of Manuscripts According to Origen's Hexapla," VT 3 (1953), 239–49.

de Vaux, Roland. *Ancient Israel: Its Life and Institutions,* tr. John McHugh. New York: McGraw-Hill, 1961.

Vesco, Jean-Luc. "La date du livre de Ruth," *Revue Biblique* 74 (1967), 235–47.

de Waard, Jan, and Eugene A. Nida. *A Translator's Handbook on the Book of Ruth.* London: United Bible Societies, 1973.

Weiss, David. "The Use of QNH in Connection with Marriage," *Harvard Theological Review* 57 (1964), 243–48.

Wolfenson, Louis B. "The Character, Contents, and Date of Ruth," AJSL 27 (1911), 285–300.

———— "Implications of the Place of the Book of Ruth in Editions, Manuscripts, and Canon of the Old Testament," *Hebrew Union College Annual* 1 (1924), 151–78.

———— "The Purpose of the Book of Ruth," *Bibliotheca Sacra* 69 (1912), 329–44.

Würthwein, Ernst. *Ruth,* Handbuch zum Alten Testament, 18, 2d ed. (Tübingen: Mohr, 1969), 1–24.

RUTH

I. A FAMILY OF SOJOURNERS
(1:1-5)

1 ¹ Once, back in the days when the judges judged, there came a famine over the land, and a certain man went from Bethlehem of Judah to sojourn on the Moab plateau, he, his wife, and his two^a sons. ² The man's name was Elimelek ^band his wife's name was Naomi^b, and the names of his two sons were Mahlon and Kilyon— Ephrathites from Bethlehem of Judah. They came to the Moab plateau, and there they settled.

³ Then Elimelek, Naomi's husband, died, so that she was left, with her two sons. ⁴ They then took Moabite wives, the name of the first being Orpah and the name of the second Ruth, and they lived there about ten years. ⁵ Now also the two of them, Mahlon and Kilyon, died, and the woman was bereft of her two lads and her husband.

^a LXX^{BL} and the Syriac lack the word for "two."

^{b–b} LXX^B omits by haplography the entire phrase. Elsewhere it joins the Lucianic group, Theodoret, and other Greek manuscripts of various families, in spelling Naomi with a final *n;* all LXX spellings have a preceding long-ī vowel. The original Greek may have been working with a variant name ending in -*īn,* but such a form eludes Hebrew explanation.

Notes

1:1. *Once, back in the days when the judges judged, there came.* Taken in combination, the five Hebrew words at the start of Ruth show unique syntax. They are *wayhī,* "and it happened," followed by "in the days of/the judging of/ the judges" followed by another *wayhī,* "and there was." OT books not infrequently begin with a *wayhī,* but only in Joshua, Judges, Ezekiel, Esther, and Ruth does a time reference follow, and only in the last two is it in terms of "in the days of." Esther, like Gen 14:1; Isa 7:1; and Jer 1:3, goes on then to name a person, thus giving an absolute chronology to the sequel. Ruth follows with a very general time reference (compare II Kings 23:22 where the meaning is similar but the syntax different) which employs a cognate relationship of an infinitive construct and a plural noun of *špṭ,* "to judge, rule." To this syntax can be compared only Gen 36:31 (followed by I Chron 1:43), "before the ruling of any king over the sons of Israel," where *mlk* is the root used and the reference is to the establishment of monarchy. After the time reference comes the second *wayhī*, virtually another story opener (see Gen 12:1 and 26:1). Many of the ancient versions found the combination redundant. LXX[BL] and some other LXX manuscripts omit "in the days of," while Syriac reads simply "in the days of the judges." However, the OL, and the LXX versions which tend to conform back to the MT, rendered the entire phrase, even though the result was clumsy Latin or Greek.

Frequently the first time reference is considered a later addition, perhaps after the fashion of the Deuteronomists. The unique sequence tells against this; structural considerations for the story as a whole urge maintaining the text as it is (see COMMENT).

went from Bethlehem of Judah. Joüon (*Commentaire*, p. 31) is probably correct that the verb controls the phrase here (thus, not ". . . a man from Bethlehem went . . ."). In verse 2 the focus will shift from places to persons. F. I. Andersen has observed in a letter to me, however, that, since the syntax allows either, the attempt here may be to identify the man by his village connection rather than by his district or generic association (see on verse 2, below).

the Moab plateau. Seven times in Ruth a form of *śādeh*, "field," is used in construct relation to Moab, at 1:1, 2, 6 (twice), 22, 2:6, and 4:3. On nine other occasions the term refers to land in Judah (see the second NOTE on 2:2). Orthographic difficulties arise only in the seven uses with Moab. In BH[3], there are three occasions where the normal singular construct form *śᵉdēh* is used, namely at 1:6, 2:6, and 4:3. The other four have the consonants *śdy*, vocalized by the Masoretes as *śᵉdēy*, ostensibly a plural construct but one unlike the normal one for this feminine word, *śᵉdot*; BH[1], based on a manuscript three centuries later than that used in BH[3], had this form at 2:6 as well. The overwhelming evidence is that the word is singular, and probably an old poetic form. The versions are unanimous in rendering singular, and various Hebrew manuscripts frequently normalize to the singular *śᵉdēh*. Qumran fragment C62a from Cave 4 (unpublished; see Introduction), gives *śᵉdēh* in 1:1 and 2, the only two places it preserves the word. Myers (MLLF, p. 9) gives ample evidence of confusion in spelling of the word in other biblical books. See also the grammars (Joüon, § § 89b, 96Bf; Hans Bauer and Pontus Leander, *Historische Grammatik der hebräischen Sprache des Alten Testamentes* [Tübingen: Niemeyer, 1922; repr. Hildesheim: Olms, 1965], § 731; cf. GKC, § 93ll.

Moabite topography is well enough known, but a problem lies with the attempt to determine what parts of Moab might be in the story-teller's mind. Closest and most easily accessible to Bethlehem would be the north portion of what can be termed "ideal Moab." This lies north of the river Arnon (modern Wādi Mōjib) and extends to a line just north of the top of the Dead Sea, a rough square twenty-five miles on a side. Included are the "plains of Moab" (Num 22:1, 33:48 ff., etc.), a part of the rift valley across the Jordan from Jericho. Stretching south from this rather well-watered and rich plot is flattish tableland, its western flank rising abruptly from the Dead Sea to a point 3300–3700 feet above the Dead Sea (2000–2400 feet above mean sea level). The tableland is marked by higher peaks such as Mount Nebo and by such key cities as Heshbon, Medeba, and Dibon among a host of Iron Age settlements. (See the results of N. Glueck's survey, *Annual of the American Schools of Oriental Research* 14 [1933–34]; 15 [1934–35]; 18–19 [1937–39]; 25–28 [1945–48]; cf. a convenient summary of the Iron Age sites in A. H. van Zyl, *The Moabites* [Leiden: Brill, 1960], pp. 61–101 and map.)

This tableland is fertile and comparatively well-watered. The abrupt rise from the Dead Sea forms a rain barrage, so that the western half of this region gets a fair rainfall (about sixteen inches per year on the average but records are not kept in the modern towns). The wind, however, is relatively unimpeded, so that it is grass crops and pasturage which flourish, rather than orchards and vines. It is clear that conditions here can differ from those in the Judean hills around Bethlehem (against Gerleman, p. 14; cf. D. Baly, *The Geography of the Bible* [London: Lutterworth, 1957], p. 61; W. Reed, *College of the Bible Quarterly* 41 [1964], 5 f.).

South of the Arnon, the higher tableland reaching above 3000 feet and finally above 4000 extends down to the Zered (Wādi Ḥesa), the natural boundary between Edom and Moab. Rainfall is less and irrigation potential in the deep wadis diminishes; this is more marginal land than the northern sector.

Does the plausibility of a sojourn in Moab extend to historical matters? The issue is unclear because biblical data on control of the northern sector is difficult to date and to interpret. Apparently Moab held the north first, lost it to Sihon the Amorite (Num 21:26–30), and certainly regained it under King Mesha in the mid-ninth century B.C.E. (the inscription on the Moabite Stone of ca. 830 B.C.E.; cf. II Kings 3:3–5). It was Sihon that Israel defeated in this area according to the accounts in Num 2:21 ff. and Deut 2:16 ff., whereupon Reuben took the territory as its allotment (Numbers 32; Josh 13:15–23). A swarm of historical problems remain. Some surround Reuben and its territory (see K. Elliger, "Reuben," in *The Interpreter's Dictionary of the Bible*, ed. G. A. Buttrick et al. [New York and Nashville: Abingdon, 1962], vol. R–Z, pp. 53 ff.). Others are connected with why Numbers 22–24, about Balak, king of Moab, and Balaam, the professional curser, should follow upon the account of the defeat of Sihon. It is possible that Moab reoccupied the northern sector during the time of the Israelite judges; that is the implication of the story in Judg 3:12–30, in which Ehud assassinates Eglon, king of Moab, especially if verses 28–30 are taken to mean that Israel pushed Moab back to the Jordan river fords only. However, Judg 11:25, in Jephthah's elaborate argument with the Ammonites, implies just the opposite, namely that no attempt was made by Moab to reoccupy this territory. Perhaps all we can say at this stage of our knowledge is that Moab and Israel had a checkered relationship, sometimes of relative cordiality (hence David's delivery of his parents to the care of the Moabite king in I Sam 22:3–4) possibly based on ancient kinship ties, and sometimes calling for the severe dictates of international struggle (hence the punishment of a recalcitrant vassal in II Sam 8:2). As for the setting of

Ruth, there is nothing intrinsically impossible, climatically or historically, about the portrayal of a Judean family finding a place to sojourn there.

2. *Elimelek*. Ruth provides the only biblical use of this name, otherwise frequently attested in the onomasticon of the Late Bronze Age. In an Amarna letter from Jerusalem (J. A. Knudtzon, *Die El-Amarna-Tafeln* [Leipzig: Hinrichs, 1915; repr. Aalen: Zeller, 1964], letter 286), dated about 1365 B.C.E., Jerusalem's ruler refers to *i-li-mil-ki*. Texts from Ugarit of the fourteenth and thirteenth centuries attest the name in native alphabetic cuneiform (*ilmlk*) and in Akkadian texts using logograms; two further Akkadian texts from Ugarit have *ili(m)-mu-lik* (J. Nougayrol, *Le palais royal d'Ugarit*, IV [Paris: Imprimerie Nationale, 1956], 215, line 27; VI [1970], 80, line 16). There is an unresolved question about the *i*-vowel between the two elements *il(u)*, "god," and *milk(u)*, "king." Is it a relic of an old case-ending, as Noth, *Personennamen*, pp. 34 ff., suggests (followed by Gerleman), or is it a pronominal suffix meaning "my"? On balance, the pronominal suffix seems more likely.

What can "Elimelek" mean? Almost certainly, the *mlk* element is the name or title of a divinity; compare, for example, Ugaritic *Mlkn'm*, "Mlk/The King is (my) delight." Elimelek, then, would mean "Mlk/The King is my god." A divine name Mlk is a distinct possibility; recall Milkom of the Ammonites (I Kings 11:5, 33; cf. vs. 7), and see on this complicated question Albright, *Archaeology and the Religion of Israel*[5], pp. 156–57, and J. Gray, "Molech, Moloch," in *The Interpreter's Dictionary of the Bible*, vol. K–Q, pp. 422 f. For our purposes, I mention only two points. First, the great likelihood is that *for an Israelite* the name Elimelek would mean "The King (Yahweh) is my god." Yahweh is given royal titles throughout Israelite history; see especially his designation as king in Exod 15:18. Second, the name Elimelek is an authentic and typical name in Canaan prior to the time of the Israelite monarchy, and it is the one name in the Ruth story that seems incapable of being explained as having a symbolic meaning pertinent to the narrative.

That makes the versional variants all the more interesting. LXX[BL] plus several other Greek witnesses give the name as Abimelek, and LXX[A] joins them in this reading at 2:1; 4:3, 9. This name is more common in the Bible, and that fact may account for its presence in a Hebrew version of Ruth from which the Greek translators worked; indeed it is quite likely to be the original LXX reading, later corrected by various Greek traditions to conform to Masoretic Elimelek. On the other hand, if an early Hebrew version had it, it may represent a genuine alternative reading. H. Bruppacher, in *Theologische Zeitschrift* 22 (1966), 17, has even dug up an old suggestion of L. Köhler (published in 1904 and not available to me), that Abimelek is original, that it means "Father of the king," and that even this name can be brought into the circle of symbolic meanings, since it looks ahead to David as a descendant. This suggestion is extremely unlikely; among other problems, it leaves us wondering where the name Elimelek arose as an alternative! It does, however, underscore the whole problem of the names in Ruth. See the COMMENT.

Naomi. This name relates to a root *n'm*, having to do with liveliness or delight. Noth, in his *Personennamen*, p. 166, takes it to be a shortened "nickname," which in its original full form would have been compounded with the name of a deity—such as "(My) delight is (god-name)" or better "Delight of (god-name)." He compares Elna'am of I Chron 11:46 and Abino'am, Barak's father, in Judges 4 and 5, along with other names in Semitic inscriptions, J. J. Stamm, in his article "Hebraische Frauennamen" (*Hebräische Wortforschung: Baumgartner Festschrift*=VT *Supplement* 16 [1967]), classes Naomi as a "profane appellative" name instead, in accord with the frequently made observation that few Hebrew names of women were compounded with god-names. Stamm goes on to speculate that the original vocalization of the name ended not in *i* but in *-ay*, comparable to a group of Ugaritic names of women with that ending (see Gordon, UT, § 8.54, and note especially *Nu-ú-ma-ya and Nu-ú-ma-ya-nu* in text 98 of J. Nougayrol et al., *Ugaritica*, V [Paris: Geuthner, 1968], 191). To this we can add Amorite names with this ending in the Mari texts, the majority of which are names of women (H. B. Huffmon, *Amorite Personal Names in the Mari Texts* [Johns Hopkins University Press, 1965], p. 135). If Stamm's proposal is correct, it would mean that Hebrew tradition had lost track of the old ending, both in the MT form and in the various Hebrew texts behind the LXX versions—all of which attest *î*. This strains Stamm's argument, and it should be noted that forms of the root *n'm* occur as epithets of heroes (Aqhat and Keret) and as an adjective for the gods (Gordon, UT, text 52), a fact which is in favor of the proposal of a shortened nickname.

Whatever the outcome of such speculations, the important thing to note is that names containing the root *n'm*, with a variety of vocalizations, were common from at least as early as 1400 B.C.E. on; the name Naomi is not contrived for the story-teller's purpose. See COMMENT.

his two sons were Mahlon and Kilyon. The Syriac and one LXX[L] manuscript persist in leaving out the word for "two," while another Lucianic manuscript omits "sons" (see COMMENT). The names of the sons are plausible for the period when the Ruth story is set. Kilyon appears in the Ugaritic onomasticon (*Le palais royal d'Ugarit*, III [1955], 37, text 15.81, line 1: *ki-li-ya-nu* and in four texts in alphabetic cuneiform); it shows the familiar *-ān* ending which becomes *-ōn* in such Hebrew names as Samson (Gordon, UT, § 8.58). It may be diminutive, "little vessel," or an abstraction, "destruction" (Joüon). LXX[B] and a mixed collection of LXX witnesses support the latter, with spellings suggesting Kilayon (cf. Isa 10:22). Mahlon (note the *ḥ*, a harsher sound than *h*) is more difficult, since it is unattested in the Late Bronze Age onomasticon or elsewhere in Hebrew. The Hebrew names Mahlah (a daughter of Zelophehad in Num 26:33 and several other passages and a Gileadite son [?] in I Chron 7:18), Mahli (a Levitic name in two generations in I Chron 6:19, 29[Hebrew, 4, 14] with I Chron 6:47[Hebrew, 32] among other references, and Mahalath (a daughter of Ishmael in Gen 28:9 and a granddaughter of David in II Chron 11:18) all suggest the existence of a root *mhl*. The ending *-ōn*, which one expects to find added to noun forms showing only the root letters rather than to already augmented noun forms (here with a preformative *m*), also points to *mhl* as the root. For this reason, derivation from Hebrew *ḥly/w*, meaning either "to be sick, sickly" or "to be sweet" (the latter assumed from Arabic attestation to lie behind existent Hebrew *Piel* forms) seems highly unlikely. Arabic *maḥala* is frequently cited by commentators, in the sense either of barrenness or craftiness. But Arabic etymologies appear particularly perilous in this group of otherwise early names. We simply do not yet know what Maḥlon and Kilyon mean.

The two names rhyme, and, as D. N. Freedman has observed to me, this is a rather common feature of legends and traditions; recall Eldad and Medad in Num 11:26–27, Jabal, Jubal, and Tubal(-cain) in Gen 4:20–22. Doubtless such rhyming helped the memory in the passing along of tradition, but that does not necessarily mean names which are linked in this manner are to be judged inauthentic or invented for the purpose of easy memory.

Ephrathites from Bethlehem of Judah. Bethlehem of Judah presumably names the town and the geographical district from which the family comes (cf. Ramoth-Gilead, Qedesh-Naphtali in Judg 4:6, etc.). Bethlehem was an established town from early in the Israelite period according to the biblical tradition, and it is probably attested as a part of the Jerusalem city-state in the Amarna period (fourteenth century B.C.E.) if the controversial reading of Knudtzon, *Die El-Amarna-Tafeln,* letter 290:16 stands (Bît-NIN.IB=Bît-Ninurta =Bît-Laḥmi); this has been challenged by J. Lewy, JBL 59 (1940), 519 ff., and more stringently by Z. Kallai and H. Tadmor, *Eretz-Israel* 9, the W. F. Albright volume (1969), 138–47, the latter proposing Beth-Horon instead. Its identification as Judahite distinguishes it from another Bethlehem in Zebulon (Josh 19:15), although it is doubtful that the story-teller is worried about confusion here; the designation Bethlehem of Judah seems standard (Judg 17: 7–9, 19:1–2, 18; I Sam 17:12).

We know little of Bethlehem's history archaeologically, except in the New Testament and subsequent eras. A topographic survey conducted by S. Gutman and A. Berman in 1969 has suggested that the general outlines of the Iron Age town stretch eastward and southward from the site of the Church of the Nativity—see *Revue Biblique* 77 (1970), 583–85 (with map). In addition, an extensive tomb deposit dated from the time of the Israelite monarchy has come to light from a site a short distance north of the church—see S. Saller, *Liber Annuus* 18 (1968), 153–80. The claim that Bethlehem was the political center for Judah prior to Jerusalem's ascendancy (M. Noth, *The History of Israel* [New York: Harper, 1958], p. 55) or that it was a focal point for anti-Jerusalem sentiment in the time of Micah (A. Alt, "Micah 2, 1–5," in his *Kleine Schriften zur Geschichte des Volkes Israel,* III [Munich: Beck, 1959], 373–81, approved by Gerleman) is based on conjecture, so far as archaeological indications are concerned. That Rehoboam fortified the town is recorded in II Chron 11:6; before that, II Sam 23:14 records an escapade of David's "mighty men" under the noses of a Philistine garrison occupying it.

A greater problem is the denotation of the term Ephrathites. Biblical evidence is slim and perplexing. David is called "the son of this (?) Ephrathite man" named Jesse in I Sam 17:12; otherwise, the gentilic with this spelling is used for people from Ephraim in the north (Judg 12:5; I Sam 1:1; I Kings 11:26). The two Calebite lists contained in I Chron 2:18–24 and 42–50a employ the names Ephrath (verse 19) and Ephrathah (verses 24, 50; cf. 4:4) for

Hezron's wife whom Caleb, Hezron's son, married after his father's death; Caleb is a descendant of Judah. At least the latter of these two lists is pre-exilic and lists a number of Judean towns as the names of offspring in the Calebite line (see J. M. Myers, *I Chronicles*, AB, vol 12, ad loc., and the studies of Noth and Albright there cited). Ephrathah, then, is in Judean territory but it is still not clear whether it names a city, a district, or a tribal sub-division. Gen 35:16, 19, and 48:7, containing references to Rachel's burial place, are notoriously problematic in that they refer to an Ephrath which one expects to lie near Bethel, explaining the name with "that is, Bethlehem." Just this also happens in Josh 15:59 in the LXX, where the entirety of the ninth province of Judah has dropped out by haplography (F. M. Cross and G. E. Wright, JBL 75 [1956], 221). Micah 5:2[Hebrew, 1] simply enjambs Bethlehem and Ephrathah, although the LXX here reads "Bethlehem, house of Ephrathah." Ruth 4:11 uses the two names in poetic parallelism (see there).

With a cue from Micah 5:2, a good case can be made for Ruth and for I Sam 17:12 that the term is ethnic, perhaps a designation for a "sub-phratry" (to use F. I. Andersen's term in *The Bible Translator* 20 [1969], 29–39), rather than geographical. Bethlehem would be one town of several where Ephrathites lived, while other than Ephrathites would also live in Bethlehem. The Genesis passages and Ps 132:6 stand opposed to this, as does the LXX on Josh 15:59; in them Ephrath(ah) is a place name. One can hazard the conclusion that Ruth represents the older state of affairs sociologically. In any event, it is clear that Ephrathah is the larger designation, viewed either territorially or from the point of view of numbers of people. Interestingly enough, the mosaic map of Madeba of the sixth century c.e. implies the same thing (see V. R. Gold, BA 21 [1958], 65 f.).

and there they settled. Qumran manuscript 4QRuth[a] joins two late Hebrew manuscripts and perhaps the Vulgate's *morabantur* (which may simply be translating the sense) in reading *wayyēšᵉbū,* "and they *dwelt.*" The rest of the tradition, including the LXX throughout, stays with the more unusual expression *wayyihyū,* "and they were" (cf. Exod 34:28, and frequently enough with this sense in other constructions). The shift may have come through harmonization to verse 4.

4. *took . . . wives.* The verb *nś'* is used here for "take," where most early Hebrew prose employs *lqḥ.* The former idiom occurs in the language of the Chronicler (Ezra 10:44; II Chron 11:21, 13:21, 24:3, and without the word "wives" but with that meaning in Ezra 9:2, 12 and Neh 13:25). The only probable preexilic use of the idiom is at Judg 21:23. To use this as a dating criterion is, however, dubious (see Introduction, p. 25).

Orpah. No entirely satisfactory explanation of this name has been proposed. Connecting it to Hebrew *'orep,* "back of the neck," implies invention by the story-teller to signal Orpah's decision to go home rather than to stay with Naomi. With four plausible names already introduced, however, we expect our story-teller to continue on the same track. Akkadian and Ugaritic offer a meaning having to do with "cloud," Ugaritic using it as the epithet for Ba'al as "Cloud-rider." The name of one of Ba'al's daughters, Ṭal(a)ya, probably means "Dew" or "Dewy," and is analogous in that it is derived from a natural phenomenon. On the other hand, Arabic *'urfa,* "mane," may offer a path to a solution as yet unclear. Most recent commentators (e.g. Joüon, Knight, Gerleman, Rudolph) speculate that the name is pure Moabite and thus obscure to us, but we do well to remember that what Moabite material we have shows minimal difference from Hebrew, so there is little refuge in this explanation.

Ruth. Of all the names in the story, Ruth's is the most tantalizingly obscure. Syriac renders *re'ūt,* "woman companion," throughout the book, but no LXX or Latin evidence supports the presence of a consonant *'ayn* in the name; for a West Semitic word to lose this guttural sound is unlikely in the extreme. A feminine name spelled *ru-ut-um* occurs in seventeenth-century Babylonian administrative texts; see W. F. Leemans, *Legal and Administrative Documents of the Time of Hammurabi and Samsuiluna* (Leiden: Brill, 1960), texts 89, 90, 122, 162, 163, and compare A. Salonen, *Agricultura Mesopotamica* (Helsinki: Suomalaisen Tiedeakatemian Toimituksia, 1968), pp. 444 f., who concludes far too much from the coincidence that Ruttum is a woman who happens to be involved in agricultural administration. Ruttum does probably derive from a general Semitic root *r'h,* but with the other names in our story showing Canaanite affiliation, this Old Babylonian evidence does little to help.

Derivations from *r'h,* "to see," or from late Hebrew *rtt,* "to tremble," are too forced, although they serve to explain certain rabbinic speculations. H. Bruppacher, in *Theologische Zeitschrift* 22 (1966), 12–18, has effectively reasserted Bertholet's derivation from *rwy,* "to drink one's fill," which has a *Piel* meaning "to satiate"; we can then posit a noun "satiation, refreshment." Support for this comes from the word *ryt* occurring in the Mesha inscription, line 12, which Albright vocalized *riyyat,* developed from presumed original *riwyat* meaning "satiation (for Chemosh and Moab)"; see BASOR 89 (February 1943), 16, n. 55; cf. Ryckmans, *Jaarbericht "Ex Oriente Lux"* 14 (1955–56), 81. This derivation would also explain a group of rabbinic interpretations. We can tentatively adopt this as the explanation of the name, and then await new information.

5. *her two lads and her husband.* Significantly, the story employs the term *yelādēhā,* whereas up to this point it has used the common word for sons, *bānīm.* The versions persist with the words they have been using to render "sons" in the preceding verses. The noun *yeled* usually designates young children in the J and E narratives of Genesis and in various episodes in Samuel and Kings (note Genesis 33 and II Samuel 12 throughout, for example, together with Exodus 2). Ruth 1:5 happens to be the only OT passage where married men are explicitly referred to with the term *yeled,* but the Joseph story, at Gen 37:30, 42:22, and 44:20, uses it of teenagers, and, most important, it designates the princes who counsel Rehoboam (wrongly, but acceptably) in I Kings 12:8 ff.=II Chron 10:8 ff. (See A. Malamat, BA 28 [1965], 41–46, 51, 54 f., reprinted in BAR³, pp. 171 ff.). The point is that it stands out here in Ruth for a crucial reason: it forms a very effective *inclusio* with 4:16, where Naomi takes a new *yeled* to her bosom.

Interestingly, the LXX, except for the pure hexaplaric witnesses, joins the Syriac and certain other versions (but *not* OL) in reversing the order: "Her husband and her two sons." Either order is understandable; the sons may be mentioned first as most recently under discussion (cf., for example, the order of Cain and Abel in Gen 4:2), or the men may be mentioned in the order of their deaths. The frequent use of chiasm in our story—the reversal of the order of a pair of words for rhetorical effect, here rounding out the circumstances from 1:2 to 1:5—argues that the MT order is preferable.

COMMENT

The story-teller opens by painting with broad brush-strokes the background for the special set of problems which will carry the plot forward. We are furnished a plausible geographical and historical setting, and introduced to six of the nine human protagonists, three of the major five. Tragedy is added to tragedy in rapid succession; all this is accomplished in five verses.

The brevity of the story's introduction may be misleading, however; there is more here than meets the eye and every word seems to have been carefully chosen. The NOTES have already pointed out a striking inclusio involving the word "lads" in verse 5 which the versions and the modern translations tend to ignore (see KJ, RSV, NEB, and the Jewish Publication Society of America rendering: all "sons"). In other ways, the versions were more "efficient" than is the received Hebrew text, for example in shortening the opening time reference or in eliminating what looks like overemphasis on the fact that there were *two* sons. This repeated use of "two," however, should not be treated lightly; the contrasts of ways in which two people act is an extremely important theme of the story, and we must have two daughters-in-law in the sequel. The story-teller's style will run to overemphasis at certain points, so the audience does well to take note of it (cf. the number of times "Moabitess" appears); efficiency is not the story-teller's aim, but impact is.

The opening phrase is a case in point. Hebrew style would certainly allow a story to plunge in at the second *wayhī*, at "there came," of verse 1, much as do the self-contained episodes in Gen 12:10 and 26:1; here is a famine starkly introduced with no indication of its cause. The preceding words provide, with 4:17b, a chronological inclusio or envelope for the story which is at the same time of immense importance for the story's purpose (even if that means only the final purpose for which the story was used). We start with the pre-monarchic situation, quite probably with a reference to the work of the so-called minor judges (see Boling, pp. 7–9) and we end with the name that effectively signals the arrival of dynastic monarchy: David. Those commentators are correct who will not seek a more exact time in which to place the story; it is not germane to search out one of the interstices of quiet within the turbulent course of events described in Judges. The opening phrase is general and vague, as befits a story, but the story is not unmindful of the historical situation in the amphictyonic period, nor of the institutions of the amphictyony. In short, the chronology makes sense but it is not to be pushed for exactitude.

There is, nevertheless, a curious emphasis on the judging of the judges. Rabbinic exegesis speculated widely, even to taking the noun as the object of the infinitive: "in the time when the judges were judged." That, it was noted, would be a time of upheaval. We have noted in the Introduction, pp. 35–36, the marked relationship by way of contrast of the story of Ruth to the one told in the last three chapters of Judges. One is tempted to push beyond the evidence and speculate about a meaning for this phrase along these lines: "Once, in a time when legal matters were properly handled. . . ."

It is enough, however, to take careful account of how scrupulous our story-teller will be about correct legal procedure and about attendant details. Notice how he points out that Elimelek and his family become resident aliens, so-journers, when they leave Judah to go to Moab. Notice the effect of the final words of verse 2: "there they settled," clearly to stay for some time. Notice that when Elimelek dies he is specifically designated "Naomi's husband"; she now moves to center stage with the legal status of widow, left with her two sons, surely guarantee enough that she would be cared for. The next dramatic step surrounds the phrase "about ten years"; given the direction in which the story will move, I am inclined to disagree with most commentators and to take this phrase as indicating the time span *after* the marriages of the two sons, rather than the entire length of the family's sojourn in Moab. There is then a striking effect as one compares the ten years of childless marriage for Ruth in Moab with the rapidity of resolution in 4:13 when she becomes Boaz' wife and immediately produces an heir.

In any case, what is established in 1:4–5 is a dire set of socio-legal circumstances, and the audience is quickly made aware of what must be resolved. Three women have now all become widows and there is now no male heir left in the family; the figure at center stage, Naomi, is in a land foreign to her and she has been away from home for at least a decade. There is drama in this tragic condition which will take the best of "judging" back home to straighten out.

How, then, is the audience to take the tragic series of events in Moab? Is this a sequence of retributions and punishment? Early Jewish exegesis certainly thought so. In the Targum to Ruth and in *Ruth Rabbah* of the Midrash, a series of speculations focuses on sin and retribution. The famine is related to the sin of Israel during the judges' period. Elimelek and his sons, all prominent leaders in Bethlehem, failed their people not only by forsaking them in their need and going off to Moab, but also by not leading them to amend their ways before the famine struck. Two Midrashic rabbis, known for their propensity to build homilies around proper names, find apparent evidence for arrogance in Elimelek's name, taking it to mean "to me shall the kingdom come" (*Ruth Rabbah* II.5). The two sons' names are also treated symbolically, Maḥlon being derived from Hebrew *mḥh*, "to blot out" and Kilyon from *klh*, "to perish." The Targum explicitly relates the death of the two sons to their transgression in marrying foreign women (in its additions both to verse 4 and to verse 5). *Ruth Rabbah*, on the other hand, keeps their death related to the earlier transgression of leaving Bethlehem for Moab, and dwells on God's patience in seeking to produce repentance in them by a series of warnings across the ten years before their ultimate retribution (*Ruth Rabbah* II.10).

There is perhaps a clue in this diversity of exegesis. It was by no means a unanimous opinion, for example, that there was something wrong in the two sons' marrying foreign women. Repeatedly the Midrash seems to be explaining that the law about admittance to the assembly of the Lord for Ammonites and Moabites in Deut 23:3[Hebrew, 23:4] does not pertain to marriage to women of these nations. Nor is there unanimity about whether the two wives had become proselytes; rather little is made of this point, and more emphasis seems to lie on the claim that both women were princesses, daughters of Eglon and descendants of Balak. Jewish tradition also makes relatively little use of the symbolic interpretation of names, the Targum indulging in this haggadic device not at all.

We are probably much nearer the truth, then, if we take the impact of the first five verses very much at face value. A family, made up of four members with authentic early Northwest Semitic names, did what some other families in biblical narratives did, namely left a land of temporary deprivation to live in a land of relatively greater prosperity (cf. Gen 12:10 ff., 26:1 ff.; II Kings 8:1 ff.; and the famine motif in the Joseph narrative). The occasion was presumably a drought; verse 6, in Section II, seems to imply a common kind of natural calamity (see COMMENT there, and one can compare the condition portrayed in Amos 4:7 [see Rudolph, p. 38]). To go to the Moabite plateau makes sense on two counts. First, the conditions on the two sides of the Jordan rift can vary appreciably. Second, there doubtless existed some sort of relationship between Israel and Moab, and perhaps even more specifically between Judah and Moab. The conquest stories imply at least partially friendly relations between Moab and Israel, in spite of the curious disjuncture geographically between Numbers 21 and 22–24 and in spite of Num 25:1–4; see especially Deut 2:8b–9, 28–29, where it appears that Moab actually did give Israel supplies. Moab's derivation from Lot in Gen 19:37 points in the same direction. And finally, David's sending of his parents to Moab for sanctuary (I Sam 22:3 f.), while it may relate to his having had a Moabite great-grandmother, quite probably builds on the reestablishment of a rapprochement.

The story, then, has a *plausible* setting. It is suggested here that plausibility is precisely what is sought, as opposed to historicity. To gain plausibility, the story-teller uses his knowledge of geography, climate, and historical background. These are not to get in the way; neither are we to be concerned whether it all happened in precisely this way.

Finally, the audience is to take note of the motif of the inexplicable calamities. Naomi, like Job in the prose story serving as the frame for the poem there, is rendered bereft of those things which provide her security and she cannot comprehend why (see 1:20–21). These two characters in OT stories are parallel, and the audience is meant to ask the question "Why?" with them. As in Job, there will be resolution of the calamities, but not a final answer to the question "Why?" And, as in Job, there is going to be some forthright complaining done before the resolution begins to take shape.

II. RETURNING HOME
(1:6–22)

1 6 She arose then, she and her *a* daughters-in-law, to return from the Moab plateau, *b* for she had heard in the Moab plateau *b* that Yahweh had seen to the needs of his people and given them food. 7 So she*c* set out from the place where she had been, her two daughters-in-law with her, *d* and they took the road to return to the land of Judah*d*. 8 Then Naomi said to her two*e* daughters-in-law,

> "Go, return each to her mother's*f* house.
> May Yahweh do with you the same kindness
> Which you have done for *g* the dead and for me*g*.
> 9 May Yahweh give you recompense,
> In that you find security,
> Each in the home of her husband."

She kissed them, and they raised their voices and wept. 10 But they said to her,

a LXX, OL, and Syriac add "two" here, in contrast to their tendency in the first five verses and in verse 8. MT has "two" in verses 7 and 8; the principle of adopting the more difficult reading favors not accepting it for this verse, because when something is expected but not there, the reading has a good chance of being original. What we should notice as well is the likelihood of a certain fluidity in textual transmission. That is, the versions are not simply interested in smoothing out what can be considered a rather redundant style; they vary reciprocally with MT on this matter of emphasizing that there are two sons and their two wives, which certainly indicates that the emphasis was in the story from the start.

b–b A small group of LXX manuscripts representing families that usually stay close to MT join the OL in omitting this entire clause. At some stage, a scribe's eye jumped from one "Moab" to the next, producing a haplography. The Armenian and part of the Ethiopic traditions omit only "in the Moab plateau," an obvious attempt to avoid redundancy. Most of the LXX witnesses (including LXX^{BL}) plus the Syriac read *they* heard"; see the NOTE.

c LXX^L: "Naomi." See the NOTE on verse 15.

d–d The Ruth Targum, usually very full in its text, omits this entire clause. The scribe's eye may have jumped from the *h* of '*mh*, "with her," to the *h* at the end of *yhwdh*, "Judah" (homoeoteleuton).

e LXX^B and most of the Lucianic manuscripts, with the Syriac, do not have the word "two." See *b–b* above.

f LXX^A and some other LXX manuscripts including minor Lucianic witnesses read some form of "father"; Syriac has, "your parents." See NOTE.

g–g Syriac: "with me and with my two sons who are dead." Compare what the Syriac does in 1:5, also reversing the order.

"No! With you we will return *to your people*."
11 To this Naomi responded,

"Turn back, my daughters'! Why come with me?
　　Have I more sons in my womb
　　　　Who could become husbands for you?
12 Turn back, my daughters, go along;
　　For I am too old to have a husband.
　　If I were to say 'I have hope!'—
　　　　If I were to have *this very night* a husband—
　　　　And if I were to bear sons,
13 For them would you wait until they were grown up?
　　For them would you restrain yourselves,
　　　　Not becoming anyone's wife?
　　No, my daughters!
　　For things go far more bitterly for me than for you.
　　Indeed, the hand of Yahweh has come out against me."

14 Again they raised their voices and wept, and then Orpah kissed her mother-in-law,* but Ruth clung to her. 15 She said,

"Look, your 'sister' has returned
　　To her people and to her god.
　　Turn back, after your 'sister.'"

16 Then Ruth said,

"Do not press me to abandon you,
　　To turn back from following you.

– Syriac: "to your land and to your people." This is an attractive reading if for no other reason than the fact that in verses 15 and 16 there are pairs of goals to which one returns. It would also make for a slightly better poetic line.

i LXX^A has here the imperative "go!" which reflects Hebrew *lēknāh*, not present in the text as we have it. We could explain its loss easily, because the word which follows where it would occur is *lammāh*, "why," which begins and ends with the same letters as *lēknāh*; a scribe's eye could easily have jumped from initial *l* to initial *l*, or from final *h* to final *h*. Myers has accepted the plus in his poetic reconstruction, with an eye to its aid to meter. But the same verbal root is in "come" in the question which immediately follows, and I doubt our story-teller, even with his love for repetition, would tolerate such an inelegant example of it. Instead, this longer reading probably represents conforming to verses 8 and 12.

j–j MT *hallayᵉlāh*, "the night," meaning "tonight," is doubtless original, but the Greek tradition had difficulties with the word. LXX^BAL and the Syriac omitted it, probably considering it indecent. OL's "today" tends in the same direction. Several LXX manuscripts apparently saw *hᵃlīlāh* in the Hebrew text they were translating (note the different *h* sound, representing a different Hebrew consonant), took it to mean "profaned," and translated with an even more explicit sexual connotation, along the lines of "if I were to be profaned by a man." (See Rahlfs, *Studie*, pp. 56 f., followed by Rudolph and Gerleman.)

k Syriac adds: "and she turned and went"; the entire LXX tradition has "and she returned to her people." See the NOTE.

For wherever you go, I will go;
  Where you lodge, I will lodge.
Your people become my people;
  Your God is now my God.
17 Where you die, I shall die
  ᶦAnd there be buriedᶦ.
Thus may Yahweh do to me,
  And thus may he add,
If even death will separate
  Me from you."

18 When she saw that she was determined to go with her, she stopped speaking to herᵐ (about it) 19 and the two of them went along until they came to Bethlehem.

When they arrived in Bethlehem, all the city was excited about them, and the women said, "Is it Naomi!" 20 She responded to them:

"Don't call me 'Sweet one,'
  Call me 'Bitter one.'
For Shadday has made me bitter indeed.
21 I was full when I went away,
  But empty Yahweh has brought me back.
ⁿWhy call me 'Sweet One'?ⁿ
  For Yahweh has testified against me
ᵒAnd Shadday has pronounced evil sentence on me."ᵒ

22 And so it was that Naomi returned, and Ruth the Moabitess her daughter-in-law was ᵖwith herᵖ, who had returned from the Moab plateau. Now as it happened, they arrived in Bethlehem at the beginning of barley harvest.

ᶦ⁻ᶦ The minor Lucianic LXX manuscripts omit this clause, but its absence would ruin both sense and meter; see the NOTE.

ᵐ LXX adds here *eti*, "further," suggesting Hebrew *'ōd*, while the Syriac explains by adding "to go back." The sense is clear enough from the context, however; my "about it" probably isn't needed either! Note that the style becomes very concise when the story makes transitions.

ⁿ⁻ⁿ LXX^BL'A begin with "and," the Vulgate with "therefore." The OL omits the entire question, possibly because the scribe's eye jumped from one "Yahweh" to the next.

ᵒ⁻ᵒ LXX^A and the minor Lucianic manuscripts omit the entire line.

ᵖ⁻ᵖ LXX^BL plus a few maverick minor LXX manuscripts omit, probably by an internal Greek haplography from *her* daughter-in-law to with *her*. The Syriac then adds an interesting Targum-like adjectival clause: "who wanted to return with her out of purity of heart."

NOTES

1:6. *She arose then, she and her daughters-in-law, to return . . . for she had heard.* Notice the effective bracket surrounding the first episode; it is closed at verse 22, when the story will revert to a singular verb with Naomi as subject. The Hebrew stays with singular verbs (literally, "she arose . . . and she returned") throughout verse 6 and on into verse 7. This is a bit unusual; after the subject has been made compound, the normal pattern is for the verb number to shift to plural, as it does in 1:1–2 and 1:7, for example. Typical among early prose passages that do this are Gen 9:23, 21:32, 24:50, 55–57, 61, 31:14, 33:7, 34:20, 44:14; Exod 15:1 (all in *J* or *E;* see GKC §§ 145s, 146f–h). As for the versions, they shift to plural verbs at various stages in the sequence. The LXX and OL have "they returned," and LXX "they had heard" (OL omits this verb); both revert to singular at the beginning of verse 7. Syriac shifts to plural at "they had heard" and Ethiopic shifts at the beginning of verse 7. In short, the progression from singular to plural is what is expected, and for just that reason the Hebrew as it stands is striking and calls for explanation. I suspect there are two purposes. The story-teller seeks to keep Naomi in the foreground until he sets the scene for her attempt to persuade the girls to go home, at the end of verse 7. Also, Naomi alone must be the subject of the verb "return" (Hebrew *šūb*), since it is not yet time to speak of either of the younger women "returning" to Judah. See the COMMENT.

7. *from the place where she had been.* The literal Hebrew ("the place which she was there") recalls the end of verse 2 (literally, "and they were there"). The sojourn in Moab is over. Joüon (*Commentaire,* p. 35) is quite wrong, then, to say that this verse adds nothing substantial to verse 6, because the rhetorical effect is superb. Our story-teller likes to use repetition at relatively long range like this to achieve effect. But further: in verse 2, it is Hebrew *šām* which expresses "there," while in verse 7 *šāmmāh* is used (usually meaning "thither," not "there"). Here the two forms mean the same thing and the variation is intentional, just as it is in Isa 34:15; Ezek 23:3, 32:22–30 (which has the short form at the beginning of units in verses 22, 24, 26, and the long form in verses 29 and 30). In Ruth, a similar effect is gained by the use of two different forms of the word for "security" in 1:9 and 3:1; the story-teller, in his subtle way, achieves a little variety even as he ties his story together with his key words.

they took the road to return to the land of Judah. With this clause, the Hebrew text finally shifts to the plural subject. The expression "to walk on/in the way" which is here rendered "took the road" uses a combination of Hebrew words which more frequently means to follow the example or practice of a predecessor (a good or bad king)—usual in the Deuteronomic histories and in Chronicles—or to follow a moral or immoral path—usual in the prophets and the wisdom literature. Fewer than twenty passages employ the idiom in the mundane meaning of "hit the road," and it happens that none but Ruth 1:7 follows it with an infinitive with preposition l^e. The obvious connotation would appear to be purposive: "they took the road in order to return" (with the vast majority of translations ancient and modern). Possible, however, is a more neutral connotation, along the lines of "the road which led back." What is at stake is the impact of the word "return"; see the COMMENT.

8. *Go, return.* Note the nice touch of reversing these two imperatives in verse 12. The combination occurs elsewhere, in Exod 4:19 (*J*); I Kings 19:15, 20; and II Kings 1:6.

each to her mother's house. The surprising word is "mother's." In Gen 38:11 and Lev 22:13, widows return each to her *fathers'* house; in Num 30:16; Deut 22:21; and Judg 19:2–3, young women whose marital situations have taken on other legal dimensions are connected to their fathers' houses. And, as has been noted, the versions frequently translated with variations on the theme "father's house." This evidence compels us, of course, to adopt "mother's" as original and to explain it!

Are their fathers dead? Since *each* is to return to a mother's house, we would have to reckon with two fatherless families, a bit of a coincidence. And then, Ruth 2:11 has Boaz mention Ruth's father (although the expression is probably part of a formula and may be irrelevant to whether her father is dead or alive). In any event, the assumption that the girls are fatherless is strained. Also questionable are a number of rationalizing explanations in the commentaries: Naomi thinks in her distress of her own motherhood (Ehrlich); mother knows best how to comfort (Keil); a hint of a matriarchal society (A. Lods, effectively opposed by Rudolph and D. R. Mace, *Hebrew Marriage* [1953], pp. 81 ff.); the midrashic claim that a proselyte legally has no father (Slotki, mentioned without approval).

It is more likely that we must reckon with a custom no longer known to us in detail. Probably Song of Songs 3:4 and 8:2 point to it, as does Gen 24:28. In Song of Songs, the lover (bride) longs to take her beloved (bridegroom) to her "mother's house," but it is difficult to be sure in the midst of this lush love poetry what custom may be involved. The picture in Genesis 24 is a little clearer. In verses 23–27, mention is made of a father's house by Abraham's servant to Rebekah, and Rebekah's response implies that there is such a thing. At verse 50, Rebekah's father Bethuel is named alongside Laban. It is as the drama turns toward the question of marriage permission for Rebekah at verse 28 that the locus changes to the "mother's house." The usual treatment in the commentaries (see, e.g. Speiser, *Genesis*, AB, vol. 1, pp. 177, 180 f.) is to assume Bethuel to be dead, verse 50 to be in need of emendation, and the mother's house of verse 28 to be the family center. With no pretense to have solved all of Genesis 24's problems, I propose that in some circle of custom, hinted at by the Song of Songs passages; Gen 24:28; and Ruth 1:8, the "mother's house" was the locus for matters pertinent to marriage, especially for discussion and planning for marriage.

If this proposal has merit, it means that Naomi's speech to the girls is neatly

rounded out; she begins by urging them to go back to their mothers' houses
and ends by picturing them each in the home of a new husband.

May Yahweh do with you the same kindness. This clause expresses an idiom
and a concept for which there is no easy English translation; see the COM-
MENT. The verb is given the full consonantal spelling of an imperfect form,
rather than the short spelling of the so-called jussive, but the jussive, expressing a wish, is clearly what is called for throughout Naomi's speech. The vowel
pointing supplied later in Hebrew tradition "read" the jussive (the $q^e r\bar{e}$
mechanism).

"With you" here is Hebrew *'immākem,* the first of seven places in Ruth
where what appears to be a masculine plural occurs with a feminine antecedent. The second such instance is "you have done" in the second half of this
verse; then there are "to you" in 1:9 and 11, "than for you" in 1:13, and "the
two of them" in 1:19b and 4:11. The standard explanation is that masculine
forms tend to supplant feminine ones in later OT books, notably in the work
of the Chronicler (Joüon, *Grammaire de l'hébreu biblique* [Rome: Institut
Biblique Pontifical, 1923], § 149b; cf. GKC §§ 135o and 144a). Myers
(MLLF, p. 20), has rightly questioned this, positing instead a "relatively early
dialectical peculiarity," but he missed a crucial feature which strengthens his
proposal. Each of the seven instances in Ruth occurs when the antecedent is
two women, Ruth and Orpah, or Naomi and Ruth, or Rachel and Leah. To
this evidence should be compared these passages (probably more are to be
found): Gen 31:9 (Rachel and Leah, and note that 31:5–6 employ the standard feminine suffix); I Sam 6:7 and 10 (a total of seven instances referring to
two cows which have just calved); Exod 1:21 (the two Hebrew midwives);
Judg 19:24 (three instances referring to the virgin daughter and the Levite's
concubine); Gen 19:9 (a similar motif to that in Judges 19, so that the antecedent of "them" is probably the two daughters of verse 8); Gen 18:20 (the sin
of two *cities,* which like most geographical designations in Hebrew are feminine); Judg 16:13 (two doorposts).

There must have been an early Hebrew feminine dual suffix which ended in
-m just as the masculine plural ending does but contrasted with the feminine
plural *-n.* Presumably the vowel pattern was the distinguishing feature. As
texts containing this old form were transmitted across the centuries, it was
generally forgotten and was replaced by the standard masculine and feminine
plural forms. But in a few places it survived. Since the Ruth text as we have it
is quite scrupulous in its correct use of gender, these relics must be regarded as
a distinct mark of archaic composition or at least of composition in a dialect
retaining an otherwise lost grammatical feature. It is noteworthy that the
forms containing it appear in the narrative frame (1:19b) as well as in
speeches. (I owe thanks to Francis I. Andersen for observation of this phenomenon and identification of most of the examples cited; see also Gordon, UT
§ 6.10).

9. *May Yahweh give you recompense, / In that you find security.* Literally,
"Yahweh give to you, and find security . . ." Here a jussive verb is followed
by an imperative attached to the conjunction "and." Most recent commentators agree with Joüon (*Grammaire* § 177h) in making the second clause in ef-

fect the object of the verb "give": Yahweh grant you to find repose. But Joüon's parallels from other OT passages are not at all convincing; in no instance is the second verb in his proposed parallels an imperative. The better analysis of the syntax here is still that of GKC § 110i, citing a group of passages where the jussive *is* followed by the imperative with "and." One of these may be Ruth 4:11 (see the sixth NOTE there). Compare Gen 12:2, 20:7, 45:18; Exod 3:10, 18:22; I Sam 12:17; I Kings 1:12; II Kings 5:10; and Ps 128:5. Frequently, as GKC points out, the imperative in this sequence expresses an intended consequence. But a problem remains: adopting this solution deprives us of a direct object for the verb "give."

At this point, the versions are suggestive. The LXX^L' manuscripts have *eleon*, "mercy," here, the same word they used in verse 8 to translate Hebrew *ḥesed*. The Syriac has *ḥsd'*, the cognate of *ḥesed*, but in verse 8 it had used *rḥm'*, "compassion." This evidence may mean that in the Hebrew texts from which these versions worked some direct object word was present; that it was *ḥesed* seems unlikely, because the style here is virtual poetry, and Hebrew prefers synonyms in parallelism to repetition of the same word. We expect a term at least partially synonymous with either the *ḥesed* of verse 8 or the "security" of the subsequent clause. Coming at the matter from another perspective, it is clear that our story-teller is very much given to using pregnant key words *twice* in his story, thus binding the story together neatly. For that reason, I am proposing that the lost direct object was a form of the word appearing in Boaz' wish for Ruth at 2:12, *maśkoret*, "reward for faithfulness, recompense." Such a term gathers up the notion of reciprocity expressed in verse 8 (Yahweh's *ḥesed* and your *ḥesed*), an important ingredient in the theology of Ruth. Some support can be gathered from Gen 15:1 and 30:18, where the word is *śākār* from the same root. (Compare the proposals of Myers, MLLF, p. 61, n. 3a).

they raised their voices and wept. All three of them? Perhaps not. Manuscript *a* from Qumran Cave 4 reads *qōlām* instead of MT *qōlān*, "their voices," which may reflect the old feminine dual again (see above, in the last NOTE on verse 8). That would mean only the two girls bewail the moment, and would make for a smoother transition to verse 10, where the two girls are the ones to speak. Notice, by the way, the opening of an inclusio which will be closed in verse 14.

10. *to her, "No!"* Retain MT without emendation (with Würthwein, Gerleman, and Ludwig Koehler and Walter Baumgartner, *Lexicon in Veteris Testamentum Libros* [Leiden: Brill, 1951–53], under *kī*, 1.7; against this are Joüon [*Commentaire*] and Rudolph). The Hebrew word *kī* is sometimes adversative (C. Brockelmann, *Hebräische Syntax* [Neukirchen: Kreis Moers, 1956], § 134a), amounting to "No, on the contrary . . . ," as in I Sam 2:16 and 10:19. There were at least two ways of saying this in Hebrew: *kī* could do it alone, as it does here, but more frequent is *lō' kī*. In verse 13, Hebrew *'al* will be used for substantially the same effect.

11. *womb.* Hebrew *mē'ay*, which is not the common term for womb, sometimes means "internal organs" in general, sometimes various parts of the gastrointestinal tract, and sometimes the location for what we might call

"gut-feelings." In three poetic passages, Gen 25:23; Isa 49:1; and Ps 71:6, it appears in parallelism with *beṭen,* the more common and prosaic word for belly, abdomen, and womb, in all three instances in contexts requiring the translation "womb." Of importance is the fact that in each of these three passages, *beṭen* is in the first or "A" position, our word in the second or "B" position. As R. G. Boling has shown in *Journal of Semitic Studies* 5 (1960), 221 ff., parallel words tend to be in fixed positions, and it is the poetic, often archaic words which are in the "B" position.

12. *Turn back, my daughters, go along.* Cf. first NOTE on 1:8. Since the imperative *lēknāh,* "go along," was written defectively (without the final *h*) here, the consonantal spelling was identical with Hebrew *lākēn,* "therefore," and that is what most of the LXX tradition translated.

too old to have a husband. How old would that be? If usual ancient Near Eastern procedure was followed, Naomi was probably married in her early to mid-teens, and had had her two sons by the time she was twenty. They in turn would have married by the time they were fifteen or so, to girls a bit younger. Ten years of childless marriage for them would bring us to the mid-forties for Naomi. Given the rigors of life in ancient Palestine, that would be years enough, almost certainly, for her to have reached the menopause. The story-teller will establish that Boaz and Naomi are of the same generation, and we can assume that Ruth was between 25 and 30 when the events in the story took place.

12–13. *If I were to say . . . If I were to have . . . And if I were to bear.* These are the three parts to the protasis (the "if . . ." clauses) of a highly complex conditional sentence. The apodosis (the "then . . ." clauses) takes the form of the pair of rhetorical questions in verse 13a. Each of the three parts contains a verb in the perfect tense, itself somewhat unusual since the hypothetical event has not occurred (see GKC § 106p), but greater interest attaches to the conjunctions which introduce parts two and three of the protasis: *gam . . . wᵉgam.* The former, with simple *gam* as conjunction, seems virtually to start the protasis anew. I can find only one good parallel to it: Ps 119:23. This verse also starts with *gam* followed by a perfect verb in a conditional protasis expressing what might happen but is not an actuality: "Though corrupt men were to sit to gossip about me, your servant meditates on your statutes" (AB). Psalm 119 is an acrostic poem, and in verses 17–24 each of the eight lines opens with a word beginning with *g*. There are not many Hebrew sentence-starting words which begin with *g* and the poet must have been hard put to it to carry it through. At verse 23, I suspect, he dug deep into the syntactic resources of the language and came up with a construction like the one found in part two of the three-part protasis in Ruth 1:12. Other pertinent passages, such as II Kings 8:1; Isa 26:12 (?); Ezek 24:5; Jer 13:26; and Mal 2:2 (?), all start with *wᵉgam* and a perfect verb, comparable to part three of the Ruth 1:12 protasis.

The important thing to notice here is the use made by the Ruth story-teller of unusual, but available, syntax. It may represent a dialect little attested in the biblical Hebrew we possess, but more likely it represents a regular potential of the language of which we happen to have a very slim number of examples. Its independence as a syntactic device makes quite possible an alternative translation to the one I have adopted at verse 12:

> "Turn back, my daughters, go along;
>   For I am too old to have a husband
>   That I might say: 'I have hope!'
> Why if I were to have this very night a husband
>   And if I were to bear sons . . ."

13. *For them . . . For them.* A much-discussed but unresolved problem is the meaning of *lāhēn* at the beginning of each of these rhetorical questions. As voweled in MT, the word is the same as the Aramaic one usually translated "therefore" at Dan 2:6, 9, 4:24, and in the Teima inscription, lines 8 and 10. On the other hand, the unanimous reading of the LXX, the Syriac, the Targum, and both the OL and the Vulgate, is "for them." Rudolph makes an important point: the Syriac version (in a dialect of Aramaic), the Targum (in Palestinian Aramaic), and the LXX tradition would have had no trouble with a familiar Aramaic word had one confronted them in the text at this point. This argues that the consonants *lhm*, not *lhn*, stood here, at least in one part of the Hebrew textual tradition in the last centuries B.C.E., meaning "for them" and referring to the hypothetical sons mentioned at the end of verse 12; alternatively, it argues that the consonants *lhn* could somehow be taken with this meaning.

Now a second consideration: *lāhēn*, "therefore," is unusual in Aramaic. There are frequent uses of a word *lāhēn* meaning "except, only, but," in Daniel and in the fifth-century Aramaic papyri from Elephantini (including the wisdom sayings of Ahiqar), and M. Lambert argued many years ago that something in this semantic area could fit the three Daniel passages mentioned at the beginning of this NOTE (*Revue des Études Juives* [1904], 274). If *lāhēn* must mean "therefore" in the three Daniel passages, it is probably a Hebrew loanword into Aramaic (so H. Bauer and P. Leander, *Grammatik der Biblisch-Aramäischen* [Halle: Niemeyer, 1929], § 68x). This in turn would open the way for accepting a proposal of Joüon which he himself rejects (pp. 39 f.) to the effect that we have here, and here only in biblical Hebrew, a particle pronounced as spelled in MT with the meaning "for this reason, therefore." His decision to reject this possibility stems from the repetition of the word in the second question, but given the poetic character of these lines this constitutes no problem in my opinion. These two possibilities, *lāhem*, "for them," or *lāhēn*, "therefore," constitute the only valid options in my opinion. We will have to reject Myers' proposal, which assumes a change in the second vowel from *ē* to *e* and produces a "to them" with a *feminine* suffix. His grounds for this (MLLF, p. 27) are "the constant confusion of gender in Ruth," but the demonstration that there are relics of an old feminine dual in Ruth (see the last NOTE on verse 8) virtually eliminates the evidence for such "confusion of gender." Likewise to be rejected are the proposals of Ehrlich and Gerleman, which seek to find an appropriate meaning for a feminine suffix.

Until new linguistic data shifts the balance, I incline to the reading reflected

in the versions. Furthermore, this word should be removed from consideration
as an Aramaism for the time being, as M. Wagner seems to agree by his failure
to include it in his study, *Die lexikalischen und grammatikalischen Aramaismen
im alttestamentlichen Hebräisch.* See the next NOTE.

   would you wait . . . would you restrain yourselves. These two verbs raise a
whole group of interesting questions about meaning and about the date of Ruth.
Both verbs are rare, the second one being unique (a *hapax legomenon*) here.
Both are commonly assessed as Aramaisms (the only two in Ruth according to
M. Wagner in *Die . . . Aramaismen*), and consequently they are taken as signs
of late composition for the book (cf. Introduction, p. 24). Both are considered
late verbs for other reasons as well. And to complicate the issue, the second
verb shows a peculiar spelling which makes it uncertain what root it comes
from.

   "Would you wait" renders Hebrew *tᵉśabbērnāh,* a *Piel* form of the root *śbr;*
see Isa 38:18; Pss 104:27, 119:166, 145:15; and Esther 9:1 for the other
verbs (all *Piel*) from this root, and Pss 119:116 and 146:5 for derivative nouns.
All of these but the Esther passage are poetic and speak of hope placed in God.
While the majority of these passages are probably exilic or postexilic in date,
the chronological placement of Hezekiah's lament in Isa 38:10–20 and of Ps
104 is by no means certain; a preexilic date is preferable for both. As for the
claim that the root *śbr* is an Aramaism, there is a grave problem. The assumed Aramaic cognate has *s* (*samekh*) as its first letter, as opposed to the
ś (*śīn*) in the biblical passages. Much later, around the turn of the era, the distinction between these two sibilants had been lost, but if we are to assume that
biblical Hebrew borrowed the Aramaic root from "Empire Aramaic," that is the
Aramaic of the Elephantini papyri and of Ezra and Daniel, it should have
borrowed the root with the sibilant *s,* not *ś.* On balance, it is much more likely
that our word is archaic and native Hebrew, while the Aramaic develops from a
parallel dialect. The occurrence here in Ruth would constitute the only preexilic
survival of the verb with a "secular" meaning.

   "Would you restrain yourselves" is a probable rendering for Hebrew
tēʿāgēnāh (as the Masoretic vowel pointing has it). This has to be a reflexive
(*Niphal*) form, but of what root? If the root be *ʿgn,* the spelling ought to show
a doubled *n,* the first *n* being the root letter and the second being the beginning
sound of the second person feminine plural ending *-nāh.* If the root be *ʿgw/y,*
as has long been proposed, the spelling should show a *y* before the ending. In
fact, some medieval Hebrew manuscripts do spell the word with this *y.* Most
recent commentaries, however, assume *ʿgn,* and point to cognate words in the
Aramaic of the Mishnah and in Syriac and to special terms in mishnaic
Hebrew. But the choice is by no means so clear-cut. In the Mishnah, there are
a number of places where the topic under debate is the legal situation of bereft
women the whereabouts of whose husbands is in doubt; here appears the
technical Hebrew term *ʿagūnāh* and other derivatives, chiefly Aramaic, of a root
ʿgn. What we have here are technical terms employed in a highly complex
legal context. The backgrounds of both the legal tradition and the technical
terminology are obscure; it is even possible that the whole business may derive
from exegesis of our one verse in Ruth! Hence it is dubious procedure to use

the mishnaic data to determine the meaning in Ruth and to decide what the original root is; it can only hint at the meaning as it has developed. It is even more dubious to claim that the late usage is significant in determining the date of the book of Ruth. As for the Syriac cognate, all it really says is that there was a Semitic root *'gn* with a meaning along the lines of "to cast down, to humiliate" in use in the early centuries c.e. Countering that, Ugaritic now attests a personal name *bn 'gw* in lists of predominantly Semitic names; no meaning is as yet clear for the *'gw* element in this name, but it is evidence for the existence of an early Semitic root *'gw*, probably as a verb which could take a god-name as its subject or object.

The upshot? Reticence. These verbs are not clear Aramaisms and cannot by themselves be used as evidence for a late date for the book of Ruth. We can be confident about the meaning of the first verb, but for the second our translation must depend upon the dictates of parallelism and context, together with the evidence of the early translations such as the LXX and the OL, both of which select verbs meaning "to hold back."

No. Hebrew *'al.* Compare Gen 19:18; Judg 19:23; II Sam 13:16; II Kings 3:13 and 4:16; these are five other places where Hebrew *'al* serves as an independent negative in speeches embedded in narratives comparable in style to Ruth. II Kings 3:13 and the probably genuine variant represented by the LXX of II Sam 13:16 have *kī* following, just as does our passage, to introduce reasons for the strong negative.

For things go far more bitterly for me than for you. An admitted paraphrase of the literal "For bitter to me much from you." The proposed translation follows from answers to two questions about this clause. First, what is the relation between this clause and the one which immediately follows? Answer: in view of the story-teller's style elsewhere in Ruth, they may well be a poetic couplet and show virtually synonymous parallelism. Second, what is the mood of Naomi's words just here? Answer: in view of the accusation, built around the very word "bitter" and directed against God in 1:20–21, the story-teller artistically has Naomi move here from reasoning with the girls to the accusing outcry of the complaint (see the COMMENT). Naomi's bitterness is an internal emotion (Ehrlich), just as the bitterness in the similar idiom of Isa 38:17 is. Naomi accuses, and she makes her case against God stronger by comparing her condition to that of her daughters-in-law. This understanding of the clause demands that *mikkem*, "from you," be an instance of the comparative use of the preposition *min* after an adjective or an adjective verb (cf. esp. Gen 26:16).

Commentators defend several alternative interpretations; in fact the reading was apparently so ambiguous that the Syriac offered two of them together: "Because I am very bitter on your account, and for me it is more bitter than (for) you." The problem here is the meaning of *mikkem;* the second Syriac alternative takes it as comparative, but the first is also possible. Francis Brown, Samuel R. Driver, and Charles A. Briggs, *A Hebrew and English Lexicon of the Old Testament* (Oxford University Press, Clarendon, 1907 and since), p. 580, 2.f, lists a number of passages where *min* means "on account of," but only in Ps 119:53 is it clearly used with persons ("the wicked") as the object of the preposition. This would yield the first Syriac alternative with the sense of "because of what you have done." Joüon correctly objects (*Commentaire*, p. 41) that such an interpretation fits the context poorly. What have the young women done to cause Naomi's bitterness? If we take "on account of you" to mean "because of the situation in which you find yourselves," we are assuming an ellipsis and giving *min* a nuance for which there is no biblical parallel.

Joüon and Rudolph assume a different sort of ellipsis. They get across the comparative degree but overburden the usual sense of *min:* "I am much too unfortunate for you (implied: to be around)." (See the objections of T. C. Vriezen in *Von Ugarit nach Qumran*, Eissfeldt Festschrift [Berlin: Töpelmann, 1958], pp. 268 f., esp. n. 8, which Rudolph in his commentary, p. 41, fails to answer adequately.)

One final note: if the two clauses here are in synonymous parallelism, a tempting but highly conjectural possibility suggests itself. In verse 21, two names for God appear in one of Naomi's complaints. M. Dahood has called attention to the likelihood that Hebrew *me'ōd*, the adverb meaning "much, many," sometimes hides an old epithet for God: the Strong One (*Psalms III*, AB, vol. 17A, p. XL, and the passages there cited). *Me'ōd* appears here, translated "far" in our paraphrase. If one were to assume that Hebrew *mar*, "bitter," is what is left of a causative verb form (such as occurs in verse 20), one could reconstruct a fine parallel couplet:

> For the Strong One has brought more bitterness to me than to you;
> Indeed, the hand of Yahweh has come out against me.

Such a reading would require a minor emendation here, but would strongly suggest that a similar parallelism once existed in verse 20, something like:

> *hēmar šadday lī*
> *mā'ēd <rāb ittī>*
> Shadday has brought bitterness upon me;
> The Strong One <has put me to trial>.

> (We might reconstruct any of several predicates in
> the second line, including the *'ānāh bi*, "testified
> against me," of 1:21.)

Obviously, speculation of this sort is dangerously lacking in controls, and the observation is made only to stimulate inquiry. Indeed, Gen 26:16, which offers comparable syntax to our passage, uses the adverb "much, many" in its familiar meaning, and sense can be made of the Hebrew of this verse as it stands. The proposed translation seems the safest in the present state of our knowledge.

14. *Again they raised their voices and wept, and then Orpah kissed her mother-in-law.* The Hebrew verb translated "they raised" is spelled without the expected root letter *aleph* (see the grammars), but the idiom is so standard that no doubt the Masoretic *qᵉrē* tradition is correct in supplying it. For the idiom "raise voice and weep" in narratives, cf. Gen 21:16 (*E*), 27:38 (*J*), 29:11 (*J*); Judg 21:2; I Sam 24:17, 30:4; II Sam 3:32, 13:36; Job 2:12; and of course Ruth 1:9. These are interesting and important contrasts between 1:9 and 1:14, however. In 1:9, the order is kissing and lamenting; here it is reversed (chiasm).

The effect is to bracket artistically the episode of persuasion. Notice also that the kiss in 1:14 goes from Orpah to Naomi, while in 1:9 it was Naomi who kissed the young women. This is just the signal needed to say that the relationship between Orpah and Naomi is here terminated; we need no further words (although the versions tend to supply them) to make clear that here Orpah takes her leave. A one-way kiss of farewell is usual in stories of the conclusion of intimate relationships; cf. Gen 31:8; II Sam 19:40; and I Kings 19:20. In Ruth, the story-teller uses what might be termed a reciprocal kiss of farewell; not until Orpah kisses her mother-in-law is what was begun in 1:9 concluded. Meanwhile, the word used for Ruth's response to Naomi's urging is thrown into even bolder relief.

but Ruth clung to her. The Hebrew word order, by putting Ruth's name ahead of the verb, points up the contrast. For the verb *dbq*, "to cling," see also 2:8, 21 and 23, and the COMMENT. The LXX uses *ēkolouthēsen*, "she followed after," rather than *ekollēthē* from *kollaō*, "to adhere," though forms and derivatives of the latter are regularly used to translate *dbq* in the LXX and are employed at 2:8, 21 and 23. Quite probably the similarity of sound in these two Greek words led to a hearing error on the part of a scribe; the Old Latin, close to the Greek tradition, keeps the more colorful nuance here with *adesit* (=*adhaesit*). It should be noted, however, that both the OL and the LXX shift to a different verb to translate *dbq* in chapter 2 (OL: *adjungere*, "to attach, join to"); does this mean that both versions sensed that there should be a special meaning in 1:14?

15. *She said.* All LXX witnesses name Naomi as the speaker, and all but one minor manuscript add "to Ruth." Naomi will be explicitly named in verse 18, and LXX^L' manuscripts name Ruth there. Note a similar tradition in LXX^L at 1:7. R. Thornhill, VT 3 (1953), 241 ff., describes eighteen such "interpretative additions" in LXX^B, ascribing them to the greater precision of the Greek language; the Hebrew language, he says, does not need to indicate a change in subject. In fact, however, Hebrew is usually explicit when the subject changes, and one senses a tendency throughout Ruth not to name the speaker, but rather to let the content of the speech identify him or her. This imparts an even greater importance to the speeches and urges the audience to focus attention on every word. See further the Introduction, p. 17.

your 'sister.' To translate Hebrew *yᵉbimtēk* as "your sister-in-law" is to avoid an interesting question and perhaps to miss something the story-teller wanted his audience to notice. All other clear occurrences in the OT of the root to which this noun is related are in Deut 25:5–10 and Gen 38:8, the first a case-law unit and the second a story; in both they constitute technical terminology having to do with levirate marriage (see Introduction, p. 27, and the COMMENTS on Sections IV and V). Specifically, the same noun that occurs here in Ruth is used in Deut 25:7 and 9 to designate a widow in relation to her husband's brother; a corresponding masculine noun designates the brother in relation to her, while a denominative verb names the action of fulfilling levirate responsibility. In Ruth this language appears to be generic rather than legal. True, the husbands of the two young women were brothers, but it is difficult to see how that has any *legal* bearing on the relationship of Ruth and Orpah.

A possible approach to a different meaning is afforded by Ugaritic *ybmt limm*, a frequent epithet of the goddess 'Anat in the Ba'al myth cycle. Albright once proposed (*apud* M. Burrows, BASOR 77 [February 1940], 6–7; cf. *Archaeology and the Religion of Israel*[5], pp. 73 and 193, n. 16) to read the epithet as "progenitress of peoples," and assigned to the root *ybm* a meaning along the lines of "create" (cf. UT, Glossary, no. 1065). M. Dahood (AB, vol. 17) has followed Albright's lead and proposed *ybm* as the verb in Ps 68:17[Hebrew, 18c], with just this meaning. It is possible that this old root eventually developed a noun meaning "fertile woman, marriageable woman," but this is highly conjectural. It happens that such a meaning would rather nicely pick up the theme of Naomi's urging in 1:8–9, 13—go home to new, fruitful marriages. However as things now stand, greater clarity about the Ugaritic term is needed before it can help us understand the Ruth term.

The proposed translation represents an attempt to stay close to the technical levirate terminology but to avoid being so specific. "Sister" should be understood to mean something like "fellow-woman in the face of prevailing conditions and custom." The idea is akin to the meaning "sister" has come to have in various social movements in contemporary America. Perhaps the LXX was on the same track when it coined *sunnumphos*, "fellow-bride, fellow-maiden" for use here and here alone.

But a suspicion lingers: did the story-teller use a word which might suggest levirate custom quite purposefully? Apparently Naomi speaks with that custom in mind in 1:11–13, only to reject it because she is too old to have more sons, and even if she could it would be too long a wait for the young women. Perhaps the story-teller chose his word to keep levirate custom in the minds of his audience, a hint of the resolution to come. If he did, he also creates irony: it is Orpah to whom the word refers, while it is Ruth to whom it will be in some sense applicable.

To her people and to her god. Since the Hebrew word for God is regularly plural in form, it is possible to read "her gods," and the LXX did just that. The Syriac has only "to the house of her kin," leaving out any mention of deity. The Targum, however, reads for "her god" the epithet "her fear." In all likelihood the singular is correct. It is the Greek tradition which makes the change to plural, out of pious concern. Note the nice progression from here to the end of 1:16: her god . . . your God . . . my God.

Turn back. Syriac and LXX[BL] attest an attractive addition here, namely "you too" following the imperative. It is good Hebrew idiom (see Joüon, *Commentaire*, p. 42), presumably reflecting a lost *gam 'att*, and may represent an independent text tradition.

16. *To turn back from following you.* By adding only the one syllable needed to express the preposition "from," the story-teller skillfully has Ruth choose the opposite direction from the one Naomi has been urging in verse 15: "Turn back, following your sister" yields to "Don't urge me to turn back from following you." At the risk of awkwardness, a translation must reflect the similarity in wording.

lodge. The Hebrew verb *lwn/lyn* rarely if ever means "live" or "settle." Apparently we are to take "Wherever you go, I will go; wherever you lodge, I will lodge" to refer to the current journey homeward to Bethlehem, and this verb to have its usual sense of "stay the night." Our story-teller is up to his old trick of using a word twice at crucial points; see 3:13!

Your People become my people; / Your God is now my God. The Hebrew is as succinct as it can be: "Your people my people, your God my God." With this couplet, however, something decisive is said; note again the verbal correspondence to what is said of Orpah in verse 15.

17. *Thus may Yahweh do to me, / And thus may he add, / If even death will separate / Me from you.* This solemn oath formulary appears only here and in eleven passages in Samuel and Kings. The first part of it was presumably accompanied by a symbolic gesture, something like our index finger across the throat. Deep behind this lay, in all probability, a ritual act involving the slaughter of animals, to whom the one swearing the oath equated himself. The best indications that this is so are the portrayals of elaborate covenant ratifications, containing solemn oaths, in Gen 15:7–17 and Jer 34:18–20. The slaughtered and split animals represent what the oath-taker invites God to do to him if he fails to keep the oath.

Note several interesting things about the formulary. First, the basic form probably ran: Thus may God (or the gods: *'elōhīm* can mean both; the verb's number determines the choice) do to me and thus may he (they) add, if/if not (*'im/'im lō'*) a specified future condition occurs. When the speaker used *'im*, "if," the subsequent words expressed what he was determined would *not* happen (I Sam 3:17, 25:22; I Kings 20:10; II Kings 6:31); when he used *'im lō'*, "if not," he was determined that what followed *would* happen (II Sam 19:14). Second, only here in Ruth and at I Sam 20:13 is Yahweh, instead of Elohim, the name of the deity; in both these passages there is a purpose for this shift from the basic form, in that there is an important emphasis on Yahweh in these passages. Third, seven of the formulary passages in Samuel, Kings, and Ruth use neither *'im* nor *'im lō'* to introduce the concluding clause; they all use the conjunction *kī* (I Sam 14:44, 20:13; II Sam 3:9; I Kings 2:23, 19:2; and Ruth 1:17) or *kī 'im* (II Sam 3:35, although many read *lī 'im* here). In this group of seven there is a variety of syntax in the concluding clause; several appear to use *kī* with the same effect as *'im lō'*, that is, *kī* is followed by what the speaker was determined would happen (I Kings 19:2; I Sam 14:44; II Sam 3:9; and II Kings 2:23 are all ambiguous). There is enough variation in this group which employs *kī*, however, for other considerations to play a part in determining the precise meaning.

Two proposals about our passage are warranted. First, since Ruth has just said in verse 17a, "Where you die, I shall die and there be buried," the oath comprising verse 17b should bear at least some relation to this assertion, especially to its last word. Sufficient archaeological data is now available concerning burial practices in Palestine in biblical times to show how it can be said that people are not separated even by death. Family tombs were the dominant feature, and after decomposition of the flesh was complete, bones were gathered in a common repository in the tomb, either in an ossuary or in a pit cut out of the rock in the floor of the tomb. A body might be placed in the tomb to decompose, or, if the family member died at some distance from home, the body could be interred at the distant spot and then the bones gathered up several months later for transport to the family tomb and deposit in the repository (cf. II Sam 21:10–14). Following Eric Meyers (*BA* 33 [1970], 10–17), we can see in this practice the background for the concept of being "gathered to one's fathers." In this sense, but not in the sense of a blessed reunion after death, Ruth's final and climactic sentence promises loyalty to death and to the grave, including the adoption of Israelite burial custom. This interpretation opposes the position of most recent commentators, who tend to find the idea "only" implied in the word order (which places the noun "death" ahead of the verb, thus emphasizing the noun): "for death alone will separate me from you." Our translation also sees the noun as emphasized. See further P. W. Lapp, *Pittsburgh Perspective* 19 (1968), 139–56; and E. F. Campbell, Jr., ibid., 22 (1971), 105–19.

The second proposal is that the story-teller purposely altered the standard form here by using the name Yahweh instead of Elohim. This is the only time the name occurs on Ruth's lips, while Naomi, Boaz, and the citizens of Bethlehem use it quite frequently in a variety of blessing and complaint forms. This final part of Ruth's dramatic avowal is climactic in another sense then: with no particular fanfare, she joins the people whose God is Yahweh.

19. *the two of them.* Again the feminine dual (cf. last NOTE on 1:8). It should be noted, however, that the infinitive construct used to say "until they came" in this verse has a feminine *plural* suffix, although with an unusual form (cf. Jer 8:7).

When they arrived in Bethlehem. Two good LXX witnesses, B and the Lucianic group, omit this clause; even more striking, the Hexapla, while having it, did not mark it with an asterisk, as it usually does when something is to be added to the Greek to bring it into conformity with the Hebrew tradition (see R. Thornhill, VT 3 [1953], 240, n. 1). Is the clause after all purely redundant? The answer must be emphatically in the negative. This sentence begins a new episode, as the opening *wayhī* (which I have not reflected in the translation as such) clearly indicates. Quite probably the Hebrew text lying behind the two shorter Greek witnesses had undergone a haplography, the scribe's eye jumping from the first Bethlehem to the second one. See the COMMENT.

was excited. Masoretic pointing makes the verb a *Niphal* of the root *hwm;* the same form of the same verb expresses the excitement in the Israelite camp when the ark of the covenant was brought in I Sam 4:5 and the rejoicing at Solomon's anointing which dismayed Adonijah in I Kings 1:45. The Greek approaches the same sense in all three places with "resound," and the Syriac captures it better with "rejoice." The reaction is certainly one more of delight than of pity; hence, the question which follows, "Is it Naomi," is not to be taken as expressing shock at what time and suffering have done to Naomi, but rather delighted recognition.

the women. It is only the feminine plural verb form which shows that it is the townswomen who surround the returning pair; at 4:14, when this "chorus" returns, they are specifically identified as "the women." Apparently, the absence of any identifying noun here is original; the LXX and OL translate the verb as plural, but their languages do not show gender distinction, so the nice touch of the Hebrew is lost in these versions. A small group of LXX witnesses employs a singular verb, making it Naomi who asks (rhetorically) "Is it Naomi," and then proceeds to answer ironically. This must be an inner-Greek development, one which in its own way conveys very well Naomi's bitterness but removes the townswomen. This is an interesting alternative, but it is difficult to see how it can be original.

20. *'Sweet one'* . . . *'Bitter one.'* Cf. the NOTE on 1:2, "Naomi"; if our analysis of its meaning there is correct, a slight twist has been given it here in order to yield the contrast sought for. The two terms appear to be adjectival substantives; it is noteworthy that *Mara*, "Bitter one," is spelled with a final *aleph* instead of the expected Hebrew feminine ending *he*, presumably an Aramaized spelling (so most commentaries, and note that many late Hebrew manuscripts do spell the name with *he*). No compelling explanation for the unusual spelling has been given; it is not technically an Aramaism (i.e., an influence from the Aramaic language), but may reflect only an orthographic change in the course of scribal transmission.

For Shadday has made me bitter indeed. See NOTE on 1:13. Shadday is an ancient name or epithet probably meaning "The One of the Mountains" as W. F. Albright demonstrated in JBL 54 (1935), 180–93, and confirmed in his more recent writing (see esp. *The Biblical Period from Abraham to Ezra*, rev. ed. [New York and Evanston: Harper and Row, 1963], pp. 13 f. and nn. 35–36). What is not yet certain is whether *šadday* is an epithet of Canaanite El or a name brought with the patriarchs from their Amorite heritage. On this and other pertinent matters, see M. Weippert, *Zeitschrift der deutschen morgenländischen Gesellschaft* 111 (1961), 42–62; F. M. Cross, *Harvard Theological Review* 55 (1962), 244–50; L. R. Bailey, JBL 87 (1968), 434–38; and J. Oullette, JBL 88 (1969), 470 f. I am also indebted for what follows to communications with D. N. Freedman.

The distribution of the name Shadday in the OT is instructive. There are six occurrences in *P* materials in Genesis (17:1, 28:3, 35:11, 43:14, 48:3) and Exod 6:3, the last being the statement of *P*'s theological axiom that it was as Shadday that God appeared to the patriarchs, only to make himself known to Moses as Yahweh. These six attestations are strong evidence that Shadday was indeed in use in patriarchal times. Then, there are thirty-one occurrences in Job, together with four in late prophetic passages: Ezek 1:24, 10:5; Isa 13:6; and Joel 1:15. The Job usage is indirect support of the contention that Shadday goes with the patriarchal period; the Job book wishes to have its hero placed in patriarchal times and archaizes to help get this across. The late prophetic passages are also archaistic, representative of a nostalgic revival.

Another group of occurrences suggests that Shadday was also in use in the period of the judges. The name appears in three premonarchic poems: Gen 49:25 (read *'ēl-šadday*); Num 24:4 and 16; and in Ps 68:14[Hebrew, 15], which is at least as early as the time of the united monarchy. With this early attestation belong three names of tribal leaders repeated in Numbers 1, 2, 7, and 10: *Šᵉdē-'ūr* (doubtless *šadday-'ūr*), *Ṣuri-Šadday*, and *'Ammi-Šadday*. The antiquity of the last of these three is confirmed by the appearance of a name on a figurine from a late fourteenth-century Egyptian tomb, which amounts to *Šaddē-*

1. A terra-cotta mold, together with a modern cast made from it, found in 1963 in the destruction debris of a tenth-century B.C.E. cultic building at Taanach in northern Israel. A class of such figurines, from a number of sites, shows a woman holding a tambourine over her left breast. Quite possibly these figurines attest the singing and dancing of the women of Israel in the time of the monarchy.

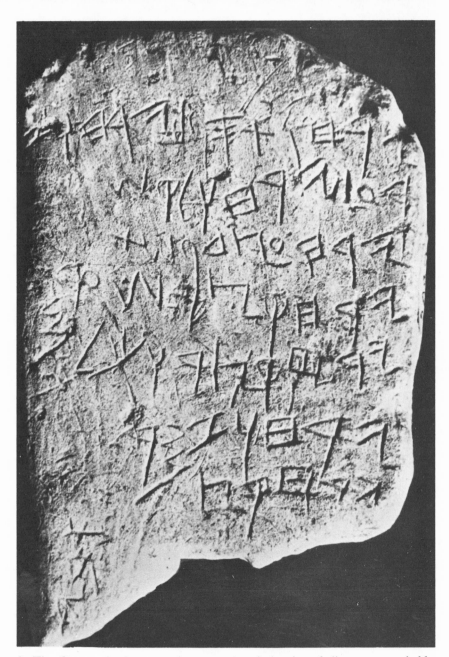

3. The Gezer calendar, a tenth-century inscription in soft limestone, probably done by a student practicing his writing. It outlines the agricultural year beginning in the fall. The fourth line reads, "His month is harvest of barley," and the fifth, "His month is harvest and festivity." These months would correspond to April–May and May–June.

2. (Opposite) Bethlehem as sketched by the masterful David Roberts in 1839. The view looks southeastward. Through a dip in the nearer hills, above the complex of buildings in the center which includes the Church of the Nativity, and also at a comparable point near the left edge, one catches glimpses of the Dead Sea. Beyond it are the hills of Moab. While Roberts' drawing emphasizes the hilliness of the landscape, the area around the village is fertile and well-cultivated.

4. A part of the frieze portraying Sennacherib's siege of Lachish in 701 B.C.E., from his palace walls in Nineveh. Notice the captive Judean women at the far left of the upper row; they wear long capes reaching from their foreheads to their ankles—perhaps the sort of garment in which Ruth carried home the grain from the threshing floor.

'*ammi* when transcribed from Egyptian orthography; the elements are simply reversed from those in '*Ammi-Šadday*. From the period of the monarchy we have two occurrences in Psalms, at 91:1 and now, as M. Dahood has shown, at 32:4 (*Psalms I, 1–50* [AB, vol. 16], NOTE on 32:4, "O Shaddai").

What these statistics suggest is that Shadday was a current name for God in the patriarchal and amphictyonic periods, and was revived in the exilic period. In between, during the monarchy, it was in virtual eclipse. Psalm 32, a thanksgiving song, and Psalm 91, a royal hymn of trust, both almost certainly preexilic, knew it, and so did the Ruth story-teller. He uses it in connection with his intent to place the Ruth story in the amphictyonic period, but it is also noteworthy that he uses it with a knowledge of its appropriateness to the context.

Its appropriateness ties to the fact that in Naomi's words and in Ps 32:4, the name appears in contexts of lament/complaint. Shadday seems to have had a special connection to judging, and to the conferring of deliverance or punishment, blessing or curse (cf. among the oldest passages Gen 49:25 and Num 24:4, 16, together with the Genesis *P* passages). Little wonder that the Job poet would adopt the name Shadday to designate Job's antagonist (see esp. Job 27:2!), against whom, like Naomi here, Job hurls his accusations of injustice.

21. *empty*. Once again, note the story-teller's use of long-range interconnectedness; the word will be picked up at 3:17.

testified against me . . . pronounced evil sentence on me. The Greek and the OL read the first verb as a *Piel* of Hebrew '*nh*, "to be bowed down," and thus translate into a good poetic parallelism: "laid me low . . . afflicted me." The MT maintained a tradition, however, in which the first verb is a *Qal* of the root '*nh*, commonly "to answer." Most recent commentators correctly work with the MT here, and agree in giving the verb a juridical flavor; compare the commandment against false witness (Exod 20:16; Deut 5:20), as well as II Sam 1:16 in which David sentences the Amalekite who had killed Saul, and probably Isa 59:12. As Talmon has correctly pointed out, in discussing the so-called Yabneh-yam ostracon (a late seventh-century B.C.E. letter written in ink on a potsherd found at Yabneh-yam on the Israeli coast in 1960), the idiom is '*nh* plus the preposition *b*ᵉ when the testimony presents detrimental evidence, '*nh l*ᵉ when the testimony presents favorable evidence (as it will, in a fine rhetorical bracketing, in Ruth 4:10–11); see S. Talmon, BASOR 176 (December 1964), 34.

If the first verb in this obviously poetic couplet has a legal nuance, so should the second one. The proposed translation draws support from Exod 5:22; Num 11:11; I Kings 17:20; and probably from Josh 24:20 and Micah 4:6. In all of these passages, the idiom involving the causative of *r*ʿ and the preposition *b*ᵉ hovers poised between God's decision and his action, between verdict and punishment. In Exod 5:22 and Num 11:11 it is Moses, and in I Kings 17:20 it is Elijah, who confront God's presumed verdict and the onset of punishment, and dare to call it into question by seeking its reversal. In our passage, some of the same tension is present, as Naomi complains about a presumed verdict and a punishment which has come to vital reality.

22. *who had returned*. By placing the accent on the penultimate syllable of

the Hebrew word, the MT makes this a perfect tense verb with a definite article prefixed. The article then becomes in effect a relative pronoun. This is not unheard of elsewhere in the OT (see the standard grammars), but it seems to be a particularly favorite syntactical device in the MT of Ruth (see 2:6 and 4:3). Final accent, on the other hand, would yield a participle with definite article, and the effect would be virtually the same. Perhaps Joüon (*Commentaire*, p. 45) is right in concluding that some emphasis is being placed on the pastness of the action by the Masoretes. In any event, the word is essential to the story and is not redundant (with apologies to Würthwein); its antecedent is almost certainly Ruth, and here the procession of uses of the verb "return" reaches its culmination (see the COMMENT).

Now as it happened, they arrived. The Hebrew is *wehēmmāh bā'ū.* The second of these words is a verb in the perfect tense, representing a shift from the string of imperfects with *waw*-consecutive which have carried the narrative, and thus suggesting a distinct break in the flow of action. The first word, *wehēmmāh,* is usually taken to be the third masculine plural independent pronoun "they," but that would leave two things to explain. Why state the pronoun explicitly when the finite verb form expresses it inherently—is some emphasis on the pronoun intended, as though it were they and not someone else who arrived? And second, why the wrong gender, masculine, when the antecedent is the pair of women? In light of what has been proposed in the third NOTE to 1:8 about a feminine dual suffix, it cannot easily be asserted that the text of Ruth betrays confusion about the grammatical distinction of gender. In fact, the masculine pronoun here would be the one and only clear instance in the book of such confusion.

The probable explanation has been pointed out to me by D. Noel Freedman. *Hēmmāh* here is not the pronoun, but the emphasizing particle found in Ugaritic epic as *hm/hmt,* and now identified by Dahood in Pss 9:7[Hebrew, 8], 23:4, 27:2, 37:9, 38:10[Hebrew, 11], 43:3, 48:5[Hebrew, 6], 56:6[Hebrew, 7], and 107:24, as well as in Isa 24:14, 35:2, and 44:9. See especially *Psalms I, 1–50* (AB, vol. 16), p. 56, and the literature there cited, and then Dahood's treatment of each of the passages cited.

Hēmmāh has here, then, much the same impact as does *hinnēh* in Ruth 2:4 and 4:1, emphasizing the entire circumstance and injecting a note of sly and good-humored wonder: "Well, what do you know, they arrived in Bethlehem for barley harvest—just the right time!"

COMMENT

With the backdrop in place, the first episode of the story can commence. But how far does it extend? To the end of the poignant exchange between Naomi and Ruth, as they resume their journey to Bethlehem (verse 18)? To the moment of their arrival at Bethlehem (verse 19a)? Or to the very end of the chapter, after Naomi's clamorous reunion with her friends of younger days?

It matters that we decide about this question. For the answer is bound up with the skill of our story-teller, who, as he successfully binds his whole story into a unity, also likes to round off each episode, giving to each its own particular emphasis. He uses his favorite literary devices, inclusio and repetition of key words, to do this. At the same time he develops important theological themes through the medium of the attitudes of his characters expressed in the words they speak. With these indicators as guides, it seems to me inescapable that the first scene extends from verse 6 to the end of the chapter.

First, inclusio. We have seen examples of this device already. An inclusio based on the word "lad(s)" links the introduction of the story in 1:1–5 to its conclusion in the final verses of the original book (4:16–17). In 1:6–22 the words "return from the Moab plateau" serve the same bracketing purpose; they open the scene with what is contemplated and close it with its accomplishment. Assuming that the inclusio is intentional, we can say that Naomi's return from Moab is not complete simply upon her arrival in Bethlehem, but must include the delightful (to the audience), if distinctly angry, outburst of Naomi as she is welcomed back.

As for the repetition of a key word, several recent commentators have pointed out the importance of the verb "to return," Hebrew šûb; see especially Hertzberg's commentary on Ruth in Das Alte Testament Deutsch and the perceptive article by Werner Dommershausen, "Leitwortstil in der Ruthrolle," in *Theologie im Wandel*, pp. 394–407, esp. pp. 396 ff. This verb (translated as both "return" and "turn back") occurs twelve times in the seventeen verses, twice as part of the inclusio just mentioned. But frequency of occurrence is less important than the way in which this verb carries the whole movement and tension of the episode. If we stay with the Masoretic inflection of the verb as a singular in 1:6 (see the NOTE there), the first appearance of "return" in the series has Naomi alone as subject. In verse 7, the subject of the verb has become plural; Naomi and the two younger women are en route to return to Judah—but it is probably the case that here the verb has more the sense of "which led back to Judah." For in verse 8, Naomi makes her first attempt to persuade the young women to "return" to their proper home in Moab, just as she is headed for hers. In verse 10, however, the daughters-in-law insist that they wish to return with Naomi to her people; this evokes her remarkable speech in verses 11–13, where the occurrences of the verb šûb must be rendered "turn back" at the beginnings of verses 11 and 12. The urging this time has its effect, at least upon Orpah; without explicitly saying so—a nice touch—the story-teller dismisses Orpah to do just what Naomi is doing: return. In verse 14, then, Naomi and Orpah alone are doing the appropriate thing, and suddenly the spotlight focuses upon Ruth, who up to this point has been simply one of Naomi's two daughters-in-law acting in concert. Naomi now presses Ruth, in verse 15, to return as her sensible "sister" has returned, but Ruth responds that Naomi should cease urging her to abandon her and "turn back." Orpah and Naomi are each on their way home (Naomi will use the verb once more in verse 21—an important part of the series to which we shall return later)—but what of Ruth? The answer comes, of course, in the climactic verse of the episode, its final one, verse 22. As the NOTE there has pointed out, the clause "who had returned from the Moab plateau" must refer to Ruth, as it explicitly does in 2:6 (but see 4:3!). Our story-teller has cleverly done even more than we expected with the phrase that functions as his inclusio; at the beginning it is Naomi who returns from the Moab plateau, but at the end it is Ruth!

This is the point at which to turn briefly to the question of proselytization. Does all this mean that Ruth, a Moabitess, is now technically a convert to Judaism? The Targum, after all, intersperses a veritable catechetical lesson into the words of verses 16 and 17: first Ruth explicitly says "I desire to be proselytized," and thereafter each line of her memorable poem of loyalty responds to instructions from Naomi concerning the practices of Judaism. But if conversion is a prominent theme in the story-teller's mind, he is far from obvious in saying so. The focus in Ruth's words is upon human loyalty and self-renouncing fidelity. Almost buried in her pledge is "your people become my people; your God is now my God," with expressions of her attachment to Naomi on either side of it. The only time in the entire book when the name Yahweh occurs on Ruth's lips comes in the oath formula in verse 17; it seems almost incidental—almost, but not quite! For it is thrown into a certain prominence by yet another example of our story-teller's use of inclusio: the dramatic exchange among Naomi and the young women which fills verses 8–17 begins with the use of Yahweh's name in a blessing formula from Naomi's mouth and ends with it in an oath formula from Ruth's. We are not to ignore what this means, but if we are to call it "conversion" or "proselytization," we shall have to do so from the theological point of view of the Ruth story. And about that this first major episode also has much to say.

For the Ruth story-teller, God's activity is intimately bound up with the mundane affairs and interrelationships of human beings. True, in 1:6 and in 4:13 the narration will refer to those "acts" of God which we would call providential. After a period of famine (1:6), Yahweh has now "visited" his people and given them food. This word "visit," Hebrew *pqd*, has profound theological overtones, for in the dynamics of the covenant relationship between God and his people it indicates the sovereign God's assessing the loyalty of his vassal people and bringing upon them either blessing for their obedience to him or cursing for their rebellion. In the background of "Yahweh had seen to the needs of his people and given them food" is the whole edifice of the covenantal model which has called forth much attention in OT study of the past two decades (as a convenient presentation of the whole subject, see Delbert R. Hillers, *Covenant: The History of an Idea* [Johns Hopkins University Press, 1969]). The striking thing about the theology of the Ruth book, however, is that it brings the lofty concept of covenant into vital contact with day-to-day life, not at the royal court or in the temple, but right here in the narrow compass of village life.

This may seem a good deal to conclude from the use of the word *pqd* in 1:6, and certainly overburdens "and Yahweh made her conceive" in 4:13. But these two passages are only the places where we encounter the narration expressing the activity of God.

It is in the conversation of the principal figures of the story that the portrayal of covenant on the local level comes to full expression. Consider Naomi's words in 1:8–9, which include one of the key covenantal terms of the

OT, Hebrew *ḥesed*. Addressing herself to the two young women, she invokes Yahweh to confer upon them the same "kindness" which they have shown to the three now dead men of the family and to her. I choose the word "kindness" advisedly, to underscore a dimension to the concept of *ḥesed* which must be emphasized as an important ingredient of covenant relationship; *ḥesed* is more than the loyalty which one expects if he stands in covenant with another person—it is that extra which both establishes and sustains covenant. It is more than ordinary human loyalty; it imitates the divine initiative which comes without being deserved.

The other uses of the word in the Ruth story show this extraordinary dimension. In 2:20, *ḥesed* will once again be God's action, as a new and promising turn of events opens a new avenue of life for Naomi and Ruth. In 3:10, on the other hand, Boaz invokes Yahweh's blessing upon Ruth because of two acts of *ḥesed* she has performed, the second surpassing the first. We must leave further development of this theme to the COMMENTS on Sections III and IV, and to the part of the Introduction dealing with the theology of the Ruth book. Suffice it to reiterate that a close intertwining of human and divine behavior is being established through the use of such pregnant terms as *ḥesed* with both God and humans as doers of it. For more probing into the meaning of *ḥesed*, see Nelson Glueck's monograph first published in 1927, entitled Ḥesed *in the Bible,* in its 1967 translation, and the important correctives in the forthcoming study by Katherine D. Sakenfeld based on her 1970 Harvard University doctoral dissertation.

The same correlation between divine and human activity is brought out again and again in the language of the Ruth story. Note, for example, the two occurrences of the term "security," the first in this same blessing of Naomi upon her daughters-in-law, in 1:9. She invokes Yahweh's blessing in the form of a rest, a stability, a condition of well-being, which she assumes will be theirs in new marriages in their own homeland of Moab. Yahweh, through human agency, is to be the author of such repose in 1:9, but it strikes the eye (or the ear!) when a very similar noun from the same Hebrew root—*mᵉnūḥāh* in 1:9, *mānōᵃḥ* in 3:1—appears in Naomi's expression of the security *she* will engineer for Ruth in the plan cooked up for the threshing floor. As for the covenant dimension, one ought not to let pass unnoticed the term *dbq*, "to cling, to cleave to," in 1:14, or the theme of "not abandoning" in 1:16 (cf. 2:20); both are prominent words in covenant terminology.

The story-teller's point is twofold. Divine will and human action go hand in hand. Further, terms which in OT theology play an important part in covenant language are displayed from the point of view of how simple human actions fulfill the aims of covenant. "Covenant" in actual name is not here, but the whole content of covenant is very much present.

How does all this relate to the question from which we started: In what sense are we to talk about conversion or proselytization here? In the Ruth book what is being portrayed is human beings doing what God's will for human interrelationship calls forth. They practice *ḥesed*. We are not told what it is that inspires them to do this, but in our story the life of integrity, of human responsibility and kindness—kindness above and beyond the call of duty—is portrayed, recommended, and shown to be attainable. What makes Ruth a true Israelite is that she, like others in the story who are generically Israelites, behaves like one. There is clearly a comprehensive character to such a view. It sees ḥesed as something within the capability of human beings of whatever lineage. In Ruth there is no miracle, no heady manifestation of God's power, no fanfare. In that sense, there is no "conversion" at all, but simply a living out of the way of Yahweh, and of the way of Yahweh's people when they are at their best—and this she had been doing already on Moabite soil according to Naomi's words in 1:8, before there was a question of "return" to Judah.

There is one further facet of this matter of Ruth's "return" which must not be missed. Clearly in chapter 1, as again in chapter 4, there is a character in the drama who contrasts with the person upon whom the audience has its eye fixed. In chapter 1, it is Orpah who is in a sense Ruth's foil. Orpah does what Naomi tells her to do, returns to her home. She returns bearing the blessing of Yahweh invoked by Naomi, to find, we are left to hope, the security Naomi has prayed for. We must be careful, then, in pushing the contrast with Ruth. Orpah is not the opposite of Ruth; she too has been commended for her ḥesed to the dead and to her mother-in-law. Orpah is a worthy woman; therefore, Ruth is all the more so. Again we are invited to look at the extraordinary in Ruth, not to focus on some imagined failure in Orpah.

Once one knows the whole story of Ruth, it is perhaps natural to focus attention upon Ruth. Her justly famous words in 1:16–17 are obviously pivotal to the first episode. But in chapter 1, one must not lose sight of the chief figure and her words and actions—and that chief figure is Naomi. The first five verses of the story have invited us to identify with Naomi, bereft of husband and sons, faced with a series of blows which seem inexplicable. Now, in the first major episode, her response to these tragedies develops step by step into an outcry, virtually an accusation, against God. The crucial words occur in the last line of 1:13 and in verses 20–21 (see the NOTES); in fact, however, all of Naomi's words in chapter 1 suggest the mood of complaint.

Naomi sets out to return to Judah. Inexplicably, the story-teller has Naomi's daughters-in-law begin the journey with her—or is it inexplicable? Perhaps the story-teller has yet one more set-back to portray, a set-back which Naomi must inflict upon herself. She must come to the realization that even these two companions must be left behind. If this be the story's intent, then even Naomi's first words of dismissal in 1:8–9 carry the undertone of complaint. The two young women can expect to find security with new husbands, but for Naomi such a prospect is out of the question. Implicit in 1:8–9, this mood becomes explicit in 1:11–13. True, this second speech is ostensibly addressed to the girls, but it is also indirectly addressed to the one whom Naomi perceives as really at fault—God! Her exaggerated picture of what cannot be points out the predicament the younger women would be in, and also gets across that Naomi is bereft, too old to bear children, hopeless, and bitter, far more bitter than the other two have reason to be. In verse 13, the rhetorical questions give way to what is clearly an accusation: all of this is from the hand of Yahweh. Once back in Bethlehem, among her old friends, Naomi's complaint bursts out even more directly. Once "sweet," she is now bitter; once full, she is now empty. The whole theme of "returning" takes on an ironic twist when she uses the causative of our key word *šūb:* Yahweh has caused me to return—empty.

The most interesting figure of speech in Naomi's words, however, is that of the legal case in the concluding couplet of verse 21. She portrays herself as defendant in a legal action in which the charges and the testimony are in effect unknown to her, in which she has been deemed guilty, in which punishment has already been meted out. Worst of all, her antagonist is God. This style recalls other Old Testament complaints in certain of the Psalms and in early narrative but most notably in Jeremiah and Job. Job's attempt to bring a case against God is well-known. In Jeremiah, parallel to the theme of suit and countersuit between God and his people (see Jer 2:4–13 with 2:29–31), the prophet himself attempts to press a legal case against God, in the face of evidence that God has failed to be just and fair. The crucial verse is 12:1, as correctly understood by W. L. Holladay in JBL 81 (1962), 49–51; it amounts to saying: "Yahweh, I will bring a case against you even though you will turn out to be innocent." The rhetorical effect of Jeremiah's suit as parallel to Israel's suit against God has been probed in an important but not easily accessible study by P. K. McCarter in *McCormick Quarterly* 23 (1970), 130–41. For our purposes here, McCarter's concluding point is significant: not only is complaint tolerated by God, but it can even be the *proper* stance of a person who takes God seriously! Anyone who ascribes full sovereignty to a just and merciful God may expect to encounter the problem of theodicy, and to wrestle with that problem is no sin, even when it leads to an attempt to put God on trial. Petulant Jonah, earnest Jeremiah, persistent Job—Naomi stands in their company.

Only as we move on into the rest of the story do we sense how many themes have been opened up in chapter 1 for resolution in the sequel. Concerning Ruth herself, most of these themes are introduced by key words, such as "security" and *ḥesed* already mentioned, which all appear again at crucial points. We can add two more such terms, whose impact of meaning is perhaps less but whose literary impact is great: "to cling" in 1:14, repeated in 2:8, 21, 23, and "to lodge" in 1:16, repeated at 3:13. As for Naomi, notice the word "empty" in 1:21, which will appear again very effectively at 3:17.

The most elaborate example of this linkage of themes is present in 1:11–13, but we encounter real difficulties in describing it. In her attempt to dissuade her daughters-in-law from accompanying her, Naomi imagines circumstances which reflect some form of levirate marriage practice, the practice by which a relative of a married man who dies before having fathered an heir takes the widow so as to sire an offspring who will be the dead man's heir and will continue his name. We have only two passages in the OT which can be used to illuminate Naomi's intent, Genesis 38 and Deut 25:5–10. The casuistic legal unit in Deuteronomy describes circumstances where brothers of the dead man are the ones who must carry out the practice. Genesis 38 portrays just these circumstances, but ends by having the father-in-law fulfill the function without his realizing it. Naomi's theoretical picture expands this in two ways. In verse 11, she implies that if she were already pregnant with sons, they could do the levirate duty. In verses 12–13 her picture is even more bizarre, to the point of a double application of levirate practice: she must find a relative of her husband to sire two sons who would in turn do the brother's duty for the two younger widows. The question will concern us further in the interpretation of chapters 3 and 4. What must be noticed now is that the story-teller has brought in a hint of a complex practice which will turn out to be applicable later in the story. He nails down the allusion to levirate marriage by introducing in 1:15 the special word "sister" (see the NOTE), which certainly must connect in some way to levirate practice.

Having focused on Naomi's return in a mood of complaint, and on the "return" of Ruth, whose unobtrusive but extraordinary loyalty will prove to be the answer both to external difficulties and to internal resentment, the first episode draws to a close. Almost playfully, but certainly with delicious irony, the story-teller brings down the curtain on Act I with Naomi complaining about her emptiness while Ruth, the very person who will bring about an end to Naomi's emptiness, stands there, apparently unnoticed. End of Act I, but not without providing the link to what lies immediately ahead: "Now . . . they arrived in Bethlehem at the beginning of barley harvest."

III. AMID *ALIEN* CORN?

(2:1-23)

2 1 Naomi had a "covenant-brother" through her husband, a man of substance, from the same sub-tribe as Elimelek, and his name was Boaz*a*.

2 Ruth *bthe Moabitessb* now said to Naomi, "I am going out to the field and glean barley spears after someone*c* in whose eyes I find favor." She*d* said to her, "Go ahead, my daughter." 3 So she set out and came and gleaned in the field after the harvesters. Now her luck brought her to the plot of the field belonging to Boaz, who was of the same sub-tribe as Elimelek. 4 Then Boaz came from Bethlehem, and he said to the harvesters, "Yahweh be with you!" They replied to him, "Yahweh bless you!" 5 Then Boaz said to his*e* young man who was overseeing the harvesters: "To whom does this young woman belong?" 6 *f*The young man who was overseeing the harvesters*f* replied, "She's a*g* Moabite girl, the one who returned with Naomi from the Moab plateau. 7 She asked, 'May I glean [   ].' "

8 Then Boaz said to Ruth,

"Hear me well, my daughter;
  Do not go to glean in another field,
  And also do not leave*h* this one.

---

a LXX*B* and manuscripts of the LXX representing all groupings except Lucianic: Boos. LXX*L*, in some other LXX manuscripts, Theodoret, and the OL: Booz. After the name, the Armenian tradition has "and he gave to Naomi a widow's house in which to live." This provides an answer to a question the story-teller chose to avoid: how were the widows to survive after their return?

b-b The Syro-Hexapla, probably in error, marks "the Moabitess" with an obelus indicating an addition in the Greek which the Hebrew lacks; but MT has it. Just possibly, this attests an early Hebrew text-form which lacked "the Moabitess."

c Syriac: "the worker."

d LXX frequently adds the name of speakers, especially since Greek does not show gender distinction in verbal conjugation. Here, only LXX*L* adds "Naomi," and then adds "Ruth" at the beginning of verse 3.

e LXX*A* and Vulgate omit "his."

f-f Vulgate omits, reading simply "who responded." Syriac omits the identifying clause and reads, "and the youth responded and said."

g LXX*BL* read the definite article.

h The spelling is curious. Expected is *ta͏ᶜabᵉrī*, but here it is *ta͏ᶜabūrī*. See comparable vocalizations in verbs in Exod 18:26 and Prov 14:3. Some Kennicott manuscripts attest the expected spelling. Could this be an archaic spelling (Myers)?

But right here attach yourself to my girls.

9 Keep your eyes on the field which they are harvesting
>And go along after them.

I am commanding the young people not to bother you.
>'Should you get thirsty,' go over to the vessels
>>And drink from what the young people have drawn."

10 ʲShe fell on her face, bowing down to the earth, and said to him,

"Why have I found favor in your eyes
>So that you take special note of me,
>Though I am a foreigner?"ʲ

11 Boaz answered, and said to her,

"It has been made quite clear to me
>All you have done forᵏ your mother-in-law,
>>After the death of your husband,
>And how you forsook your father and your mother,
>>And the land of your kin,
>>And came to a people which you did not know previously.

12 ˡMay Yahweh grant your action due recompense
>And may your payment be full from Yahweh the God of
>>Israelˡ
>Under whose wings you have come to seek refuge."

13 And she said,

"May I continue to find favor in your eyes, my lord.
>Because you have comforted me
>And because you have spoken to the heart of your
>>maid-servant.

ⁱ⁻ⁱ Another spelling problem. The root is ṣmʾ, and in most forms retains the *aleph*. Here and at Judg 4:19 the *aleph* is missing, and the verb is vocalized as though it were a third weak (*lamed-he*) verb.

ʲ⁻ʲ Syriac freely: "And she fell upon her face to the ground, and bowed down to him, and said, 'Because of this I have found grace in your eyes, to consider me when I am a stranger.'" The word-play (see NOTE) is thereby dissolved and missed.

ᵏ Hebrew ʾet, "with," but here in the sense proposed. The LXX tradition shows confusion in rendering an ambiguous situation in the Hebrew, some manuscripts using the dative, some *meta* with genitive, "along with," and one *meta* with the accusative, "after, next after."

ˡ⁻ˡ Syriac freely and tersely: May the Lord God of Israel recompense you and may he give you your wage."

Why, as for me, I am not even as (worthy as) one of your
    maid-servants!"

14 And Boaz said *m*to her*m* at eating time,

"*n*Draw near*n* here and partake of the*o* bread,
    And dip your morsel in the sour wine."

So she sat beside the harvesters, and he heaped up for her some
parched grain, and she ate and was satisfied *p*and had some left
over.*p* 15 Then she rose to glean, and Boaz commanded his young
people,

"*q*Also between the sheaves she shall glean;
    Do not bother her.*q*
16 And even pull out some for her from the handfuls,
    *r*And leave it behind*r*;
    And she shall glean
    And you will not rebuke her."

17 So she gleaned in the field until evening, and when she had
beaten out what she had gleaned, it came to about an ephah*s* of
barley. 18 She lifted it up and went to the city, and her mother-in-
law saw what she had gleaned; then she *t*brought out and gave*t* to
her what was left over*u* from her satisfying meal. 19 Her mother-in-
law said to her,

"Where did you glean today
    And where did you work?
    May the one who had regard for you be blessed."

m–m MT lacks the expected *mappiq* in the *he* of the word meaning "to her," a
grammatical peculiarity attested also at Num 32:42 and Zech 5:11.
    n–n Hebrew *gōšī* for expected *gešī*; cf. Josh 3:9; I Sam 14:38; II Chron 29:21;
Bauer and Leander, *Historische Grammatik*, p. 367, proposed an analogy to *bō'ī*,
"come," but this explanation is weak. Together with the vocalization of the verb
noted at *h* in verse 8, we may have indications of dialect variation.
    o LXX*L*: "my bread"; OL: "your bread."
    p–p The OL and one minor LXX manuscript lack the final verb. Vulgate: "and she
carried away a left-over"; is the Vulgate anticipating verse 18?
    q–q Vulgate: "even if she wants to reap with you, do not deter her."
    r–r LXX*B*: "and she shall eat"; three minor Lucianic manuscripts then show con-
flation: "and leave it and she shall eat it." The explanation probably lies in the similarity of the Greek words *phagetae* and *apheta*.
    s The OL apparently misconstrued Hebrew '*ēpāh* or one of the variety of Greek
transliterations of the word (*ōiphi, uphi, iphe*, etc.). As a result, OL has "and it happened when she had toted up the barley," and has no indication of the measure. It re-
peats this whole phrase after "gleaned" in verse 18.
    t–t Syriac simplifies to one verb: "gave."
    u LXX*L'* adds "to eat."

So she told her mother-in-law with whom she had worked, and said, "*The name of the man with whom I worked today is Boaz.*"
20 And Naomi said to her daughter-in-law,

> "*Blessed be he by Yahweh*
> Who has not forsaken his *hesed*
> With the living and with the dead!"

And Naomi said to her,

> "The man is closely related to us
> He is one of our circle of redeemers."

21 Then Ruth, the Moabitess, said,

> "There's more! He said to me,
> 'With the young people who are mine you stay close
> Until they have finished all *the harvest which is mine.*' "

22 And Naomi said to Ruth her daughter-in-law,

> "It is better, my daughter, that you go out with his young women;
> Then they will not be rough with you *in another field.*"

23 So she stuck close to Boaz' young women to glean, until the completion*z* of the barley harvest and the wheat harvest. Then she stayed (at home) with her mother-in-law.

v–v Syriac rearranges the word order so that Boaz comes first in Ruth's words, diminishing the effect. See the NOTE.

w–w One de Rossi manuscript, the Syriac, and the OL: "Blessed is Yahweh."

x–x Syriac and Vulgate lack these words and use simply a possessive pronoun for "who are mine" earlier in the verse.

y–y Syriac: "in the field of someone you don't know."

z MT reads *Qal, keḷōt;* LXX seems to have read *Piel, kalḷōt,* although the difference in meaning between the two conjugations is minimal in the infinitive construct syntactical construction. LXX*L'* employs the indicative, "they completed."

NOTES

2:1. *Naomi had . . . through her husband.* Literally, "to Naomi . . . to her husband."

"covenant-brother." The Hebrew consonants are *myd',* to be vocalized *meyuddā',* the *Pual* participle form of the familiar root *yd',* "to know." Jewish scribal tradition, however, read a noun from the same root, namely *mōda',* and some thirty-nine Kennicott manuscripts show the consonants for this vocalization, *mwd'.* It is generally accepted that *meyuddā'* designates a close

friend, an intimate, in the seven (if ours be included) passages where it occurs in the OT. *Mōda'*, which appears elsewhere only in Prov 7:4, is taken as a designation of a blood relative. At Ruth 3:2, to round out the picture, there occurs the only instance of another noun derivative of root *yd'*, the noun *mōda'atānū*.

Faced with the generally accepted meanings, with the thirty-nine Hebrew manuscripts showing *w* for *y*, and with the fact that the LXX uses the same term to translate here and at 3:2, most commentators adopt *mōda'* and the meaning "relative." But then why did consonantal *myd'* intrude here? Surely the book of Ruth is about kin responsibilities. Can this be a clue to an archaic societal picture?

One of the passages in which *mᵉyuddā'* occurs is II Kings 10:11. This is the report of Jehu's purge of the house of Ahab, in the course of which he exterminates, according to MT and LXX^B, "all his big-shots (*gᵉdōlāw*) and his *mᵉyuddā'īm*, and his priests." The LXX^L' manuscripts, however, read this way: "all of his *gō'ᵉlīm* [English: "kinsmen"], and his *mᵉyuddā'īm*, and his big-shots and his priests." Recent studies of the LXX, spurred on by the discovery of the Qumran scrolls, have led text critics to pay much closer attention to what this "proto-Lucianic" family attests, especially in certain places in Samuel and Kings. (For details, see the summation in the first chapter of J. D. Shenkel, *Chronology and Recensional Development in the Greek Text of Kings*, and esp. the work of Thackeray, Barthélemy, and Cross which he cites.) Throughout II Kings, the Lucianic family attests the existence of a Hebrew text rather independent of, and in some places superior to, the mainstream Hebrew text form which becomes the MT. At II Kings 10:11 a superior reading seems to be preserved. The list of Jehu's victims neatly joins two natural pairs, first those with close social ties and second those in prominent political and religious posts. For our purposes, the striking thing is the juxtaposition of two terms we find in Ruth, the *gō'ᵉlīm* and the *mᵉyuddā'īm*. Note the interweaving in Ruth: the story-teller introduces Boaz at 2:1 as a *mᵉyuddā'*, then has Naomi refer to him as "one of our *gō'ᵉlim*" in 2:20, only to have her at 3:2 refer to him as "of our *mōda'at*"; thereafter the term *gō'ēl* takes over completely.

On the basis of the proto-Lucianic reading in II Kings 10:11 we must choose the "written" text in the MT rather than the "read" text of the scribes. We are also led to recognize that the meaning of the term lies very close to that of *gō'ēl*, "kinsman." A hint of its original connotation comes from the recent demonstration that the verb *yd'* is an important part of treaty/covenant terminology in pre-Israelite Canaan and in Israelite theology (see esp. H. B. Huffmon, BASOR 181 [February 1966], 31–37, and, with S. B. Parker, BASOR 184 [December 1966], 36–38). Huffmon shows that *yd'* is a reciprocal action in a treaty relationship between overlord and vassal; each "knows" the other, that is, recognizes the other as partner in treaty. Note well that this language is characteristic of treaties between unequals.

Can words from the root *yd'* also apply to the kind of covenant relationship existing between persons on a par with one another? That is what I want to propose for our word *mᵉyuddā'*; hence the translation "covenant-brother." In the five passages where the term appears other than in Ruth 2:1 and II Kings

10:11, it indicates a very close relationship. In the bitter lament of Psalm 88, the poet concludes a series of accusatory cries at verse 8[Hebrew, 9] by blaming God for causing him to be shunned by his closest allies, his covenant-brothers; in the final verse of the psalm, he is still accusing: "You have made lover and friend shun me; my one and only $m^eyuddā'$ is Darkness" (after M. Dahood, *Psalms II, 51–100*, AB, vol. 17, pp. 301–7). In Psalm 31:11 [Hebrew, 12], there is a progression from adversaries to neighbors to "covenant-brothers." In Psalm 55:13[Hebrew, 14] the term is parallel with *'allūp*, a rare word which can be used to describe the relationship between husband and wife (Prov 2:17) and that between Yahweh and Judah (Jer 3:4). Finally, Job 19:14 uses the term in parallelism with $q^erōbay$, "ones near me," the very term placed in Naomi's mouth at Ruth 2:20 parallel to "our $gō'^elīm$."

These parallels help us to see the developed use of the term more than its original connotation. In fact, we have nothing certain to indicate that a real semantic distinction existed between $m^eyuddā'$ and $gō'ēl$ at the time of the composition of the Ruth story. I suspect, however, that the story-teller confronts us here with an archaic term belonging to a societal structure that reaches beyond blood ties. It adds the dimension of covenant responsibility to that of family responsibility.

To all this, one final word. The story-teller shows here not only his interest in custom and terminology, but also his interest in word-play. The root yd' is one of his key words, especially in chapter 3 (see 2:10, 11, 3:2–4, 11, 18, 4:4). Once more we see him as a master of literary effect.

a man of substance. The idiom *'īš gibbōr ḥayl* here probably combines several meanings found in other biblical passages which employ it. H. Tadmor, *Journal of World History* 11 (1968), 18, n. 33, develops the military connotation of the expression in studying II Kings 15:20 (cf. I Chron 5:24, 8:40, and the numbers in the first Judean exile of 597 in II Kings 24:14–16). The same passage also suggests their comparative wealth. On the other hand, Gideon in Judg 6:12 and Jeroboam in I Kings 11:28 are *gibbōrē ḥayl*, apparently because of their diligence and/or good reputation (so also Kish, at I Sam 9:1). In this connection, we dare not detach this description of Boaz from the expression *'ēšet ḥayl* which he himself will use to compliment Ruth in 3:11. The translation "man of substance" has just the right ambiguity to cover the term in the Hebrew!

the same sub-tribe as Elimelek. While $m^eyuddā'$ has pointed to a covenanted relationship, it is now made clear that the man is at least a distant relative of Elimelek; in F. I. Andersen's terms, he belongs to the same "phratry" or sub-tribe, a unit larger than the extended family (*bēt 'āb*) but smaller than the tribe (Andersen, *The Bible Translator* 20 [1969], 29–39, esp. 34 ff.; cf. R. de Vaux, *Ancient Israel: Its Life and Institutions* [New York: McGraw-Hill, 1961], entries under "clan" in the general index). See NOTE on 1:2, "Ephrathites. . . ."

Boaz. The LXX and OL transcribe this name "Booz," a spelling which could support a Hebrew combination *bō 'ōz*, "in him is strength." Two LXX[L] manuscripts underscore the theme of strength by adding "in strength" after "Boaz/he said" in 2:4 and 8. Another possibility is to vocalize *b^e'ōz*, "in the strength of . . . ," and to analyze the name as a hypocoristicon—a short "nickname"—of a sentence name such as "In the strength of Yahweh I rejoice." Noth, in his *Personennamen*, p. 228, invokes instead the Arabic root *bġz*, and proposes "of keen spirit" as the meaning; Rudolph prefers this etymology and proposes "lively, vigorous." The former option ascribes strength to deity; the latter describes an attribute of the person himself. If, as many assume, the names in our story were invented or at least selected to fit the characters of their bearers, Noth and Rudolph would seem to have the better of the case. As we have seen, however, there is reason to think that the names in Ruth are authentic, and this should be especially true of a man who was the direct ancestor of David. Probably, Boaz was an authentic personal name characteristic of the early Israelite period, whatever its meaning.

An even more interesting question relates to the correspondence between Boaz' name and that of the pillar at the left of the entry to the Solomonic temple (I Kings 7:21; II Chron 3:17). R. B. Y. Scott has plausibly proposed that the pillar Boaz was designated by the first word of a dynastic formula inscribed on it, and suggests that the formula read "In the strength of (*bᵉ'ōz*) Yahweh shall the king rejoice," or the like (JBL 58 [1939], 148–49, accepted by Albright, *Archaeology and the Religion of Israel⁵*, p. 135). This assumes, as most everyone would agree, that the Solomonic temple was a royal chapel closely tied to the Davidic dynasty. It would also mean that the dynastic formula was itself closely tied to the Davidic dynasty and its ideology, and does not antedate the establishment of the Israelite united monarchy. Consequently, Boaz the man could hardly carry a name derived from the formula, if he indeed was the great-grandfather of David.

But what about the reverse possibility? In 1959, S. Yeivin put forward the stimulating hypothesis that the pillars at the dynastic chapel were named after Solomon's ancestors (*Palestine Exploration Quarterly* 91 [1959], 21–22). Few have felt this hypothesis to be strong, although Rudolph notes it and rejects it primarily because Yeivin could not point out a known Solomonic ancestor with a name corresponding to the other pillar at the temple doorway, Jachin (*yākīn*). But Yeivin does note that this name, and sentence names compounded with the verb it represents, are attested in Israel. Indeed, one turns up in the Davidic line in the form *yᵉhōyākīn* (Jehoiachin), also known as *yᵉkōnyāh*, the name of the king deposed and exiled in 597 B.C.E. Yeivin's hypothesis deserves to be kept alive—and I am glad to acknowledge that D. N. Freedman, who also thinks so, is the one who pointed out to me its continued viability.

2. *I am going out.* The Hebrew uses the so-called cohortative first person, which can express a request for permission or a firm determination. There follows the particle *na'*, regularly described in the grammars as an expression of polite deference, a precative. In fact, however, its actual usage does not bear this out. A recent, superb teaching grammar, that of T. O. Lambdin, *Introduction to Biblical Hebrew* (New York: Scribner, 1971), pp. 170 f., describes it as a means of establishing "a logical consequence, either of an immediately preceding statement or of the general situation in which it is uttered." The translation here given is meant to suggest that Ruth, having

taken stock of the general situation, states her determination to set about meeting it (see the recent German commentaries: "I want to go out," as compared to recent English translations, such as NEB: "May I go out," or RSV: "Let me go").

the field. The word is the same as that used for the Moabite "plateau" in the first chapter. Here in Judah, it refers to all the land under cultivation around the town, divided into plots (see 2:3 and 4:3) belonging to the various townspeople.

in whose eyes I find favor. "To find favor in the eyes of" is a frequently used idiom, almost always in the elevated prose of dramatic narratives. Of forty instances, thirty-two occur in speeches, as does this one. It seems always to be used by a person of inferior status to a superior, thirteen times by a person before God. Indeed, it may be used as a criterion for determining who holds the dominant position in a relationship where there might be reason for doubt (e.g. Jacob to his son Joseph in Gen 47:29, David to Jonathan in I Sam 20:3, 29, and to Nabal in I Sam 25:8). Of great interest is the way in which the Ruth story-teller uses it three times in chapter 2 (see verses 10 and 13), each time with a slightly different effect. Here, it suggests that Ruth sets out to glean with the intention of requesting permission from the harvesters. See the COMMENT.

3. *So she set out and came and gleaned.* It is conceivable that this succession of three verbs represents a conflation of ancient recensions, since the LXX[B] and LXX[L], supported by the Syriac and the Vulgate, do not include the second verb. Some of the same superfluity of verbs is present in 2:7, but terseness is not necessarily a mark of our story-teller, especially as he leads into a new scene (cf. 3:3 and the first NOTE there). We hardly need follow Slotki, who suggests that she practiced coming and going so as to familiarize herself with the new (to her) practice!

There is another important thing to notice: the three verbs, each imperfect with the so-called *waw*-consecutive, are a sort of summation of the action; they do not constitute a statement that all three actions have taken place before we go on to the "and her luck brought her" opening of the drama. The story-teller does the same thing here as he did at 1:6, which is tantamount to saying, "Here is what this episode is about and here is how it happened. . . ." This style of the story-teller is crucial to a proposal for the understanding of verse 7; see the second NOTE there.

her luck brought her. Both verb and noun are built from the root *qrh*, "to befall, happen." The LXX translators dutifully reflect the Semitic structure by using a Greek noun derivative of the verb, even though they had to stretch the noun's meaning a bit, since it usually meant "calamity!" The notion of chance or accident is not usually a nuance of the Hebrew root's meaning; on the impact of its usage here, see the COMMENT.

4. *Then Boaz came.* The string of imperfects with *waw*-consecutive in verse 3 is interrupted by a clause beginning *wᵉhinnēh bōʿāz bāʾ*, an example of a frequent construction in Hebrew narrative style making it "graphic and vivid, and enabling the reader to enter into the surprise or satisfaction of the speaker or actor concerned" (Brown, Driver, and Briggs, *Lexicon*, p. 244a).

The verb in such clauses can be either participle or perfect tense, and it so happens that the verb *bā'* here is the form for both. The versions opt for the perfect tense, but another consideration supports the participle. Within the larger category of *wᵉhinnēh* clauses there is a sub-group employing the participle only, used when a scene has been set and then just the right thing happens, with little or no lapse of time, and with a distinct hint of wonder at the cause. One of the best examples is Ruth 4:1. Another excellent instance is Gen 24:15, where, after Abraham's servant has set up in his prayer the test by which he will identify the right wife for Isaac, lo and behold, along comes Rebekah. Other examples occur in II Sam 18:31 and I Kings 1:42, while something of the same tone is in II Sam 15:32, 16:1 and I Kings 1:22 (all these from the "Court History of David"). The impact in Ruth 2:4 is that Boaz' arrival came not long after Ruth herself had come to the field, but long enough after (as the sequel indicates) for the overseer to have formed a positive impression of Ruth, hence at just the right time. Furthermore, the audience is led to feel that Boaz' arrival is another facet of Ruth's good fortune in hitting upon the particular portion of the field where she is working.

Yahweh be with you! Compare Ps 129:8 and Judg 6:12. In the latter passage what started out as a greeting becomes the subject of a challenge on the part of Gideon: "Pardon me, sir, but if Yahweh *is* with us, why has all this happened to us?" (Boling, *Judges*, AB, vol. 6A ad loc.; cf. Joüon, *Commentaire*, p. 48, optative here in Ruth, but indicative in Judg 6:12).

5. *to his young man.* Beginning with this "young man" there follows a stream of occurrences of words designating "young people": *na'ar* for the overseer, *na'ᵃrāh* for Ruth, *nᵉ'ārīm* for the workers both male and female or sometimes only male, and *nᵉ'ārōt* for the young women who participate in the harvest. As he does frequently elsewhere, the story-teller bunches numerous uses of the same root in this episode of the story. References to the young people will stop in 3:2, but the word *na'ᵃrāh* will make one more climactic appearance, at 4:12. The emphasis upon youth will also have its impact at 3:10, where, with another facet of his characteristic deftness, the story-teller will use a different word (see second NOTE on 3:10).

To whom does this young woman belong? The form of the question, which may seem a bit odd, must be allowed to stand, despite the fact that a group of LXX manuscripts (*not* LXXᴮ or LXXᴸ') joins the OL in recasting the question into the simpler "Who is this young woman?" (Note the Syriac: "What is the good of this young woman?" Two OT stories provide instructive commentary: the interrogation of the Amalekite slave in I Sam 30:13 f. and Jacob's anticipation of his encounter with Esau in Gen 32:17 f.[Hebrew, 18 f.]. In both cases, a series of questions is asked and in each case the answers do identify the person questioned, but *only in such a way as to carry the story forward.* Thus, in I Sam 30:13, David asks the captured slave "To whom do you belong? Where are you from?" and learns in response that he is an Egyptian youth, slave of an Amalekite. The answer is something more than "name, rank, and serial number," for it leads directly to providing David the opportunity to find the Amalekite camp and take it by surprise. It is doubtful that the question "To whom do you belong?" was based on a prior recognition that the man was a slave. Rather, it is a question which probes circumstances.

In Gen 32:13 ff., Jacob prepares an elaborate gift of animals and sends them ahead to meet Esau, instructing his servants how to answer the questions Esau will probably ask: "To whom do you belong? Where are you going? Whose are these (animals you are driving) before you?" They are to answer: "To your servant Jacob. They are a present sent to my lord Esau." The answer is more or less pertinent to the questions but the focus is on the gift and its intended effect. Indeed, most translations make it an answer to the last question only; see Gen 32:19 in Speiser, *Genesis*, AB, vol. 1: "Your brother Jacob's; it is a present. . . ." Once again the questions are probing into circumstances.

The same is true here. Boaz' question is more general than simply one of identification. It invites the answer which in fact it receives, namely information about Ruth which will move the story forward. A good paraphrase might be "Where does this young woman fit in?" It is the first of a series of three vital questions used by the story-teller; see 3:9 and 3:16.

6. *She's a Moabite girl.* The Hebrew provides no definite article here, nor does the OL, but the LXX and Syriac do. For the Hebrew text the clause immediately following will provide the definition, which in turn presumably triggers Boaz' memory of having heard about her. The Hebrew text is the more difficult reading, and should be retained.

the one who returned. Again the definite article on a perfect verb, according to the Masoretic accentuation (see NOTE on 1:22 and compare 4:3, where Naomi is the person returning).

7. *May I glean . . . ?* The cohortative form recalls immediately 2:2 where, it was maintained (see the first NOTE), the force is one of determination. There is no difficulty in having the same form function here as a polite request for permission; the context requires it.

[*the fourteen remaining Hebrew words of verse 7*]. It is likely that the precise meaning here will permanently elude us. The bracketed blank space may help the reader to see where things stand before these words and where they stand after them. Somehow the intervening words provided the transition. An idea of the complexities involved can be gained by comparing a literal rendering of the entire Hebrew verse with a highly influential attempt to make sense of the words, that of Rudolph.

MT: "She said, 'And I shall gather (or: let me gather) among the sheaves after the reapers.' So she came and stood from then the morning and until now; this is her (sitting/resting) the house a few."

Rudolph: "She said 'And I shall gather blades behind the reapers,' then she went out and has been on her feet from morning until now; only just now has she taken a brief break."

Notice the following problems and proposed solutions.

1) Because Boaz will arrange for Ruth to glean between (Hebrew, *bēn*) the sheaves in 2:15, it is incongruous to have Ruth request and receive permission to glean among (Hebrew, *bᵉ*) the sheaves here. Rudolph therefore follows Joüon in revocalizing MT's *'ᵃmārīm* to *'ᵃmīrīm*, the plural of *'āmīr*. This noun occurs elsewhere in the OT only as a singular collective, in four pro-

phetic similes (Amos 2:13; Jer 9:21; Micah 4:12; and Zech 12:6); the meaning in the prophetic similes is itself "sheaves," but Joüon suspects that the plural (of the usual singular collective) suggests isolated spears or blades of the barley. The preposition *b*ᵉ is then to be taken as "participative," as it was on the word *šibbolet*, "barley spears," in 2:2, which requires no equivalent in translation (we might say, "work at the stalks"). Perhaps the Syriac and Vulgate offer an easier way out; they simply eliminate "and I shall glean among the sheaves" (Gerleman accepts).

2) To translate *watta'ᵃmōd* with "has been on her feet=has persisted" is to stretch the meaning of the verb *'md*, "to stand," rather seriously. Rudolph, sensing this, is friendly to a proposal of Houbigant made in 1777 to change to *watta'ᵃmōr*, a verb cognate with the noun just discussed, meaning "to glean stalks" (cf. a unique *Piel* form of this root in Ps 129:7).

3) Rudolph takes Hebrew *mē'āz*, usually "from then," to mean simply "from," invoking Exod 4:10, Lachish Letter 3.7, and possibly Ps 76:8. M. Dahood has argued convincingly that this word means "from of old" in Ps 76:8 (*Psalms II, 51–100*, AB, p. 220; cf. *Psalms I, 1–50*, AB, p. 278). The other two places follow *mē'āz* with a suffixed infinitive construct in what is probably a syntactically fixed combination: "from the time of your speaking to your servant" (Exod 4:10); "from the time of your sending (word) to your servant" (Lachish Letter 3.7). The case is very weak, therefore, to read here "from the morning." An alternate proposal is to emend *mē'āz* to *mē'ōr*: "from the light of" the morning. Another possibility is to assume that there existed alternative readings in two early Hebrew recensions, one having "from then and up to now" and the other "from the morning and up to now"; conflation of the two would result in the MT reading. Finally, note the LXX "from early morning until evening," an impossible reading if we are to understand that the text is describing the events of a single day; there lie ahead a break for a meal and then more gleaning until evening (verse 17).

4) Rudolph proposes that there was a second *'attāh*, "now," in the original text and that it dropped out by scribal haplography. This second *'attāh* he then joins to *zeh*, "this," in an adverbial combination: "only just now." Such an idiom is attested in II Kings 5:22 and I Kings 17:24. Such haplographies certainly did occur in scribal transmission, but the resulting text here is slightly awkward.

5) Rudolph revocalizes the consonants *šbth* from *šibtāh* of the MT ("her sitting" or "her resting") to *šābᵉtāh* from the root *šbt*, "to rest." Many others propose the same change, and this is one of the cornerstones of the ingenious solution offered by D. Lys, VT 21 (1971), 479–501. (The chief value of Lys' article is its catalogue and comparison of some nineteen varying translations.)

6) The following word in the Hebrew text is *habbayt*, "the house." Because it shares two consonants with *šbth*, Rudolph proposes to delete it as a dittography. This drastic measure would help immensely, because "the house" here is very hard to fit into the picture. Was there a house at the field where the workers could get a few minutes in the shade (so KJ and the Targum)? Was it a toilet (so W. Reed, *College of the Bible Quarterly* 41 [1964], 8)? Had Ruth gone home, and if so, why is Boaz able to address her in the following verse?

Two solutions offered by the versions suggest how early translators sought to resolve the matter. The LXX reads "she has *not* stopped in the *field* a little," and the Vulgate, "*not* for a moment has she returned home." The negative in these two translations is not attested in the other versions or in the MT.

What can be made of all this? Clearly there was a confused text present before the ancient translators did their work. Only a combination of errors, progressing by stages and compounding the confusion, can account for what we now have. It is even doubtful whether we can assert what most commentators do, namely that whatever the original reading the portrayal was of a girl both polite and diligent. Perhaps one more thing can be said, as a stimulus to further wrestling with the problem. B. Zimolong, in a brief note to ZAW 58 (1940–41), 156–58, urges a closer attention to the context, especially to verse 8, and proposes that the final word in verse 7, "a few, a little," be taken as a description of what Ruth had been able to glean up to the time of Boaz' arrival.

Looking at the context *preceding* this verse, there may be another clue. Ruth has said she will go to glean after someone in whose eyes she finds favor. The story-teller will, of course, see to it that this motif is picked up. It is, in verses 10 and 13. Favor is found in Boaz' eyes. The question can be asked, then, whether it is necessarily certain that Ruth had received permission to glean from the overseer and had begun working before Boaz arrived. Perhaps, in fact, we should take the beginning of the verse to mean that she had asked but had not received her answer, because the owner of the crop had not yet arrived, and in the overseer's view the owner alone was the one to grant it. We can then take *watta'᷈mōd* in its literal and regular sense: "she arrived and has stood" waiting for permission before she begins and not leaving until she has tried to secure it. This proposal requires the understanding of the beginning of verse 3 given at the first NOTE there: "she set out and came and gleaned" is a summary of the action which the whole episode spells out. Her luck had brought her to the "right" field, but she had not as yet secured permission. If this proposal has merit, it may explain the distinctly languid pace of the first seven verses of chapter 2, with its attention to the greetings between owner and workmen, and the drawn-out exchange between Boaz and his overseer. The impact is to underscore her patience and determination. But once Boaz gets clear on the matter, as he notices the young woman "standing there," he at once gives the permission in the sequel, perhaps with a bit of irritation at his scrupulous overseer (so Freedman). If so, once again a righteous person's behavior transcends proper, but uninspired, correctness.

Fortunately for the story, the radical disruption of the text in verse 7 appears not to lead to confusion about the progress of the drama. Let the reader of the Bible note well, however, that a hundred conjectures about a badly disrupted text are all more likely to be wrong than any one of them absolutely right!

8. *Hear me well.* Literally, "Have you not heard?" The Hebrew negative rhetorical question, assuming the strongly affirmative answer, is a frequent feature of story style. See 2:9, 3:1, 2.

to glean. Oddly enough, the Masoretic vocalization makes this a *Qal* of the verb, while in the eleven other occurrences of the verb in this chapter it is vocalized as a *Piel.* E. Jenni, *Das hebräische Pi'el* (Zürich: EVZ Verlag,

1968), pp. 188 f., notes that the *Qal* of this verb normally expresses a comparatively effortless gleaning from a large available supply, while the *Piel* has the nuance of difficult and hence thorough work. That fails to account for this one *Qal*, however. For it, Jenni points out that this is the only occurrence in Ruth which follows a negative, and negation makes the emphasis on the result (and hence, presumably, the difficulty) superfluous. I am not persuaded we have the reason as yet.

in another field. Probably better than "in the field of another" (Ehrlich). The Syriac offers a bizarre variant: "Have you not heard the proverbial saying: 'Do not glean in a field which is not your own'?" Perhaps the phrase looks ahead to things to come, or even to 4:3 where we will be left without explanation of how it happens that Naomi has a portion of the field to sell.

And also do not. The word *gam*, "also," seems superfluous, and distinctly not poetic. Here, and at the two instances of *gam* in 1:12 (see the NOTE on 1:12–13), LXX[B] fails to use its usual *kaige* to render *gam*. The language in Boaz' mouth has often been recognized to be rather heavy and archaic. Perhaps this is a quaint manner of speech.

But right here. Joüon is wrong to find this redundant. Boaz speaks a balanced rhythmic prose as do the women. The word *kōh* in this locative sense is confined, as S. R. Driver, *Introduction to the Literature of the Old Testament,* rev. ed. of 1913 (repr. New York: Meridian, 1956), note on p. 454, points out, to classical prose. Cf. esp. Gen 31:37; Num 23:15; and II Sam 18:30.

attach yourself. That root is *dbq*, the pregnant key word introduced at 1:14. At 1:14 and 2:23, it is followed by the preposition *bᵉ*; here and at 2:21 it is followed by the preposition *'im*, "with," the only places in the OT displaying that syntax. Joüon notes that these two instances are in Boaz' words (the second when Ruth is quoting him). Here is another mark of Boaz' special style of speaking.

The orthography of the form is interesting: *tidbāqīn,* with the so-called paragogic *nun*. This is probably a mark of archaic style; see Myers, MLLF, pp. 17 f. There are four of them in second feminine singular verb forms in Ruth, all in speeches: 2:8 (an imperative addressed to Ruth), 2:21 (Ruth, but quoting Boaz), 3:4 and 18 (Naomi).

my girls. We have pointed out in the first NOTE on verse 5 the heavy use of nouns based on *na'ar.* This is the first occurrence of a plural feminine noun designating a part of the harvesting team. It will reappear in 2:22 and 23 in an interesting way (see NOTES there). Joüon (*Commentaire,* pp. 52 f.) is properly surprised that so little specific mention is made of the feminine contingent among the harvesters, and especially that Ruth is not instructed to sit with the other women at the time of eating in verse 14. It appears that we must take most if not all the masculine plural endings on the nouns "harvesters" and "young people" to include both sexes. Then, when the story-teller uses a feminine plural, we are probably being reminded (as so often in the Genesis patriarchal stories) of the importance of protecting the "elected" woman from harm and even the possibility of the wrong marriage for her.

9. *Keep your eyes on the field.* The MT preserves simply "your eyes on the field" without any verb or conjunction, which is surprising in Ruth because of

the overwhelming tendency to begin sentences with w^e, "and," plus a verb. As it stands, the MT raises the question of whether the words make up a complete sentence, or represent a clause to be subordinated to what follows: "(Keeping) your eyes on the field where they harvest, go after them . . ." Perhaps we have to do instead with an imperative, with a pronominal suffix, of the verb *'yn*, attested in Ugaritic and now being found in biblical passages. M. Dahood has found a *Hiphil* of the root at Ps 65:6, and compares I Sam 2:27, 18:9 and Ecclesiasticus 14:10 (*Psalms II, 51–100*, AB, vol. 17, NOTE on 65:6, "show us"). This proposal requires that the first clause in this verse be an independent, not a subordinate unit.

which they are harvesting / And go along after them. The verb *yiqṣōrūn*, "they are harvesting," uses the *masculine* plural form; the final prepositional phrase uses the *feminine* plural suffix. It is clear that the action indicated by the verb *qṣr* is the comprehensive one of harvesting: sickling the stalks, gathering them into sheaves, and binding them. This is done in concert by a team of both men and women, the women presumably performing the gathering and binding. The shift in gender is therefore understandable.

I am commanding. Literally, "Have I not commanded?" another rhetorical question as in 2:8 (see the first NOTE there). The LXX[BL] here has *idou*, "behold," while at 2:8 it reflects the Hebrew negative question precisely. The hexaplaric LXX manuscripts conform to the Hebrew.

to bother you. The verb *ngʿ* is usually related to its object by a preposition; only here and at Gen 26:29 and Isa 52:11 does it take a direct object (Joüon, *Grammaire*, § 125b). Quite possibly the assonance of this word to *pgʿ* of 2:22 is intentional; see second NOTE there.

the vessels. Some of the harvesters would have brought water jars to the field as a general supply for all. (This may well have been women's work, so that the masculine plural on "young people" may again reflect mixed gender.) Because water is not explicitly mentioned in the MT, Joüon (*Commentaire*, pp. 53 f.) speculates that the drink was wine, but the verb employed at the conclusion of the verse is used exclusively for drawing water. The OL, Vulgate, and Syriac fail to mention vessels.

10. *Why have I found favor in your eyes.* See the last NOTE on 2:2 and the COMMENT. The interrogative word is *maddua'*, not the more frequent (and perhaps less precise) *lāmāh*, "why?" It is not clear that special precision is needed here. Possibly the story-teller is capitalizing on the assonance of *maddua'* with forms of the root *ydʿ*, "to know," used frequently in this story (see second NOTE on 2:1).

So that you take special note of me, / Though I am a foreigner. The word-play between the first and last words, and the assonance of all three, makes this unit a pure delight: *lᵉhakkīrēnī wᵉ'ānōkī nokrīyāh.* The first word is a *Hiphil* of *nkr*, and usually has slightly different meanings from that needed here, such as "to identify, to recognize someone formerly known, to acknowledge" (see, e.g., 3:14). In meaning, the occurrence at Ps 142:4[Hebrew, 5] comes the closest: "no one takes note of me." In short, the first word is the one bent semantically to allow the word-play. Myers, MLLF, pp. 19 ff., uses the comparative frequency of the long form of the first person pronoun *'ānōkī* over the short form *'ᵃnī* as a criterion for judging the comparatively early date of Ruth; a preponderance of the long form should point to greater antiquity, and in Ruth odds are 7 to 2 in favor of the long form. Here in 2:10, however, the choice of the long form is probably dictated by assonance with the words surrounding it.

11. *It has been made quite clear.* The Hebrew is *huggēd huggad,* a familiar syntactic device for emphasis employing an infinitive absolute form before the indicative of the same verb. Josh 9:24 uses the same expression; the Gibeonites had been made all too fully aware that there was no opposing the Israelite conquest. The precise nature of the emphasis might be iterative ("I've been hearing it from all sides") or an indication of its impact ("I have been impressed by what I've been hearing").

The forms, *Hophals* of *ngd,* are very much a mark of classical Hebrew prose. Of thirty-five instances, none are in *P* materials, while three are distributed throughout the product of the Isaianic "school" (at 7:2, 21:2 [a late oracle], and 40:21 [Deutero-Isaiah]). All the rest are in *J, E,* Deuteronomy, and the Deuteronomic History, six in the Court History of David.

And how you forsook. The Hebrew has no explicit expression here for "how," but the LXX states it explicitly: *pōs.* This is hardly necessary, as Joüon shows, citing I Kings 18:13 as displaying similar syntax (*Commentaire,* p. 55; *Grammaire,* § 118j).

previously. How prosaic the English is compared to the Hebrew, literally, "yesterday and the third day." The idiom displays considerable variety in its spelling, and in its employment of prepositions and adverbial adjuncts. Only at Exod 5:8 does it appear exactly as it does here (note Exod 5:7 and 14 with variation). However varied, the idiom belongs almost exclusively to the prose of *J* and *E* and the Deuteronomic historian (note it in casuistic law, at Exod 21:29, 36; Deut 4:42, 19:4, 6).

12. *May Yahweh grant your action due recompense.* The meaning here is clear enough, but the Hebrew is syntactically uniquely terse when one compares it to similar passages. Here, MT reads *yᵉšallēm yhwh poʿᵒlēk,* that is, verb-subject-direct object (with no preposition or mark of accusative). The full form of the syntax when God is the subject of this verb is probably "recompense to (*lᵉ*) X according to (*kᵉ*) his/your/their Y," where Y is most likely evil, rarely good, and only on three occasions the neutral *poʿal,* "deed, action, work" (here and at Jer 25:14 and 50:29). The full form occurs at II Sam 3:39 and Jer 25:14. Variations occur: Deut 7:10 lacks the final "according to" element, while the echo of that verse in Jer 32:18 includes the final element as the direct object: "recompensing the fathers' iniquities to (Hebrew, *'el,* not *lᵉ*) the bosom of their sons."

There are two interesting considerations. First, LXX^L' has *soi,* "to you," as does the OL (*tibi*) and the editor's hand in Theodoret's exegesis of Ruth. Given the standard formula, this stands an excellent chance of being an original reading at least in one of the early Hebrew recensions of our story: "May Yahweh recompense *to you* your action." (Cf. the Ugaritic idioms in letter salutations, recently discussed by S. Loewenstamm, BASOR 194 [April 1969], 52–54, and the literature he cites). Second, attention should be called to the final word of this short blessing. Brown, Driver, and Briggs, *Lexicon*, states that the noun is poetic (correct) and late (incorrect!). The verb *p'l* is an archaic word, used in Exod 15:17 and Num 23:23 (eleventh-century poems), Ps 68:28[Hebrew, 29] (see W. F. Albright, *Hebrew Union College Annual* 23 [1950–51], 31–39), and Deut 32:27 (at least ninth-century; see G. E. Wright, in *Israel's Prophetic Heritage*, eds. B. W. Anderson and W. Harrelson, [New York, Harper, 1962], esp. pp. 26 f., 36–41, 58–65). It also appears in the early tenth-century Ahiram inscription and the late tenth-century Eli-Ba'al inscription from Phoenicia. As for the noun, it occurs in Deut 32:4 and in what may be the original snippet of the Levi blessing by Moses in Deut 33:11 (see F. M. Cross and D. N. Freedman, JBL 67 [1948], 204, n. 29). Then, there are a number of occurrences of the root in exilic and postexilic writing. Once more we are confronted with archaic diction which will have a renaissance in the period beginning around 600 B.C.E.

your payment. Hebrew, *maśkurtēk*. The same word is used literally for wages in the Jacob-Laban stories at Gen 29:15, 31:7, 41, the only other places where this particular form occurs. Another noun from the same root, *śākār*, shows the same combination of literal and figurative meanings; see Gen 30:28–33, 31:28 compared to Gen 15:1 and 30:18. Note also Jer 31:16; Isa 40:10 and 62:11, where forms of the roots *śkr* and *p'l* (see preceding NOTE) appear together; especially in Deutero-Isaiah a new use is developed for a noun, *pe'ullāh*, as Yahweh's "reward."

Under whose wings you have come to seek refuge. The imagery recalls most explicitly that of Deut 32:37 and Ps 91:4; the latter is the only place to use the preposition "under" as our passage does. See also Pss 17:8, 36:7[Hebrew, 8], 57:1[Hebrew, 2], and 61:4[Hebrew, 5], and the thorough exploration by G. E. Mendenhall, *The Tenth Generation*, pp. 32–68. The Ruth story-teller will produce a marvelous effect, intrinsic to his theological message, by using the word *kānāp*, "wing," once more, at 3:9.

13. *May I continue to find favor.* The progression beginning in verse 2 and continuing in verse 10 is here brought to its conclusion. This sentence is both a statement of thanksgiving and, because it uses the imperfect verb, an expression of confidence about future well-being; cf. I Sam 1:18, where Hannah responds in this fashion to Eli after he has blessed her, and to II Sam 16:4, where Ziba does the same after David has bestowed on him all of Mephibosheth's belongings.

Because you have comforted me. Most frequently used for the act of consoling one who mourns, this *Piel* of *nḥm* also designates comfort of the oppressed or distressed. It is hardly likely that Ruth is referring back to the loss of her husband; the best commentary on its meaning is provided by the clause parallel to it which follows.

And because you have spoken to the heart. I would not be at all averse to seeing the "and" deleted (with Myers) in this manifestly poetic line. To speak to the heart of someone, although it occurs but nine times in the OT, can mean several different things. In Gen 34:3; Judg 19:3; and Hosea 2:16, it means to persuade, to entice a woman; in Gen 50:21, where it parallels a use of *nḥm* as it does here, and in Isa 40:2, it means to comfort, to relieve. In narrative

5. The Solomonic city gate at Gezer, viewed from inside town. Notice the low foundations for benches in the left foreground which faced an open plaza inside the gate.

6. A view of one of the side chambers within the Gezer city gate. The chamber is lined with the foundations for plastered benches on which people could sit as they deliberated a legal matter.

(Opposite above)

7. Plan of the city gate of Dan, in use from the late tenth century at least through the ninth. One entered from the right, into a rectangular plaza; in its northwest corner were benches, and just at the entrance of the inner gate was what appears to be a judgment seat.

(Opposite below)

8. The large hewn blocks which served as benches within the plaza of the gate at Dan.

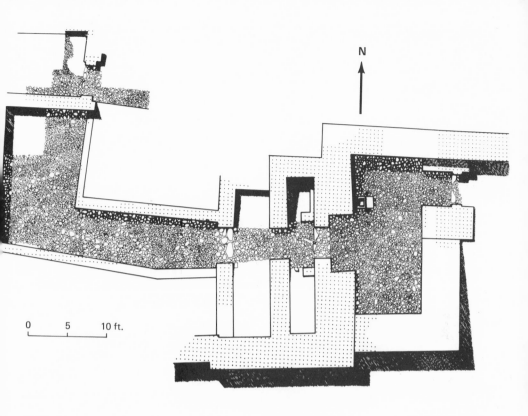

9. The foundations of a structure which was probably a ceremonial judgment seat for cases decided at the city gate, located just to the right (north) of the entrance to the inner gate at Dan. Two ornamented sockets, of an original four, which probably supported the posts holding up a canopy over the structure, flank the foundation.

contexts in II Sam 19:8; II Chron 30:22, 32:6, it refers to the encouragement the king gives to his people. On balance, one favors the second of these three. But it would not be at all unlike our story-teller to have a double meaning lurking here. In chapter 3, he will do much of the same sort of thing.

your maid-servant. Here and at the end of the verse, Ruth uses the term *šipḥāh;* at 3:9 she will call herself Boaz' *'āmāh.* Joüon has suggested that *šipḥāh* is more deferential than *'āmāh,* representing an even lower rung on the social ladder; he invokes I Sam 25:41 in support, but the reading there is suspicious enough to raise doubts. In fact the terms seem to be almost precise synonyms: note for example that the designations are intermingled but with *'āmāh* predominating in the Abigail-David episode in I Sam 25:24–41, are again intermingled but with *šipḥāh* predominating in the story of the wise woman of Tekoah in II Sam 14:6–19. Just possibly, *'āmāh* is a characteristic of E in various Genesis passages while *šipḥāh* is J's word. (See the discussion of this in A. Jepsen, VT 8 [1958], 293–97.) But I propose a much more obvious reason for the use of *šipḥāh* here; it is cognate with the word *mišpāḥāh,* "sub-tribe" in 2:1 and 3. Our story-teller is running true to form.

D. N. Freedman has reminded me of a bit of evidence which may pertain to our understanding of Ruth's deferential words here and in 3:9. Over a century ago, a damaged inscription was found on a tomb facade nearly buried beneath a home in the village of Silwan, across the Kidron valley from the temple mount in Jerusalem. N. Avigad was the first to make cogent sense of it, in an article in IEJ 3 (1953), 137–52. It is the epitaph of a Judean royal steward of about 700 B.C.E., the time of King Hezekiah and the prophet Isaiah; indeed, it quite possibly belongs to the steward Shebna mentioned in Isa 22:15–16. It reads: "This is [the sepulcher of . . .]*yahu* who is over the house. There is no silver and no gold here, but [his bones] and the bones of his *'āmāh* with him. Cursed be the man who will open this!" Avigad translated *'āmāh* here as "slave-wife." Surely this is correct; it is more likely that the *'āmāh* was indeed a beloved slave-wife than that she was buried with her lord simply in order to serve him in the netherworld! At the least, we can conclude from this inscription that an *'āmāh* could aspire to marriage with her master. Given this hint, it is not surprising to learn the outcome of Abigail's almost obsequious reference to herself as both *'āmāh* and *šipḥāh* in I Sam 25:24–41—namely that she becomes David's wife. Nor is it difficult to assume that Ruth's deferential terms for herself in 2:13 and 3:9 give hints to an attentive audience of what is to come.

Why, as for me, I am not even as (worthy as) one of your maid-servants. This rendering is by no means certain. The LXX, OL, and Syriac all show no negative, resulting in "I will become (OL: I am) one of your maid-servants." An easy way to bring the Hebrew into agreement with this is to posit an asseverative *lā/lū* in a place of the negative *lō'* (with F. Nötscher, VT 3 [1953], 375), and explain the extra *aleph* as a dittography from the word following. With Rudolph, however, one seems on surer ground by seeing this as an even greater expression of humility than the previous line. This is reinforced by the presence of the explicit pronoun *'ānōkī.* It is as though Ruth, having used the deferential term *šipḥāh* just previously, has her thought triggered to the realization that she cannot even claim that status: "and now that I think about it, I'm not even a *šiphāh* of yours" (see Joüon, *Commentaire*, p. 57). Myers' proposal simply to remove the pronoun to serve the metrical cadence can only lead one to ask why it was at a later stage put in.

14. *at eating time.* Most commentators see this as attached to what precedes, not to Boaz' words, although the LXX and the OL do attach it to his words. Joüon's argument (*Commentaire,* pp. 57–58) is especially important: the dramatic effect of Ruth's words concluding verse 13 would be utterly shattered if Boaz' immediate reply to her were that she come at once and concern herself with such mundane matters as eating. As she did to Naomi in 1:17, so here, she literally leaves Boaz speechless.

Draw near here. The effect is to invite but at the same time to suggest a slight distance. In other words, the story-teller appears to have Boaz respect Ruth's deference and modesty. The verb is from the root *ngš;* among many contexts where a note of deference is suggested, see the occurrences in the Joseph story (Gen 43:19, 44:18, 45:4, 48:10–13), the cluster of six usages in Gen 27:21–27, together with I Sam 14:38 where the same adverb (*hªlōm*) is used with the same spelling of the imperative. The OL, however, is more forward: draw near to me.

in the sour wine. It is clear that *homeṣ* is liquid or semiliquid, and that it tastes good. Note Num 6:3, where the Nazirite is to vow he will not not drink *homeṣ* of wine or *homeṣ* of strong drink. In Ugaritic economic texts, the word appears with wine (e.g., in the ration list, UT 1099:27, 28, 35). In Ps 69:22, however, it designates a drink a thirsty man would not want; the Gospel accounts of drink offered to Jesus on the cross (Mark 15:36; Matt 27:48 [cf. vs. 34]; and John 19:29–30) may take their rise from this psalm, but they manifest a discrepancy as to Jesus' attitude toward the offer. It is enough to assume that it was a refreshing sour drink. The Syriac, presumably mistakenly, reads *halbā'*, "milk," through a scribal error on an original *hallā'*, "(wine) vinegar." Comparison to contemporary drinks or spreads among Arabs (G. Dalman, *Arbeit und Sitte,* III [Gütersloh: Bertelsmann, 1933], 18, doubts there really is a valid comparison) advances our knowledge little.

beside. How near to the harvesters did Ruth sit? Presumably not among them, because the preposition is the unusual *miṣṣad,* "at the flanks of" (see the use with mountains at I Sam 20:25, 23:26). The selection of this preposition seems again to underscore Ruth's modesty.

heaped up. This is largely a guess, because the root *ṣbṭ* occurs only here in the OT, and the versions tend to cloud rather than clarify the issue. One line of evidence is afforded by a noun *mṣbṭm* in the Ba'al-Anath cycle from Ugarit (UT 51.I.25), which probably means tongs; this would support some such idea as "passing over" the roasted grain. By one line of reasoning, the LXX reading may indicate the same idea. It translates *ṣbṭ* here and *ṣᵉbātim* (note the different *t*-sound representing a different Hebrew consonant) in verse 16 with forms of the same verb root. If the LXX were based on a Hebrew text which had forms of *ṣbṭ* at both places, we could link that root to Akkadian *ṣabātu,* "to grasp or seize." In fact, however, the verb the LXX coins means "to heap into a mound"; this in turn points toward Hebrew *ṣbr,* a root occurring in seven very diverse OT passages which have to do with heaps (see Gen 41:35, 49: heaps of grain; Exod 8:10: heaps of dead frogs; etc.). The Vulgate complicates matters further by rendering "she heaped up barley for herself." The decisive argument at this stage seems to be that the Greek coins a word which suggests heaping. At least to one early witness, heaping was the connotation, and it accords with the conclusion of the verse, where Ruth, having eaten her fill, has a surplus.

parched grain. Although the impression may be gained that it was being prepared during the break for a meal, it is clear that this food, *qālī,* was stored in quantity and was something of a staple; see I Sam 25:18, where Abigail brings five *seahs* or about a bushel of it as part of her lavish gift to David and his men (based on the measurements worked out by R. B. Y. Scott in BAR³, p. 352), and I Sam 17:17, where Jesse has his son David take an ephah (about three-fifths of a bushel) of it for the provisioning of his elder brothers. Dalman, *Arbeit und Sitte,* III, 265 ff., claims that the OT practice pertained to wheat (as opposed to barley?), but this cannot be substantiated, and does not help us to decide whether the harvesters were eating the produce of their current work or some of last year's leftovers.

15. *between the sheaves.* Or possibly "among the sheaf-binders" with the OL, especially if the Hebrew of verse 7 (see the second NOTE there) is allowed to stand.

Do not bother her. The verb, a *Hiphil* of *klm* implies nothing as specific as molestation, although the LXX translates with a verb meaning "to disgrace, to shame." It may well be, then, that the term carried a nuance which underscores Boaz' determination to protect Ruth from improper advances from the men. If, on the other hand, we take the masculine plural *neʿārīm* in this verse as young people of mixed gender, rather than as young men, the connotation of Boaz' command to them is very nearly "do not deter her." The Vulgate reads just that, and the sense is close enough to the Hebrew that we do not need to resort, as Joüon does (*Commentaire,* p. 60), to assuming Jerome had a form of *klʾ,* "to restrain," before him.

16. *And even pull out.* The Hebrew is *weḡam šōl tāšōllū;* it has long puzzled commentators because a derivation from Hebrew *šll,* "to spoil, plunder," seems impossible. The problem is further complicated by the versions. The Syriac omits all of verse 16 (as repetitive of 15?), while the LXX goes in two divergent directions. LXX^B gives *two* verb phrases, both reflecting the Hebrew idiom of combining an infinitive absolute (actually here an infinitive construct) with its finite verb, literally, "Lifting, lift up for her; also casting, cast aside for her . . ." Note that this reflects the Hebrew *gam,* "also," at a point between the two verbs. It is not at all impossible then, that LXX^B, along with a few other LXX manuscripts, reflects a Hebrew recension which contained synonymous parallelism making of this part of Boaz' speech another example of the semipoetry encountered frequently throughout the book. LXX^Lʹ, on the other hand, shows only one verb, *sōreusate,* "you shall heap up." Conceivably this represents Hebrew *sll* and would then attest a Hebrew version in which a hearing error had led to a writing of the wrong sibilant sound (Gerleman, but with too much confidence).

All of this throws little light on our verb *šll* here. An Arabic cognate *šll*, used chiefly of drawing a sword, seems the best clue to follow. The word *šl* in a letter found at Ugarit (*Le palais royal d'Ugarit*, V [1965], text 114=UT 2114), although the letter speaks of the devastation of threshing floors and vineyards, must be connected to the more common Hebrew *šll*, "to plunder."

the handfuls. That is, the amount of grain the sickler grasps with his left hand as he cuts with his right, a guess governed by the context. The assonance of the Hebrew word, which occurs only here in the OT, with the verb "heap up" in verse 14 has been discussed in the fifth NOTE on that verse.

17. *about an ephah.* The preposition *kᵉ* before *'ēpāh* probably means "approximately," as it frequently does in the OT. A very attractive alternative has been proposed by S. Talmon, BASOR 176 (December 1964), 33, in his study of the seventh-century Yabneh-yam ostracon to which we have referred before. In this ostracon, a harvester in the forced-labor battalion seems to argue that he has delivered the exact amount of harvest required of him, using the preposition *kᵉ* to indicate the exactitude, a so-called *kaph veritatis*. Talmon wonders whether the same meaning should be applied here: just an ephah. If so, the emphasis would lie on the remarkable fact that Ruth had gleaned exactly an ephah, and would enhance our marveling at the way Ruth's fortune in hitting upon Boaz' field has paid off. That marveling is provoked, whichever alternative one chooses.

The ephah is the dry-measure equivalent of a *bat*. W. F. Albright computed the capacity of a "bath" from a jar with *bt* inscribed on it found at Tell Beit Mirsim. His figure is about twenty-two liters or 5.8 gallons (U.S. measure). This archaeological datum serves as the basis for R. B. Y. Scott's calculations of measures of capacity in BAR[3], p. 352. Another system, followed by most German commentaries, traces the ephah back to the calculated capacity of a Persian *maris*, and would yield a set of values just under twice as large. As it happens, this set accords rather well with Josephus' measures for the "bath" (*Antiquities* 3.8.3, 8.2.9). In either case, we should heed Scott's double warning that the base of calculation is not certain, and that we do not know what variations developed throughout the biblical period. The amount Ruth carried home was rather impressive for a gleaner, but we are not called upon to add to her list of virtues that she was as strong as an ox. At most, her load would have weighed 47.5 pounds, while Scott's calculations (which I prefer) would be about twenty-nine pounds.

18. *and her mother-in-law saw.* The MT points the verb as a *Qal*, and the LXX tradition is unanimous in supporting it. The Syriac and Vulgate, however, read a causative: "and she showed her mother-in-law. . . ." Two Hebrew manuscripts collated by C. H. H. Wright, *The Book of Ruth in Hebrew* (London: Williams and Norgate, 1864), have the *Hiphil* voweling, and two others (Kennicott) show *'et,* the sign of the direct object, before "her mother-in-law." Most recent commentators follow their lead and read the *Hiphil,* thereby keeping Ruth the subject throughout the verse. Two considerations tell against this decision, in my mind. In the first place, while the Ruth text as we have it is rather sparing in its use of the sign of the direct object, it uses it where needed to avoid confusion. Its absence here, except in the two

manuscripts mentioned above, ought to be taken seriously (so also Joüon, *Commentaire*, p. 62). Second, we ought not to be concerned by a change in subject in midstream (the term is used advisedly). The Ruth story moves at varying pace. It can linger over an episode, using repetition and intricate syntax structures. But when it moves, it moves rapidly. Consider the rapid sequence at the end of verse 14 and beginning of verse 15: "and she ate and she was satisfied and she had some left over and she rose up to glean and Boaz commanded. . . ." A similar rapid change of subject in a sequence of five verbs takes place in 4:13 (see first NOTE). In 2:18 the words move so rapidly that at two points a verb has no direct object where we would expect it (with the first verb and with "and she brought out"). The matter hardly deserves extended discussion, since either reading yields good sense, but the proposed reading is an indication of the story-teller's sense of pace. As a bonus, of course, we get a glimpse of Naomi in wide-eyed astonishment as her daughter-in-law returns with an abundant supply of barley.

from her satisfying meal. A paraphrase for the sake of English. The Hebrew is probably an infinitive construct with possessive suffix, literally, "from her being satisfied." A noun "abundance" is attested in Hebrew, and the spelling would be identical. In any event, the point is to recall the final two words of verse 14; they are neatly given a reverse (chiastic) order.

19. *Where did you glean today / And where did you work?* The synonymous parallelism is again evident, although the text as we have it connects the two questions with the conjunction "and." Two different and relatively rare words express the interrogative "Where?": *'ēpōh* and *'ānāh*. Both are much less frequent than the usual *'ayyēh*, but Brown, Driver, and Briggs, *Lexicon*, points out that *'ayyēh* is never used with verbs. Our passage is the only one in the OT to use two of the three available words for "where" in parallelism.

'Ānāh is usually assumed to have the so-called *he*-directive on it, indicating movement and calling for the translation "whither?" But it means simply "where" in Gen 37:10; II Kings 6:6; and Isa 10:3. A similar phenomenon occurs with the word *šām*, "there"; it can take a similar ending and become *šāmmāh*, "thence," but there are occasions where this longer form means simply "there" (Gerleman points to the final word in the book of Ezekiel). Indeed, our story-teller uses this longer form at 1:7. This may be a hint of a dialect usage in Ruth.

As for the word *'ēpōh*, is the story-teller indulging his fancy for assonance? The sound is very much like the word *'ēpāh* he used in verse 17!

To translate "work" for the frequent verb *'śh* gives no problem; the story uses it three times in this sense in this verse. LXX[L] however, has, "Where have you done this work?" which provides the verb with a direct object. One maverick LXX manuscript adds instead "today," giving a complete synonymous parallelism.

May the one who had regard for you be blessed. This unusual blessing form occurs elsewhere only at I Kings 10:9=II Chron 9:8 and at Prov 5:18. The usual form is *bārūk X lᵉ Yahweh* (see 2:20 and 3:10). Here the word order places *bārūk*, "blessed," last: *yᵉhī makkīrēk bārūk*. The unusual order may have been selected to place the emphasis on *makkīrēk*—surely the story-teller wants his audience to see that Naomi has used the same root (*nkr*) which Ruth had used at 2:10. (See COMMENT.) This is a fine touch, and we should not assume that Ruth has given any answer to the questions asked by Naomi before Naomi pronounced the blessing. Naomi has not yet learned of the coincidence; the size of the gleaning is enough to call forth the first blessing.

A highly interesting variant, almost certainly an expansion but a rather early one, is attested by the Lucianic family with Theodoret; literally it reads at the conclusion of the brief blessing, "for he has satisfied a hungry soul, as he has done with that which he has done." The first part of this is a quotation from Ps 107:9, and one LXX witness, not usually found with the Lucianic family, stopped with the quotation only. The Greek itself may be in error in the second part, after the quotation; Rudolph suggests "as he had done with the one with whom you worked." Just how far back into Hebrew tradition this expansion may have gone we cannot tell, although it appears that a first stage had simply the quote from Ps 107:9, the second stage the further expansion. See the Introduction, pp. 39–41 on the value of the versions.

So she told her mother-in-law with whom she had worked, and said, "The name of the man with whom I worked today is Boaz." The text sounds redundant in the extreme, so that one is attracted to the LXX (with Syriac and OL) reading: "And Ruth told her mother-in-law where she had worked and said. . . ." This is a direct answer to the question Naomi first posed, while the MT offers an answer tangential to the questions (cf. 2:5 and 3:13), but directly pertinent to Naomi's blessing. There are two reasons for accepting MT rather than LXX: How does one answer a question about where she has been gleaning except by identifying the owner of the field (so, implicitly, T. H. Robinson in the notes to Ruth in BH³)? As far as redundancy is concerned, one must claim that the story-teller has suddenly slowed his pace once more, so as to gain effect. It is hard to imagine how he could pack more words into the description of Ruth's return, before she finally says the climactic word: Boaz! The audience has known this all along, but the dramatic suspense lies with the recognition that Naomi has not.

20. *Who has not forsaken his ḥesed / With the living.* There is genuine ambiguity here as to the antecedent of "Who"; is it Yahweh or Boaz? N. Glueck, in his classic study *Ḥesed in the Bible*, pp. 35 and 40 f., claimed that the clause modifies Boaz, and compares II Sam 2:5. The Greek retains the ambiguity and may even be said to support Boaz as antecedent, because it usually adds a name when a change of subject occurs. It is true that Boaz has done acts of *ḥesed* in chapter 2 and will yet do more, but the much more likely antecedent is Yahweh. Compare Gen 24:27: "Blessed be Yahweh, the God of my master Abraham, who has not forsaken his trustworthy *ḥesed* with my master." The same verb "forsake" occurs, but the preposition is different: *'et* here in Ruth, *mē'im* in Genesis 24—probably a variation of no consequence. Furthermore, Naomi's expression of praise seems to be quite general, because the word for "the living" is a masculine plural. If the frame of reference is simply the well-being of the women who are left alive, one would expect a feminine plural.

He is one of our circle of redeemers. The consonants of the MT are *mg'lnw*, vocalized as the preposition *min* and the singular noun with suffix.

Valiant attempts have been made to explain the singular noun with a preposition that is most easily taken as partitive: "one of." For example, Ehrlich proposed the preposition as "approximative," yielding "he is, so to speak, a relative of ours" (cf. Staples, AJSL 54 [1937], 62 ff.). But seven manuscripts collated by Ginsburg and forty collated by Kennicott join the LXX and Syriac in reading the plural. What is needed here is a plural term which corresponds to the situation surrounding $m^e yuddā^c$ in 2:1 (see the second NOTE there). The sequel demands that there be a group of people who bear responsibility in circumstances involving covenant associates and kin; see 3:2 and 3:12.

21. *the Moabitess.* The LXX and OL have "to her mother-in-law" and leave out "the Moabitess." The Syriac and Vulgate leave the gentilic out without substitution. The only defense for its appearance here is that Ruth is about to state the long-range boon that Boaz has granted her, she being a foreigner. It is conceivable that the story-teller wants once more to remind us of the remarkable circumstances. If it is redundant to have "the Moabitess" expressed, it is equally redundant to repeat "to her mother-in-law."

There's more! Hebrew *gam kī* is a rare expression found in the OT only in Hosea 8:10, 9:16; Isa 1:15; Ps 23:4; Prov 22:6; and Lam 3:8. In these passages, the complex conjunction means "even though" or literally "also when." The LXX seems not to have had a clear idea of the idiom, and so rendered it literally *kaige hoti;* the OL uses no connective at all. We are left to translate it according to the sense.

With the young people. Once more we are confronted with the problem of gender; the MT uses masculine plural as does LXX[B], but the OL and some LXX manuscripts use feminine doubtless to bring it into conformity with Naomi's words in verse 22.

Until. The Hebrew uses the rare combination *'ad 'im* here, attested elsewhere only in Gen. 24:19, 33 and Isa 30:17. As Joüon (*Commentaire*, p. 65) has pointed out, our story-teller usually uses *'ad* plus the infinitive construct to express "until X happens"; see 2:23, as well as 1:19 and 3:3. Boaz' language is curious, even when it is quoted by Ruth.

who are mine . . . which is mine. There is a correspondence of sorts between the two parts of Boaz' words as Ruth presents them: Stick close to the young people who are mine / until they complete the harvest which is mine. Boaz is depicted to us as a man of rather turgid speech; repetition for him does not seem to imply special emphasis (this against Rudolph's proposal to delete these words as "false repetition").

22. *It is better.* Or simply: "Good!" followed by emphatic *kī*, yielding "Fine, my daughter; then by all means go out. . . ." Notice this usage at 3:13. Joüon (*Commentaire*, p. 65) and Rudolph both compare II Sam 18:3, where David's military men counsel that it is better for him to stay in Jerusalem and support them than for him to take the battlefield. The Vulgate uses *melius*, "better," but the other versions reflect simply "good."

with his young women. Naomi introduces the gender distinction, and much has been made of this, perhaps too much. Naomi's counsel parallels quite closely that of Boaz in 2:8, especially if we retain the word "another" at the end of the verse (Rudolph deletes it). It is acceptable to say that the reasons of Naomi and Boaz are parallel, but there is one crucial change: where Boaz used *ng'*, "bother" (vs. 9; see NOTE on "to bother you"), Naomi uses *pg'*, a much stronger and more violent word, at least as we have it attested in the prose of the Deuteronomic histories. Beside "to meet, encounter," *pg'* is regularly used to mean "strike down, attack violently" (see e.g. I Sam 22:17–18 and I Kings 2:25–46). Naomi's instructions do appear to place more emphasis on Ruth's personal safety, although no other use of the word in the OT suggests sexual assault. Nevertheless, by this slight change of verb, from *ng'* to *pg'*, the story-teller may be nudging his audience along to think about the protection of the "elect" woman, a theme prominent in the patriarchal stories. At the same time, we should recall that *pg'*, Naomi's word here, was on Ruth's lips in 1:16—"Do not press me to abandon you."

23. *the barley harvest and the wheat harvest.* From Deut 16:9–12 it is clear that from the beginning of barley harvest to the end of wheat harvest was normally seven weeks, culminating with Pentecost. Of course, the precise time of year would differ from low altitudes to higher, and from south to north, but the span would run roughly from late April to the beginning of June. This is in accord with the famous schoolboy's practice text called the Gezer Calendar (illustration 3) dating from about 925 B.C.E. (see the translation by W. F. Albright in *Ancient Near Eastern Texts*, p. 320, and his treatment in BASOR 92 [December 1943], esp. 25 f.; see also the illuminating reconstruction of the agricultural year based on this calendar by G. E. Wright, *Biblical Archaeology* [Philadelphia: Westminster, 1962], pp. 183 ff.). In fact, however, the seasons do not follow this schedule in modern times. Thanks to the efforts of Munira Sa'id of the Albright Institute of Archaeological Research in Jerusalem, I learn that barley in the region around Bethlehem now is harvested in late June, and wheat in early July, an observation which fits rather well with my own observations in the northern hill country, around Shechem. The discrepancy is not easy to resolve, although modern agricultural techniques, which appear to favor slowing down the growing process and have introduced new strains of these cereals, may have something to do with the shift.

A curious question remains. If Ruth gleaned throughout the entire late spring harvest, can the usual reading of 3:2, that the scene at the threshing floor involved barley, be correct? Was barley left for threshing until after the wheat had also been gathered? The apparent discrepancy led Gunkel, *Reden und Aufsätze*, p. 75, to see the reference to wheat harvest as an addition (cf. A. Bertholet in E. Kautzsch et al., *Die Heilige Schrift des Alten Testaments*, II, 4th ed. [Tübingen: Mohr, 1923], 410). As a better way out of the difficulty, see the translation and the second NOTE on 3:2.

Then she stayed (at home) with her mother-in-law. MT has *wattēšeb 'et ḥᵃmōtāh*, but a very few Hebrew manuscripts read *wattašob 'el ḥᵃmōtāh*, "and she returned to her mother-in-law." The Vulgate reads this way, making the verse the opening of chapter 3. But Rudolph is surely right that MT should be retained. Here, as at the end of each scene, a summarizing statement is needed which also points ahead. Now that harvesting and gleaning are over,

Ruth no longer goes out each day; for the moment, "the tale once more has come to a standstill" (Gerleman).

COMMENT

The second episode involves all of chapter 2, with three interconnected scenes. The first (verse 2) and last (verses 18–23), involving Ruth and Naomi, surround the more measured scene in the field. The story-teller uses his favorite devices to knit the scenes into a unit. For one thing, the verb "glean" keeps up a steady beat from verse 2 to verse 23. Another link is the designation of Ruth as "the Moabitess" in 2 and 21, while her Moabite origin is the subject of verse 6. Again, from verse 5 to the end of the chapter there is repeated use of words in the cluster "young man/young woman/young people/ young women." An effective link is created between verse 1 and verse 19: the audience is told about Boaz and his relationship to Naomi at the start, but the two women do not put his name and his relationship to them together until the end of verse 19 and in the words of Naomi in verse 20. Another link between scenes is the marvelous bit of word-play by which Naomi uses in verse 19 the very verb that Ruth used in verse 10, translated as "take special note of" in 10 and "had regard for" in 19 (see second NOTE on 2:19). Also, as he did at the end of the first chapter, the story-teller brings this episode to its end with a summary sentence which points toward the next episode, when harvest is over and threshing begun. All of these literary signals invite us to look for themes emphasized within chapter 2, while at the same time to be alert to the development of the overall story.

The first thing that happens is that the story-teller makes a brief appearance on the stage as narrator to introduce us to Boaz. Some of what is stated in this introduction is repeated in verse 3, but there are three important things told us in verse 1 and there only: that Naomi, as Elimelek's widow, has some sort of connection to Boaz; that the connection is tied up with the term here translated "covenant-brother"; and that Boaz is "a man of substance" in terms both of wealth and worthiness (see the NOTE).

The remainder of chapter 2, and indeed all the rest of the story, will tell us what Boaz' being a man of substance means (and will also, of course, link Ruth to him by a corresponding term in 3:11). What is harder to identify is the nature of the connection between Naomi and Boaz, for it belongs to the realm of Israelite custom at the village level, a realm not nearly so well known to us as we could wish. Family ties, doubtless extending outward for several circles, are part of the picture, although we will never be told exactly what familial relationship Boaz had to Elimelek. Another ingredient is the range of responsibility bound up in the function of the $g\bar{o}'\bar{e}l$, "redeemer." The NOTE on verse 1, "covenant-brother," has proposed still another dimension, that of responsibility inherent in covenant ties, relationships entered into voluntarily rather than through the accident of blood connection. This proposal of a covenant dimension is in part conjectural. I make it to free us from the narrow definitions of levirate marriage and redemption as they are usually derived by scholars from other OT passages and attested customs of surrounding cultures. The important thing to see here is that there is a distinct ingredient of good will, of willingness to help, indeed of determination to care for the widow and the destitute, which is fundamental to the Ruth story.

We must of course return to the concept of redemption in treating chapters 3 and 4, but two words in chapter 2 will have already set the stage for that concept's range. I submit that an element of magnanimity is introduced by the word translated "covenant-brother"; already at 2:1 it is made clear to the audience that the relationship between Naomi and Boaz depends upon the exercise of magnanimity. The same need for magnanimity is presumably inherent in the synonymous term in Naomi's words at 2:20, which I have translated "circle of redeemers." This whole matter can be stated the other way round: the Ruth story is basically about extraordinary caring and concern, kindness that is above and beyond the call of duty. There are people in this story whose actions display this "plus" factor, but there are also words. One of these words is ḥesed, as was suggested in the COMMENT on Section II, and will be seen again later. The two designations of a community, "covenant-brother" and "circle of redeemers," also suggest the "plus" factor. Together they point to the heart of the story.

While Boaz' membership in a circle rightfully responsible for Naomi is one facet of their relationship, chapter 2 also relishes another facet, that together they represent the senior citizens of the story. This is shown in several ways. It is from their perspective that everyone else even so much as mentioned in the action of chapter 2 is young. Boaz' foreman at the harvesting is a young man. He in turn calls Ruth a young woman, while Boaz refers to Ruth as a young woman in 2:5, and regularly speaks of his harvesters as young women (girls) or young people (masculine plural, presumably including youths of both sexes). In 2:22, Naomi takes up the chorus, with a wry bit of motherly advice: you'll do better to stick with the girls rather than with the whole group of young people! Both Naomi (at 2:2 and 22) and Boaz (at 2:8) address Ruth as "my daughter"; in verses 8 and 22, this form of address accompanies some firmly stated advice, almost imperious in tone. Also, commentators have frequently pointed out a certain old-fashioned style in their words. Myers, in his study of the book's form and style, lists ten examples of archaic or at least dialectal spelling (MLLF, p. 20, augmented by taʻᵃbūrī on p. 17), every one of which occurs in a speech of Boaz or Naomi. It is these two who ask the series of three questions containing enigmatic syntax in 2:5, 3:9, and 3:16. Boaz' speeches particularly are ceremonial and rather turgid.

What purpose is there behind these devices? One senses that the story-teller means to give his characters a certain credibility in this way. Perhaps also there is a need, especially in the case of Naomi, to underscore the truth of her own assertion in 1:12 that she is too old to have a husband. As for Boaz there may even be a question about his ability to sire a son (see the last NOTE on 4:11). There may be a quite different explanation: perhaps it is just good, story-telling style to have one or several of the crafty older generation whose wisdom and experience make them capable of thinking out the clever schemes which will provide the drama in the subsequent chapters. In any event, senior citizens they are, and the audience should appreciate them as such. The development of the portrayal of Ruth will take place in connection with them, alternating from one to the other.

First, then, let us consider Ruth with Naomi. In chapter 1, the audience witnessed how determined Ruth can be; by the power of her own loyalty and attachment to Naomi, she has overcome her mother-in-law's objections and rendered her speechless. At the onset of chapter 2, Ruth, on her own initiative, sets about providing for the two of them; it is doubtful indeed that Ruth in 2:2 is really asking permission from Naomi to go to glean. In chapter 2, Ruth in relation to Naomi is a diligent younger companion, strong enough to do the gleaning, considerate in bringing home not only the fruits of her work but also the leftovers of her meal at the field, and exuberant in reporting her adventures and accepting Naomi's reaction and advice.

In relation to Boaz, however, Ruth is deferential almost to a fault. The words which carry this tone more than any others are "to find favor in someone's eyes." When Ruth first uses them, in verse 2, we are not, I think, to conclude that she has selected a target; verse 3 makes that very doubtful. Rather, Ruth is setting out to take advantage of a well-prescribed custom, that Israelites not pick their fields clean, precisely so that unfortunates may glean (Lev 19:9 f., 23:22 and Deut 24:19). The clear implication in 2:2, made explicit at the beginning of verse 7, is that Ruth will ask permission. The second NOTE on verse 7 has even speculated that Ruth did not begin to glean until Boaz himself had given permission. This is unusual, for the guidelines in Leviticus and Deuteronomy mention no need for the poor to ask permission to glean. However, the perspective of these guidelines is from the landowner toward the poor, while the perspective in our story is from the poor toward the landowner. Something is being said here about the character of a young woman in an alien society. Her circumstances, bound up as they are with Naomi's, require more than ordinary kindness from whoever is willing to help; to correspond with this, she is more than ordinarily scrupulous about the customs of her new home.

We are back again with the story-teller's emphasis on the extra, the more-than-required. Boaz will prove to be one who can give more than is legally required; the only way Ruth can act correspondingly is to be a more-than-ordinary recipient. She is after all a foreigner and a woman, and, as her mother-in-law warned her in 1:11–13, with next to no prospects in Judah. When "she fell on her face and bowed down to the earth," an elaborate but by no means unheard of act of deference, it is a genuine response to what is only the first of a series of kindly actions which Boaz will take on her behalf. When she expresses wonder that she has found favor in his eyes—the second use of this idiom (2:2 and 2:10)—Boaz responds that he has heard of her extraordinary deed in leaving home and family to return with her mother-in-law. One magnanimous act, one act of *ḥesed* as Boaz will call it at 3:10, gives impetus to another; it was Ruth's act which began the sequence of correspond-

ingly gracious acts. And so Boaz invokes Yahweh's blessing on her for her
deed. To that blessing Ruth responds with humility, and with the expression of
hope that she will go on finding favor in the eyes of "my lord."

One word about Ruth's character as it has been unfolding in the story. It is
inherent in biblical thought generally that a person's actions and words offer a
true picture of the person's character. Hebrew stories do not have characters
with hidden motives and concealed agendas, or if they do, the audience is explicitly told about it. The ancient audience would have received Ruth as her
words and deeds have portrayed her. If the modern audience does not receive
her in this way, it is liable cynically to conclude that she is a scheming
woman trying to butter up a vain old man. It is clear that, for all his sense of
drama and for all his intent to portray and recommend behavior attainable by
all people, our story-teller is not writing a modern-style soap opera. His characters are to be taken at face value and without devious motives. This is important to realize here in chapter 2, and all the more important for understanding chapter 3 correctly. What is at issue here is men and women, old and
young, living out publicly the sort of lives the story-teller commends.

All the action takes place in the presence of the unobtrusive chief character
of the entire story, the God who is the only person present in all of the scenes,
but always in the shadows. Take, for example, the matter of Ruth's "luck" in
2:3. The Hebrew term involved here is only rarely to be taken as meaning
"luck" or "chance"; few things if any happen by chance, according to biblical
thought. The best comparable passage is the serio-comic story of the test
which the Philistines concoct to determine whether or not their possession of
the Ark of Yahweh is the reason for various troubles they have been experiencing (I Sam 6:1–12). The conditions of the test come at verse 9: will the
test show the troubles to be due to Yahweh—or to chance? The audience
knows perfectly well who is responsible; indeed the previous chapter has told
them specifically. In Ruth, the question is handled more subtly, but the audience knows it is hardly by chance that Ruth came to Boaz' field.

Chapter 2 affords other opportunities to observe the story-teller's theological perspective. Especially important are the blessings in Yahweh's name occurring in 2:4, 12, and 20. They affirm Yahweh's ultimate responsibility for
well-being, for *shalom,* in society; they pertain to what calls forth Yahweh's
blessing upon persons and upon peoples; they portray the correspondence between Yahweh's will and the wills of his people.

At 2:4, Boaz and his workmen exchange conventional greetings invoking
Yahweh—conventional, but suggestive of an ordered and tranquil domestic
scene in which Yahweh's name is readily and properly on the lips of his people. Compare the opposite circumstances in Ps 129:8, where enemies of the
Psalmist, of Zion, and thus of Yahweh, are never again to be greeted with a
similar set of blessings in Yahweh's name. There is more than mere conven-
tion to these greetings; there is affirmation of a condition of well-being, of
shalom.

The other two blessings, of Boaz upon Ruth in 2:12 and of Naomi upon
Boaz in 2:20, are anything but conventional. Each is a specific response to the
report of specific human deeds of an extraordinary sort. Each states an affir-

mation about God appropriate to the occasion. Each adds a dimension of praise of God to its approval of the acts of human beings.

In 2:12, Boaz' blessing of Ruth comes immediately after his recapitulation of her record of magnanimous loyalty to Naomi. It is imperative to realize that there is no mechanical doctrine of reward and punishment here; what is here is a confident affirmation that God's blessing follows upon righteous living. In terms of the now well-known covenant formulations of the OT, God first favors his people on his own initiative, then requires that they live in accord with their status as his people, and then responds with blessing or curse to their obedient or disobedient living. Human righteous acts do not incur God's favor, they live out God's favor. God's people do acts of *ḥesed* not in order to deserve God's grace, but in order to respond to his grace. God's blessing is then a response to the response, one of which his people may be confident but of which they cannot be mechanically sure. To put it more directly with reference to Boaz' blessing of Ruth, his words really are a prayer, a petition, and not a statement of doctrine.

The best indication in the Ruth story that there is nothing automatic about God's blessing is the theme of Naomi's complaint. We saw in chapter 1 the depth of discouragement Naomi felt at how the sweetness of her life had turned sour and her willingness to hurl this state of affairs at God. Blessing for her seemed at a great distance. But at 2:20, the situation begins to alter. As with Boaz' blessing at 2:14, Naomi's here comes immediately after she learns that the specific acts of kindness Ruth has received came from Boaz. Her blessing is for Boaz, but it takes the form of praise to Yahweh as the one who, in spite of her complaint, still does act in *ḥesed* among his people.

Ḥesed in the human scene is evidence of God's *ḥesed*, his faithful magnanimity. This correspondence is a particular characteristic of the story-teller's theology, one we have noted before and will encounter again. Boaz invokes God's blessing upon Ruth only to become himself the agency for the fulfillment of that blessing; the God he invokes is the one under whose wings she has come to seek refuge, but it will be the "wing" of Boaz, in 3:9, which brings her due recompense. Naomi praises the God who still acts with *ḥesed* because Boaz has so acted, and it will be the *ḥesed* of both Boaz and Ruth which will bring Naomi fulfillment. We can say that persons act as God to one another in our story. If that be so, how striking it is that Ruth falls on her face and bows to the earth—worship language in most instances in the OT—before Boaz, and responds to his blessing of her in Yahweh's name by calling him "my lord."

IV. THE ENCOUNTER AT THE THRESHING FLOOR
(3:1–18)

3 1 Then Naomi, her mother-in-law, said to her^a, "My daughter, have I not been seeking security for you, so that things may go well for you? 2 Now is it not so that Boaz is one of our covenant circle, with whose girls you have been? Notice, he is winnowing (the grain of) the threshing floor near the gate this very night. 3 Now^b bathe and anoint yourself, don your cape, and go down to the threshing floor. Do not make yourself known to the man until he has finished ^ceating and drinking^c. 4 And when he lies down, note the place where he lies, and go and uncover his legs and lie down. Then he will tell you what you are to do." 5 She said to her, "All that you say^d I shall do."

6 So she went down to the threshing floor and did everything her mother-in-law ^ehad commanded her^e. 7 Boaz ate ^fand drank^f, and his heart was merry, and he went to lie down at the far end of the grainheap; then she came quietly, uncovered his legs ^gand lay down^g. 8 Around midnight, the man shuddered and groped about;

^a Throughout the chapter, as throughout the entire book, the LXX in general and the Lucianic family in particular (LXX^L here: "to Ruth") make explanatory additions. Only where they are controversial are they pointed out, usually in the NOTES.

^b LXX^B begins the verse *su de*, "but as for you."

^{c–c} LXX^B and most Lucianic witnesses reverse the order; cf. the same phenomenon in 1:5, and the Syriac at 3:10.

^d The *qᵉrē* of MT, a large group of Hebrew manuscripts, some LXX nonhexaplaric manuscripts, Syriac, OL, and other dependent versions add, "to me." The chapter has many such expansions; other additions of the same kind, attested by various witnesses, occur at 3:9, 11, 15, 16, and 17.

^{e–e} MT: anomalous *ṣiwwattāh* for expected *ṣiwwathā*, often explained as a contraction. Instead, probably what happened is a development from *ṣiwwathā* to *ṣiwwattā* (by backward assimilation of the *h* to the *t*) to *ṣiwwattāh* (showing the full spelling of the final long *ā* vowel.)

^{f–f} LXX^{BL'} lack "and drank"; Syro-Hexapla marks with an asterisk (Origen added it to the Greek on the basis of the fuller Hebrew text).

^{g–g} LXX^B plus one vagrant LXX witness lack "and lay down." A secondary hand added to the main OL manuscript a second "at his feet."

and *here was* a woman lying next to him! 9 He said, "Who are you?" and she said, "I am Ruth your maid-servant. Now spread your 'wing' over your maid-servant, for you are a redeemer." 10 And he said,

> "Blessed may you be by Yahweh*, my daughter.
> *You have made your latter *hesed*
>   Better than the former,
>   In not going after the younger men
>   Be they *poor or rich*.
> 11 And now, my daughter, do not fear.
>   All that you say I shall do for you,
>   For all the assembly of my* people know
>   That you are a worthy woman.
> 12 Now it is certainly true that I am a redeemer
>   But there is also another redeemer
>   Nearer than I.
> 13 Spend tonight (here), and in the morning
>   If he will do the redeemer's part,
>   Well and good, *let him redeem*,
>   But if he does not want to do the redeemer's part,
>   I will redeem you
>   *As surely as Yahweh lives*.
> Lie down until the morning."

14 So she lay down next to him until the morning, and she arose before* one man could recognize another, for he said, "Let it

---

h–h Syriac, Vulgate, and Targum read a verb, "he saw," for the particle *hinnēh*, "behold," probably interpreting rather than attesting a variant (against BH³).

i LXXᴮ adds "God." The minor Lucianic witnesses read "the Lord your God." BH³ is incorrect in saying the OL supports the addition of "God."

j LXX and Syriac supply a logical connective, "because," here; doubtless an interpretive addition, this does not attest a lost Hebrew *ki*.

k–k Syriac reverses: "rich or poor." Cf. textual note *c–c* above.

l Syriac "our" for "my"; a nice touch but hardly original.

m–m Two Lucianic LXX witnesses: "*I* will redeem you," an inadvertent anticipation of what lies ahead.

n–n Syriac lacks the oath. The scribe of LXXᴮ appears to have heard two different possibilities, and writes them both: *zē kurios su ei kurios*, "live, Yahweh, you are Yahweh."

o MT consonants for "before" are *btrwm*, but the vowels are those of the common word *beṭerem*. No satisfactory explanation for the extra *w* has been given; Rudolph's relic of a lost word *bdbrw*, "at his command," is far-fetched indeed.

not be known that the woman came ᵖto the threshing floor"ᵖ.
15 Then he said,

> "Present the wrap which is about you;
>   Get a good hold on it."

She held it firmly, and he measured out six *šāʿār*-measures, and set it
upon her; then he went into the city. 16 She went to her mother-
in-law, who said, "How do things stand with you, my daughter?"
So she told her all that the man had done for her. 17 And she said,

> "These six *šāʿār*-measures he gave me,
>   For he said,�q 'You shall not go empty
>   To your mother-in-law.' "

18 And she said,

> "Sit tight, my daughter,
>   Until such time as you know
>   How the matter will fall out.
>   For the man will not rest
>   Until he has brought the matter to conclusion todayʳ."

ᵖ⁻ᵖ OL, "to me"; Vulgate simply, "here."

q For the second time in the chapter (see verse 5 and textual note ᵈ) "to me" is
read but not written. Here a somewhat different group of versions give support.

ʳ Two LXX manuscripts and the Vulgate lack "today."

NOTES

3:1. *My daughter, have I not been seeking.* In 2:8–9, Boaz addressed Ruth
with two negative rhetorical questions, accompanying the first question with
"my daughter." Here and in the next verse Naomi uses two negative rhetorical
questions and the appellative "my daughter." It is stylistic devices like these,
more than any explicit statement (see 3:10), which suggest Boaz' age; he and
Naomi are made to belong to the same generation by the simple device of
having them talk the same way. The verb here, however, is not a perfect as at
2:8–9, but is imperfect, suggesting the active and continuing effort of Naomi.

security. The audience should recall Naomi's words in 1:9, where she prays
that the two young widows should find security in the homes of new husbands.

so that things may go well for you. Almost certainly a "final" clause, here
taken as expressing result, in spite of the fact that the clause is introduced by
the relative conjunction *'ᵃšer.* The relative conjunction can tempt the translator toward "a rest which will be good for you," but this is decisively blocked
by the fact that the combination of the *Qal* of the verb *yṭb* and the preposition
lᵉ invariably expresses an impersonal construction in biblical Hebrew: "it may/
will go well for you." See Deut 4:40 and 6:3 for the same syntax (with *'ᵃšer*)
over against the more common construction with the conjunction *lᵉmaʿan* (e.g.
in Deut 6:18).

2. *one of our covenant circle.* MT, *mōda'tānū*, a unique feminine noun from *yd'*, "to know." The spelling of the first person plural suffix, *-ānū* for *-ēnū*, is itself an anomaly (see the grammars), but it need not detain us. The interest lies rather in the connotation of the word. It seems to me inescapable that we be guided by the terms *mᵉyuddā'* in 2:1 and *mg'lnw*, "one of our circle of redeemers," in 2:20 (see the NOTES on these words). Reverting to the Hebrew consonants of our term, *md't*, we must posit that they are, or contain, a feminine abstract noun naming the larger entity of which *mᵉyuddā'* designates a single member. Furthermore, on the basis of *mg'lnw*, we must presume the original presence of the preposition *min* in its partitive sense "one of," attached with the usual assimilation of the *n* sound. Thus, if the original word here is a *mem*-preformative noun, the attachment of *min* would yield consonantal *mmd't*, and we would have to assume a loss of one *m* by haplography. It is also possible that the original noun was made up of the consonants *d't* only (there exists a common Hebrew noun *da'at*, "knowledge,"); the *m* preserved in the Hebrew consonantal text would then represent the preposition.

Let the reader be clear: this is highly conjectural. It places heavy reliance on the "interlocking" style of the story-teller, which compels consistency with the terms in 2:1 and 2:20. We are in the vicinity of the correct meaning with the proposed translation.

the threshing floor near the gate. The usual translation is something like the RSV's "he is winnowing barley at the threshing floor," which represents a more radical departure from the text than is usually admitted. The MT reads, literally, "he is winnowing the threshing floor of the barley."

At 2:23 we had already recognized a certain problem arising: if Ruth gleaned throughout both barley and wheat harvest, why is Boaz just getting to winnowing the earlier crop? It is conceivable, I suppose, that the Israelite farmer cut his crop before the grain was fully ripe and left it to dry for a time before threshing and winnowing. But our story-teller had Ruth "beat out" what she had gleaned in her first day of work, which suggests the barley was ripe. The general circumstances, then, place a strain on the correctness of the word "the barley" here.

The Hebrew syntax also makes "the barley" dubious. The word *goren*, "threshing floor," is marked as the direct object of "winnowing" and is in a construct relationship with *haśśe'ōrīm*, "the barley." The second word of a construct chain is expected to modify the first in some way, but it is not clear how that is meant to happen here. Is it "the barley threshing floor," as though there were separate threshing floors for each kind of grain? Even if we accept Joüon's proposal (*Commentaire*, p. 67) to read "threshing floor" as metonomy for "the *product* of the threshing floor" we remain in syntactic difficulty; for then "barley" would presumably have to stand in apposition to "the product of the threshing floor," but the Hebrew construct chain does not normally express this kind of thing.

The proposed translation gives an alternative containing several advantages. It involves reading *śe'ārīm* for MT *śe'ōrīm*. The two sibilant consonants *š* and *ś* are written with the same Hebrew letter, and were distinguished in

Hebrew orthography only in the medieval Masoretic period. Thus, at Gen 26:12, where MT uses *šᵉʿārîm* (here with the meaning of a measure of some sort—see Ruth 3:15), the LXX and Syriac read "barley." At II Kings 23:8, many commentators suggest reading *šᵉʿîrîm*, "demons," for *šᵉʿārîm*, "gates." R. G. Boling, in *Judges*, AB, vol. 6A, NOTE on 7:13, suggests a word-play between "gate-fighters" and the "moldy barley-loaf" which bounces through the Midianite camp in the dream of the soldier. Another elaborate word-play between the two words "barley" and "gate" is to be found throughout II Kings 7:1–20, especially in verses 1 and 16–18. In short, then, confusion of the two words is very easy to understand, and so is word-play between them. The gate will assume great importance in what follows (see 3:11, 4:1, 10–11, and the pertinent NOTES), just as barley has played its role up to the end of chapter 2. Given the story-teller's love for word-play as well as for giving hints of things to come, it is not surprising to have him introduce the gate in 3:2, close to his last use of barley in 2:23.

The combination of threshing floor and gate accords very well with the picture drawn in I Kings 22:10, where the confrontation between the prophet Micaiah and the court prophets of Ahab takes place at "the threshing floor of the entrance of the gate of Samaria" (literally, so as to suggest the long construct chain). This passage was the starting point for an informative exchange between Sidney Smith and John Gray (*Palestine Exploration Quarterly* 78 [1946], 5–14; 84 [1952], 110–13; 85 [1953], 42–45 and 118–23) concerning the location and purpose of threshing floors. With their work in mind, what can be said with confidence about gates and threshing floors?

First, a threshing floor was probably located close enough to the city gate to allow ease of carrying the grain into town and ease of keeping watch over the grain during the threshing and winnowing operations. Second, the threshing floor was probably an open space, large enough for many to thresh and winnow at the same time, which was sufficiently exposed to the prevailing west wind to take advantage of it for the winnowing process. Note well: only directly against a high city wall at the east edge of town would there be too much protection and hence not enough wind. Third, certain public occasions, especially judicial hearings, could properly be held at the threshing floor near the gate; this is the case in I Kings 22 and in a passage from the tale of *Aqht* found at Ugarit, text A v:4–8. In this passage, Dan'el sits "in the 'nose' of the gate under the *'adrm* (meaning disputed) which was/were at the threshing floor, judging the case of the widow, adjudicating the claim of the fatherless." Still another hint of the juxtaposition of the winnowing site and the gate is afforded by Jer 15:7: "I have winnowed them with a winnowing fan, in the gates of the land . . ." (against J. Bright, *Jeremiah*, AB, vol. 21: "in the outlying towns").

There is still another bit of archaeological data which is only beginning to come into focus. The American excavations at Gezer in 1971 turned up what is apparently a granary in the acropolis region at the highest point of the *tell* and near its western edge, dating to the twelfth century B.C.E. Outside the granary, there had accumulated a layer as much as four feet deep of charred wheat and barley, identified by microscopic analysis. The hypothesis being advanced is that this resulted from burning the threshing floor periodically; see W. G. Dever et al., BA 34 (1971), 129. Similar layers of charred debris, which will soon be submitted to the same analysis, are to be found at Tell el-Ḥesī (Eglon), Lachish, Shechem, and Dothan, all roughly of the same date or a little later in the Iron Age. This datum may suggest that some threshing and winnowing was done inside the city walls, or it may indicate that the threshing floor lay just outside the city to the west, whence its chaff and some of its grain would be blown into the city where it was burned to drive out vermin and rodents.

One final consideration: I Kings 22:10 uses the word "gate" in the singular, as will the remaining passages in Ruth. Here in 3:2, however, the word bears the masculine plural ending. That the plural can be used for the gate structure as such is shown by II Sam 18:24. Here David takes his place "between the two gates," that is, in one of the recesses of a double- or triple-entry gate, as he awaits news of the battle against his beloved rebel son Absalom. That David is within the gate structure is made clear by the fact that the watchman on the roof of the gate tower calls down word of the approach of the messengers. The multiple-entry gates found at such sites as Gezer, Dan, Megiddo, and Hazor fit well into this picture—see the COMMENT on 4:1–12.

Was Bethlehem a walled town? While it seems likely that it was, we have no archaeological information as yet. Once again, what must be noted is that the story-teller has authentic knowledge of the conditions of the early monarchic period, and uses the details with precision.

this very night. Hebrew, *hallayᵉlāh,* "the night, tonight." The LXX, Syriac, OL, and Vulgate all use the demonstrative "this," a perfectly justifiable rendering of the Hebrew. If the story-teller means simply to designate the time when winnowing is most likely to be taking place, he has apparently chosen the wrong term; his designation should be pertinent to the hours from about 2:30 to 6:30 P.M., when the constant and dependable west wind blows over the Palestinian hill country. Joüon (*Commentaire,* pp. 67 f.) followed by most recent commentators cites Josh 2:2 ff. as evidence that "the night" can mean at least a part of the afternoon. When Jericho's king is told that Israelite spies have been in the city "tonight," he confronts Rahab, who admits that the spies came to her home but left before the city gates were closed, at dark. This Joshua passage is a slim basis for understanding the impact of the word here. The Ruth story-teller has used *hāʿereb,* "the evening," at 2:17, to refer to the end of the work day; one would think this would be the more appropriate term here.

All in all, we probably do best by taking our cue from Josh 2:2 and thinking of the twilight hours, but we will do well also to keep in mind that the word "tonight" orients the audience toward the scene which is about to unfold in the dark of the night.

3. *Now bathe. . . .* Naomi's instruction of Ruth is expressed not with the expected imperative but with a series of perfects with *waw.* It is common enough to have an instruction begin with one or more imperatives and then continue with perfects; see, for example, Joab's instruction of the wise woman

of Tekoah in II Sam 14:2–3 (three imperatives followed by three perfects). Rarer is a series which starts off with perfect with *waw*. A complicated example occurs in I Sam 10:2–8, as Samuel portrays to Saul a sequence of events about to take place, interspersed with instructions to Saul (fourteen perfect verbs with *waw*, with several imperfects appearing after the midpoint of the sequence, but no imperatives until verse 8, after thirteen of the fourteen perfects!).

As the MT in 3:3 stands, there is a symmetry to the verb sequence which may well be intentional. First come four perfects with *waw* ("wash . . . anoint . . . don . . . go down"), the last of them showing what may be an archaic feminine second person ending *ī* (see the list of certain instances in Myers, MLLF, p. 11, all from Jeremiah and Ezekiel—archaizing?). After these four come a negative imperative ("don't let it be known") and an imperfect (literally, "and it shall be when he lies down"). Then comes another group of four perfects with *waw* ("take note . . . come . . . uncover . . . lie down"), the last again with the archaic feminine *ī*. Whether the symmetry is intentional or not, Naomi's instruction is expressed in unusual and quite possibly early Hebrew syntax. By the way, for an imperfect to intrude in the series of perfects appears to be acceptable. We have seen that it happens in I Sam 10:2–8, and Rudolph has added II Sam 5:24, as he refutes Joüon's claim that we should emend the imperfect to a perfect and thus make the series uniform. If anything, one suspects that uniform syntax is later than mixed syntax.

anoint yourself. The LXX^L' has highly interesting readings here. The mainstream Lucianic group adds after this verb "and rub yourself with myrrh." The minor Lucianic witnesses substitute this phrase for "anoint yourself." Possibly we have in the main group a conflation of two old readings; I judge it equally possible that the fuller reading was in some old Hebrew text, perhaps with the verb *nsk* parallel to the verb *swk* attested by the MT; both carry the connotation of "pour," the latter more explicitly for anointing. In any event, the Lucianic witnesses bring myrrh into the picture. This would make much clearer the implication that Ruth was to make herself enticing; see the use of myrrh in Song of Songs 1:3, 13, 3:6, 4:14, 5:1, 5, 13; in the wedding Psalm, 45:9; in the beauty regimen of Esther 2:12; and in Prov 7:17.

your cape. The q^erê MT gives a plural, while the consonants indicate singular. The versions divide, Syriac, Vulgate, and the Targum reading plural, the LXX singular. The plural is used frequently enough in the OT to mean simply "clothing" but not necessarily at any place to mean dressy clothes (but see Gen 35:2, 45:22; II Sam 12:20). The singular recommends itself to most recent commentators and is adopted here. Probably the story-teller is referring to just this garment again, but with a different Hebrew word in the mouth of Boaz at verse 15.

and go down. The verb is to be taken quite literally; the threshing floor is down from the city (but cf. LXX: "go up!"); in 4:1 Boaz must go up to the gate. Invoking the phenomenon of "semantic polarization," whereby a word can have a meaning virtually the opposite of its familiar one, some have sought to place the threshing floor uphill from the city and to take the verb to mean "go up" (see H. G. May, *Journal of the Royal Asiatic Society* [1939], 75–78). This is far-fetched here, and relates to the broader purpose of the author to show a sacral activity lying behind the present story. See the Introduction, p. 7.

4. *and uncover his legs*. The Hebrew is *wᵉgillīt margᵉlōtāw* (note the assonance); here and in 3:7 *margᵉlōtāw* designates what Ruth uncovers, while in 3:8 and 14 the same noun designates the place where Ruth sleeps. *Margᵉlōtāw* appears elsewhere in the OT only at Dan 10:6 where it is paired with "arms" and must mean "legs." This noun is etymologically related to the common noun *regel*, "foot," which can serve as a euphemism for the penis or the vulva, either as sexual organs or as the urinary opening (see Judg 3:24; I Sam 24:3; II Kings 18:27=Isa 36:12; Isa 7:20; Ezek 16:25; and in all probability, Exod 4:25; Deut 28:57; and Isa 6:2). The versions were clearly troubled as they sought to interpret correctly, doubtless because they recognized the possible inference that Ruth uncovered the entire lower body of Boaz. Consider LXX "reveal the (place) at his feet"; Vulgate: "remove the coverlet which hides the place at his feet"; Syriac "draw near and lie down near his feet" (no reflection of a verb "to uncover"); OL: "cover yourself to the feet"; and modern renderings such as NEB: "turn back the covering at his feet."

The question is whether the story-teller meant to be ambiguous and hence provocative. It seems to me that he did; therefore the intentional ambiguity of the translation "legs," which leaves open the question of how much of his legs (see the COMMENT).

5. *All that you say*. The verb is imperfect, and hence is taken by Joüon to be a general statement of obedience, citing II Kings 10:5, where Ahab's retainers in Samaria indicate their willingness to undertake whatever Jehu plans. Rudolph, in opposition, cites II Sam 9:11, where Ziba assents to a specific instruction from David. The clinching comparison, however, is to Ruth 3:11, where Boaz assents to Ruth's claims upon him. What Ruth is assenting to in 3:5 are the specific steps in Naomi's plan, however drastic or dangerous they may appear to be. The Latin and Greek versions, by using the past tense, "all that you said," are simply reflecting the sense.

6. *did everything*. The Hebrew is *watta'aś kᵉkōl*, "she did according to all." Freedman has suggested the attractive alternative that we read the *kᵉ* here as the *kaph-veritatis*, an indication of exactitude (see the NOTE on 2:17). The translation would then be "and she did everything exactly as her mother-in-law had commanded her." The impact would be particularly effective, because Ruth does do exactly what Naomi told her to do—up to a point. Then, where Naomi had said "he will tell you what you are to do," Ruth instead tells Boaz what he is to do.

7. *his heart was merry*. The combination of *lēb*, "heart," with some form of the root *ṭwb/yṭb*, "to be good (in a multiplicity of senses)," means a general sense of euphoria and well-being, such as occurs at the end of harvest (Isa 9:2). When wine induces this feeling, it sometimes means a state of sufficient drunkenness for one to make bad decisions, as Nabal does in I Sam 25:36 and Xerxes does in Esther 1:10, or to be incapable of defense, as with Amnon in II Sam 13:28. Just as readily, however, the expression suggests a positively evaluated exuberance, as in I Kings 8:66; Prov 15:15; and Eccles 9:7. It is the

circumstances which dictate whether the state of having a "good heart" is dangerous or not; see the ambiguity in the drama of Judg 19:6, 22. Boaz need not be drunk, but there is just a slight hint either of a further obstacle to be overcome, or of an intention to take advantage of a mellower-than-usual condition, in Naomi's plan (note that she counsels to wait until he has eaten and drunk in 3:3, but with no mention of a merry heart).

quietly. Hebrew *ballāṭ*, one of a group of words with a variety of spellings most of which contain an *aleph* (*ballā'ṭ*, *lᵉ'aṭ*, etc.). The basic meaning of the root without preposition (so Joüon, *Commentaire*, p. 71) may be "gentleness," but it is not clear whether the root is *l'ṭ* or simply *'ṭ*. Three Ugaritic occurrences of a word *'uṭ* are all in ambiguous and broken contexts. In any event, the best parallels to the Ruth usage are Judg 4:21, where Jael approaches the sleeping Sisera *ballā'ṭ*, tent peg at the ready, and I Sam 24:4 [Hebrew, 5] where David snips off the corner of Saul's mantle *ballāṭ*.

8. *Around midnight.* Literally, "in the half of the night." Compare Exod 12:29 (*J*), the time when God smites the firstborn, and Judg 16:3, when Samson transplants the city gate of Gaza.

shuddered. The Hebrew root *ḥrd* occurs almost always in contexts where people tremble in fear of the unknown or of threatening, awesome circumstances. We have had no indication of fearsome circumstances here, so the best we can do is to assume the same physical reaction, shuddering, but probably here in response to the unexpected cold.

groped about . . . next to him. Oswald Loretz, in *Studies Presented to A. Leo Oppenheim* (University of Chicago Press, 1964), pp. 155–58, makes a strong case that the three occurrences of the root *lpt* in Hebrew (Judg 16:29; Job 6:18; and here) are consistent with one another and with Akkadian *lapātu*. All contain the idea of touching, grasping, even striking, actions done with the hand. Thus, the *Qal* of the verb in Judg 16:29 portrays Samson gropingly grasping the pillars of the Dagon temple. For Job 6:18, Loretz proposes a figurative idiom: caravans "hitting the road." The available Arabic cognate of the root has a different meaning, having to do with turning one's head or gazing to the side. Neither of these meanings would fit very well a situation where Boaz has to sit up and bend forward to see someone lying at his feet (note the reserve with which Rudolph, p. 55, defends "bend forward"). If our decision at 3:4 is correct, that Ruth was to uncover Boaz' legs and lie beside him, then his hand would encounter her as he groped about for his mantle, to cover himself from the cold.

If so, the versions did not understand the word. All continue the notion of trembling inherent in the preceding verb, either toward being disturbed or toward being astounded.

9. *Who are you?* In contrast to the same words at 3:16, this question asks directly for identification. The LXX is clear here on the question, while at 3:16, it will betray confusion. On the other hand, the Syriac reads "What is the news of you?=How are you?" which would be more appropriate for 3:16. Doubtless under the influence of 3:16, five Hebrew manuscripts collated by Kennicott and de Rossi add "my daughter" after the question, thereby dispel-

ling the air of anonymity and shadowy movement which the story-teller has so effectively created (see the COMMENT).

your maid-servant. Here the noun is *'āmāh*, while Ruth had called herself "your *šiphāh*" in 2:13 (see the NOTE on "your maid-servant" there). While there may once have been in Hebrew a clear legal distinction between the two terms, there does not seem to be any difference between them in Ruth. A. Jepsen, VT 8 (1958), 293–97, in proposing a legal differentiation between *'āmāh* and *siphāh*, acknowledges their virtual identity of meaning and opposes their use as criteria for separating *J* from *E* in the Tetrateuch. For the book of Ruth, what must be said is that once again the story-teller uses synonymous words in parallel situations for rhetorical effect, and, as the NOTE on "your maid-servant" in 2:13 suggests, quite possibly to give a hint of the future.

spread your 'wing' over your maid-servant. This translation points up the word-play between Yahweh's wings in 2:12 and the "wings" or "corners" on Israelite garments (Deut 22:12; Ezek 5:3). There is a question here whether "wing" is singular or plural; a number of Hebrew manuscripts and the MT vowel tradition read plural, while the versions join the consonants of MT in reading singular. The singular is almost certainly correct, if we are guided by Deut 22:30[Hebrew, 23:1], 27:20; and Ezek 16:8, all of which pertain to marital custom. Especially significant is the Ezekiel passage, which concludes an elaborate metaphor portraying Yahweh's election of Israel in terms of marriage: "Then I passed your way and saw you, and lo your time was the time for love, so I spread my wing over you and covered your nakedness, and I pledged myself to you, and I entered covenant with you—so says Adonay Yahweh—and you became mine." The exact correspondence of terminology between Ezek 16:8 and Ruth 3:9 is strong evidence that Ruth's request of Boaz is marriage. Commentators frequently invoke ancient and modern Arabic custom as further evidence that the placing of a garment over a woman is a symbolic claim to marriage; see especially W. Robertson Smith, *Kinship and Marriage in Early Arabia*, rev. ed., 1903 (repr. Boston: Beacon, 1963), p. 105, and A. Jirku, *Die magische Bedeutung der Kleidung in Israel* (Rostock: Adler, 1914), pp. 14 ff.

for you are a redeemer. In the NOTES on 2:1 ("covenant-brother"), 2:20 ("He is one of our circle of redeemers"), and 3:2 ("one of our covenant circle"), I have argued that Naomi knew of the existence of a circle of redeemers or confederates. But did Naomi and Ruth know anything about the order in which these men would be expected to act; that is, who was the nearest relative? It is possible that they did know, and that Ruth asked Boaz to marry her without assurance that civil custom would in fact lead directly to that. Her approach would then be a ploy to force him to act, to start the wheels rolling toward marriage whether to another person or to himself. Support for this interpretation would come from the fact that Ruth calls Boaz "a redeemer," not "the redeemer" or "my/our redeemer." Also, notice that Boaz gives Ruth assurance that he will do all that she has asked before he mentions the existence of a nearer redeemer, which seems to suggest that her request could be answered by marriage to another as well as by marriage to Boaz.

What is much more likely is that the two women simply did not know the order of redeemer responsibility. They only knew that the responsibility existed and that Boaz was one to approach. Ruth's action has put Boaz on the spot, and that is what it was intended to do. Boaz now must act, and of course he will do so in accordance with what righteous human behavior calls for.

10. *Blessed may you be by Yahweh.* See 2:20 and the second NOTE on 2:19. This blessing form follows a worthy action on the part of the one so blessed; cf. Gen 24:31 and I Sam 23:21, for example.

In not going after the younger men. The combination "to go after" (Hebrew, *hālak 'aḥᵃrē*) has a wide variety of meanings of which we need note only two. It can mean aggressive harlotry, as in Prov 7:22, especially when prophets use harlotry as a metaphor for Israel's idolatry. This can hardly be the meaning here. Better guides are Gen 24:5, 8, 39 and I Sam 25:42, stories in which Rebekah and Abigail follow after messengers sent to bring them for marriage to Isaac and David respectively. Apparently Ruth had received marriage proposals—the Targum is surely in error with its addition, "to commit fornication with them"—probably from the youths who harvested Boaz' crop (hence the definite article, which the LXX lacks). If so, the story-teller neatly suggests the attractiveness of these young men by shifting from *nᵉ'ārīm* used throughout chapter 2 to *baḥūrīm*, implying the choiceness of the young men.

11. *All that you say I shall do for you.* The precise words of Ruth to Naomi at 3:5 (see the NOTE there) except for the important additional "for you."

all the assembly of my people. Literally, "all the gate of my people." At 4:10, a similar expression occurs: "from the gate of his place," while in 4:1 and 11 the gate is the location of the complex legal transaction centering on Boaz and the nearer redeemer. With excellent insight, the LXX uses *fulē* at 3:11 (one manuscript has *sunagōgē*) and 4:10, *pulē* at 4:1 and 11; the first Greek word denotes a body of men linked by blood ties, while the second is the usual word for gate. In similar fashion, OL (*tribus*), Syriac (*šrbt'*, "family, tribe") and the Targum with its addition ("the gate of the great Sanhedrin") recognize that there is a special meaning here of the term "gate." Undeniably, it means something like, "the legally responsible body of this town." Under no circumstances should we claim that the LXX meant to write *pulē* when it wrote *fulē* (against BH³ and Gerleman). That the word "gate" could designate the legal body of a city or town is strongly supported by a frequent usage in the book of Deuteronomy. These are the occasions when Israel is commanded to care for the sojourner, the Levite, the fatherless, the widow and the poor who are "within your gates, within one of your gates." Regrettably, the RSV and NEB translate with "within your towns" or "your settlements," but it is clear that these unfortunates are the responsibility of the body politic; the translation should be "under your legal care." This point deserves more extensive demonstration than is possible here. The passages in question are Deut 5:14, 12:12, 14:21, 27–29, 15:7, 16:11, 14, 18, 17:2, 5, 8, 18:6, 23:16[Hebrew, 17], 24:14, and 26:12. See also Prov 31:23, 31.

you are a worthy woman. The Hebrew is *'ēšet ḥayl*, which recalls the description of Boaz in 2:1 (see the Note there on "a man of substance"). Here *ḥayl* says nothing about wealth or social status, but emphasizes the quality of Ruth's person. The best exegesis of that quality is provided by the magnificent acrostic poem in Prov 31:10–13, which begins with the very words *'ēšet ḥayl* (see Introduction, p. 34). How effectively the story-teller hints that these two people should marry, just before the final complication is introduced!

12. *Now it is certainly true that.* The Hebrew is difficult; there are simply too many introductory words: *we'attāh kī 'omnām kī 'm.* The Masoretes placed no vowel point on *'m* (that is, they read as though it were not there), although the consonants were fixed in the tradition. Furthermore, most of the LXX tradition fails to reflect *we'attāh*, "and now," and commentators have noted that the same word begins the preceding verse, suggesting some support for the impulse to emend it away.

The first three words should all be retained, however. Deletion of "and now" would be arbitrary, especially since Boaz' speaking style is purposely made redundant by the story-teller. As for *'omnām*, with its congeners *'umnām* and *'omnāh* it is regularly an introductory word (see S. Talmon on *'mn* in the Yabneh-yam ostracon, BASOR 176 [December 1964], 34–35, and compare Jesus' words "Truly, truly, I say to you"), but often enough it is preceded by another adverb such as *gam*, "also," or *'ap*, "also, indeed," or by the emphatic particle *kī* (I Kings 8:27; Job 36:4). The proposed translation adopts the emphatic meaning for the first *kī*.

On the other hand, *'omnām* and its congeners are rarely followed by the conjunction *kī*, "that," even in places where modern languages might mislead the translator into looking for it (for example, Num 22:37); exceptions are Job 9:2 and 12:2. The "that" in the proposed translation is simply implicit in *'omnām*. For this reason, and because *'m* was already recognized as a problem by the early Jewish tradition, it is best to follow the LXX and Joüon, *Commentaire*, pp. 74–75).

W. Staples, AJSL 54 (1937), 62 ff., in developing his theory that only one person at a time was properly designated "redeemer," takes the *'m* to be a negative (this is possible) and translates along these lines: "But now, as a matter of fact, I am really not (your) *gō'ēl*, but you do have a *gō'ēl*, one who is more closely related (to you) than I." The general implausibility of Staples' whole theory, in view of our reading in 2:20 and in view of 4:4, 6, makes the proposal fruitless (so also Rudolph, p. 55).

13. *Spend tonight (here).* Hebrew, *līnī hallay'lāh.* For reasons lost to us, the scribes of some Hebrew manuscripts wrote the *l* and/or the *n* of the first word in an enlarged size. Joüon speculates the scribes wished to attract attention to a defect in the text, perhaps a lost but needed word; he proposes *pōh*, "here" (cf. Num 22:8; Judg 19:9). True, with most occurrences of the verb *lyn*, "to lodge the night," is a statement of the place where the lodging is to occur (e.g. Gen 24:23, 25; Judg 19:4–20 [eight times]; II Sam 17:8, 16, 19:8), but at Gen 24:54 and Judg 19:6 the place is not stated but implied. The reason for the enlarged letters escapes us. But note the same verb at 1:16, and see the COMMENT.

Since the verb by itself means "spend the night," the explicit "the night" may seem redundant. Read "tonight, this particular night" and compare Num 22:8; II Sam 17:16 and 19:8.

Well and good. Hebrew, *ṭôb*. The Haggadic tradition takes the word here as the name of the nearer redeemer, but the Targum stands with all the other versions in reflecting simply "good." Compare I Sam 20:7; II Sam 3:13; I Kings 2:18; and possibly Ruth 2:22 (see the NOTE on "It is better" there).

does not want to do the redeemer's part. Compare Deut 25:7–8 within the law statement on levirate responsibility. There the verb *ḥpṣ* in the sense of "want, wish" is also used, but instead of the technical term *g'l* as the infinitive following, Deuteronomy uses *lqḥ*, "to take." There are striking differences of vocabulary between Deut 25:5–10 and Ruth 3:12–4:12, just as there are certain similarities. See the COMMENTS on this section and the next.

As surely as Yahweh lives. A paraphrase of *ḥay Yahweh*, a standard oath formula occurring some thirty times in Judges, Samuel, and Kings, five of these in the Court History of David (II Sam 9–20; I Kings 1–2[?]); by contrast, it does not appear in the Pentateuch, and appears but once in the work of the Chronicler, in the Micaiah story taken from the Kings source (II Chron 18:13=I Kings 22:14). Hosea condemns its hypocritical use in Israel (4:15), while Jeremiah looks ahead to a time when it will be properly used by former Ba'al worshipers, that is, when men will do their oath-taking in Yahweh's name instead of in Ba'al's. The two prophetic passages imply that one using the oath is expected to mean what he says: as sure as Yahweh is the living God, you can count on what I promise (note the interesting variation which adds an oath by the life [*nepeš*] of the recipient of the promise, I Sam 20:3, 25:26; II Sam 11:11, 15:21; II Kings 2:2, 4, 6, 4:30).

The standard order begins with the oath and then follows with the promise, introduced by the particles *kī* or *'im* or both. Here in Ruth, the order is inverted. Boaz' promise is that he will see to the matter of redemption, to which he adds the authority of the Yahweh oath. The only narrative passage comparable is I Sam 20:21 where Jonathan adds the Yahweh oath to his statement of the meaning of his signal: "for it is peace for you and there is no problem, as surely as Yahweh lives."

14. *next to him.* The consonants are *mrgltw*, clearly the same word as the one designating Boaz' legs in verses 4 and 7, but lacking the *y* before the *w* of the usual spelling of the suffix form. Ruth is to resume the same place to sleep as she had taken in verse 8. It is inescapable that this position is next to Boaz; see the NOTE on 3:4 and the last NOTE on 3:8.

and she arose. The MT feminine is retained, as the versions indicate. The LXX Lucianic tradition is explicit that Ruth is the subject of the first verb of verse 14, "she lay down," and the entire LXX tradition explicitly makes Boaz the subject of the following "for he said." There is no need to follow Joüon in making Boaz the subject of "arose," nor to accept Rudolph's more elaborate suggestion that *bidbārō*, "at his behest," has been lost. The story-teller is getting across the idea that both Boaz and Ruth take the initiative in the progress toward resolution of what has now become their common cause. The Syriac reading is curious and worth noting: "And she rose in the morning when it was still dark, while a man could not recognize his neighbor, and she said to him: 'No one should learn that I came to you at the threshing floor.'"

could recognize. The story-teller, perhaps not inadvertently, uses the same word here as he did twice in 2:10 (in word-play) and again in 2:19.

Let it not be known. The impersonal construction, employing the *Niphal* of *yd'* is attested certainly only here and in Pharaoh's description of his dream to Joseph at Gen 41:21: "It would not have been known that (the lean cows) had eaten (the fat ones)." Dahood has disposed of another possible instance in Ps 74:5 by achieving effective parallelism with the use of a root *d'k* (*Psalms II, 51-100*, AB, vol. 17, first NOTE on 74:5).

15. *Present the wrap.* The verb is an oddity. Ostensibly an imperative of a root *yhb*, it is usually translated "give" because of the cognates in Aramaic, Syriac, Ethiopic, and Arabic. The biblical usage is frequent enough (over thirty times spread through all kinds of literature), but aside from one probable *Qal* participle in Ps 55:22[Hebrew, 23], it occurs only in the forms of *Qal* imperatives. Some of these have virtually an adverbial meaning, "now then," but the majority take an object (see for example Gen 29:21 [*J*], 30:1 [*E*], 47:15-16 [Joseph story]; II Sam 11:15 [Court History]). The subsequent imperative "grasp, get a good hold on" is virtually redundant (the LXX[BL'] and the Syro-Hexapla omit the imperative), a characteristic of Boaz' speech at other places.

It is difficult to say what the article of clothing is here. The Hebrew word occurs only here and in the catalogue of clothing in Isa 3:18-23. Dalman, *Arbeit und Sitte,* V (1937), 332, proposes a head shawl, perhaps the long, narrow one shown on the women in Sennacherib's wall relief of the capture of Lachish (see illustration 4 and G. E. Wright, *Biblical Archaeology*, p. 193. Since our story-teller enjoys using synonyms for the same entity, the "wrap" is more likely the same as the "cape" in 3:3 (see the third NOTE there).

Get a good hold on it. The Hebrew combination *'ḥz b-* is used more frequently in prose and in early passages than is *'ḥz 't* (with the accusative mark) and has a stronger implication. See among other places Gen 25:26 (Jacob holding fast to Esau's heel); Exod 4:4 (Moses' taking the serpent by the tail); Judg 16:3 (Samson's grip on the Gaza city gate), 20:6 (the Levite holding his dead concubine's body to cut it up); II Sam 20:9 (Joab holding Amasa by the beard as he prepares to stab him); and I Kings 1:51 (Adonijah's grip on the horns of the altar, in fear of Solomon's retribution—parallel to *ḥzq* in verse 50).

he measured out six šā'ār-*measures.* Brockelmann, *Hebräische Syntax,* p. 77, collects a number of passages including Ruth 3:15 where a numeral and a commodity are given without indication of what he terms a "self-evident" unit of measure. For Ruth 3:15, the self-evident measure of barley is an ephah, the same measure as in 2:17. But the reckoning of the weight of an ephah (at the standard 0.6 kilograms per liter) is either 47.5 or 29 pounds, depending on the system followed (see the NOTE on 2:17). Six ephahs would weigh 285 pounds on the older calculation, 174 pounds by Scott's calculations; certainly more than Ruth could carry. Brockelmann's "self-evident" measure is in no way self-evident! Perhaps, then, we should turn instead to the '*ōmer*, comparing Exod 16:18 where the manna is being measured by this unit. An '*ōmer* is one-tenth of an ephah, and the result would mean that Ruth receives here three-fifths of what she had garnered in a day's work in 2:17. Since this is to be a supply sufficient to care for Naomi, the amount seems too small. Besides, as Joüon (*Commentaire*) and Rudolph point out, the word '*ōmer* is of masculine gender, but the numeral here is the one used with feminine nouns. These two commentators select instead the *sᵉ'āh*, one-third of an ephah; the resulting load of barley would be two ephahs, 95 pounds on the traditional system, 58 pounds on Scott's system.

Attractive as this last calculation is, the translation suggests an entirely different attack on the problem. I proposed at 3:2 to read "gates" (*šᵉ'ārīm*) for "barley" (*šᵉ'ōrīm*), thus leaving it unclear what crop was being winnowed. On the basis of Gen 26:12, I propose here to do the same, but with a different meaning for *šᵉ'ārīm*. In Gen 26:1–11, we have the second *J* story of a patriarch's attempt to pass off his wife as his sister in the face of threatening circumstances in a strange land, Isaac and Rebekah before Abimelek of Gerar. After the discovery of the stratagem, "Isaac sowed in that land, and he came up with one hundred *šᵉ'ārīm* in that year, for Yahweh had blessed him." The versions translate "barley" here, but the *š* should be retained and dealt with as the more difficult reading (so Speiser, *Genesis*, AB, vol. 1, NOTE on 26:12). This must be a measure of some sort, unknown to us elsewhere unless it be the unit we need in Ruth 3:15. If Isaac raised one hundred such units (of what commodity?) in a season, then for Ruth 6 per cent of that amount could well be correct, and would be a generous gift.

and set it upon her. See the same verb, *šyt*, in 4:16, which Joüon says has more of a nuance of delicacy than would *śym*, another word of virtually the same meaning.

then he went into the city. A number of Hebrew manuscripts (seventeen collated by Kennicott, twenty-one more by de Rossi) have the feminine form of the verb, as do the Syriac and Vulgate. Three Lucianic manuscripts state Ruth's name explicitly as the subject, but another Lucianic witness states Boaz and so does the Targum. Chapter 4:1 begins by having Boaz "go up" to the gate, apparently starting from the threshing floor and reversing the direction of Ruth's "going down" in 3:3 and 6. On the other hand, the majority of the LXX witnesses fail to indicate a change in subject from the preceding verb, but all will add "Ruth" as the subject of "and she came" at the beginning of verse 16. The masculine form, making Boaz the subject, seems best here.

Nevertheless, the variation among the versions, including the divergence within the Lucianic family, may suggest that both readings were available from well back in the history of the story's transmission, each preserved in a divergent text.

16. *How do things stand with you, my daughter?* The question is literally simply "Who are you, my daughter?" Recall 3:9, where Boaz puts the same question in a situation where identification is in fact needed; there he did not add "my daughter," but its presence here means that Naomi is not asking for identification. That her question is correctly carried in the tradition is evident

from what the versions did. The Syriac (with its offspring, the Armenian) has an answer to the literal question "Who are you?": "And she said to her, 'I am Ruth.'" LXX^B fails to reflect the question at all, but a variety of attempts to render it by other LXX witnesses all tend to support the form of the question as MT preserves it. Completely unexpected is the reading in manuscript *b* found in Qumran Cave 2, *"What* are you? (see the Introduction, p. 40).

Most commentators compare Amos 7:2, 5, "As what (=how) can Jacob stand?" and posit what Rudolph calls an accusative of condition for the interrogative pronoun. J. Gray points to the similar usage in the wail over Ba'al's death in the Ugaritic Ba'al cycle: "Ba'al's dead!—What (*my*) becomes of the people? Dagon's Son—What (*my*) of the masses?" (H. L. Ginsberg's translation in *Ancient Near Eastern Texts*, p. 139; UT, texts 62:6–7 and 67:23–24). Recognizing the necessity to paraphrase, we can safely adopt a translation such as the one given here.

17. *These six* šāʻār-*measures*. See the third NOTE on 3:15.

empty. Here is one of the most effective of the story-teller's long-range inclusios, for it is the very word Naomi used in describing herself in her mournful complaint at 1:21. The story is moving toward resolution, now, of some of its most salient motifs. With a single word, the resolution of one part of Naomi's plight is accomplished. The story-teller chooses to place the word not in Boaz' mouth while he and Ruth are still at the threshing floor, but in Ruth's mouth as she reports to Naomi a part of the conversation we were not in on earlier. This technique, by the way, is used by the story-teller in 2:7 and 2:21; thus he keeps the story free of repetition and gives each scene its own contribution to the developing dramatic effect.

18. *Sit tight*. As it was in 2:23, the story is brought to a stand-still, at least for a few moments, by a form of the root yšb. See the last NOTE on 2:23.

How the matter will fall out. A minimal paraphrase of the combination 'ēk yippōl dābār, which involves a unique use of the common verb npl; the slavishly literal translation in LXX^B suggests that it was not an easy idiom to convey, especially in view of the curious lack of a definite article (later in the verse, the same noun has the article). The LXX^L manuscripts translate to the sense, "the matter will be/come to be/happen," using the definite article and the verb "to be." Syriac lacks any reflection of the clause. Of interest is the Targum's expansion: "Until you know *how it is decreed from heaven and* how (the) matter will be made clear." Divine agency is made explicit in this part of the sentence, as contrasted to Boaz' agency in the balancing second half of the sentence. Are we not to see the same hidden hand behind "how the matter will fall out" as controlled the "luck" in 2:3? See the COMMENT and the Introduction on the theology of the book.

Until. Hebrew kī 'im expresses "until, unless" after a negative preposition (Joüon, *Grammaire* § 173b); see especially Gen 32:26[Hebrew, 27]. See D. R. Hillers, *Lamentations*, AB, vol. 7A, NOTE on 5:22: "The clause following kī 'im states a condition that must be fulfilled before the preceding statement can or should be in effect: 'Not A unless N.'" Earlier in our verse here, "until" is expressed by 'ad 'ašer, "up to such a time as."

he has brought the matter to conclusion today. Syriac: "Until the verdict is passed down for him today," an anticipation of what is to come which may convey rather well the implication in the Hebrew.

COMMENT

Chapter three contains the climactic events of the whole Ruth story. At no other point does dramatic tension and suspense reach such a pitch. And once the scene at the threshing floor is over, even though there will be one more suspenseful episode, the audience knows that things will work out well. The necessary commitments have been made, and in this story, where righteousness prevails, commitments are certain to be fulfilled.

The structure of this episode is very similar to that of the previous one: a main scene moving at measured pace and involving Ruth and Boaz, bracketed by two somewhat shorter scenes (verses 1–5 and 16–18) involving Ruth and Naomi. Certain key words recur frequently, knitting the scenes together, and one dramatic sentence, "all that you say I shall do," connects the opening with the main scene (verses 5 and 11).

Meanwhile, the technique of reusing signal words at long range, a special form of inclusio, serves to link this episode to the two preceding ones, as some of the problems raised in the earlier part of the story begin to be resolved. Notice, for example, "security" (3:1 with 1:9), *ḥesed* (3:10 with 1:8 and 2:20), "wing" (3:9 with 2:12), "worthy woman" (3:11 with "man of substance" which employs closely comparable Hebrew vocabulary in 2:1), and "empty" (3:17 with 1:21). To these crucial terms we will return below, but for now the point to be seen is the craftsmanship of the story-teller.

Here, however, the story-teller uses his craft in another and special way, to show that for the moment events will operate in a profoundly different atmosphere. For one thing, he establishes and develops a marked sense of mystery, secrecy, privacy. This is the only episode in which Naomi, Ruth, and Boaz have the stage to themselves. There is no "chorus" to give the action a public, open setting—no neighbor women of Bethlehem, no team of young harvesters, no quorum of elders and bevy of onlookers at the city gate. Not even an Orpah, or a foreman of the harvesters, or a nearer kinsman interferes with the action. The three key figures are in charge: they plan and carry out their actions apparently so much on their own initiative that the audience may well wonder—and this is important—whether even the God who works from the shadows has for the time being averted his gaze and is not in control of what is going on. The darkness of midnight and the dimness of the pre-dawn hide both persons and events. No one seems able to recognize anyone else (verses 3, 9, and 14)! As if to heighten the sense of privacy—I see no other artistic reason for it—the story-teller uses "the man" and "the woman" instead of the names Ruth and Boaz (verses 8, 14, 16, and 18). Notice these signals of mystery as well: Boaz goes to lie at the far end (literally the "corner") of the threshing floor; Ruth approaches the sleeping man quietly; the man gropes in the dark for his mantle; the woman leaves the threshing floor before there is light enough to reveal to anyone that she has been there.

Together with the air of mystery there is built up a carefully contrived ambiguity; it revolves around whether Ruth's act in approaching Boaz under such compromising circumstances will result immediately in sexual intercourse. The story-teller clearly means to have his audience reckon with this possibility. Naomi's instructions to Ruth in verse 3, for example, can be taken to mean that Ruth goes to the threshing floor prepared "so to speak as a bride" (Hertzberg)—but they don't have to mean that. David makes quite similar preparations before going to the temple to worship, after learning of the death of his first son by Bathsheba (II Sam 12:20); Joab instructs his message bearer, the wise woman of Tekoah, *not* to anoint herself with oil but rather to act like a mourner when she seeks her audience with David in II Sam 14:2. The circumstances at the threshing floor are ambiguous, purposefully so.

The indicators of this ambiguity swarm throughout the episode. Consider the matter of uncovering Boaz' legs; the NOTE on 3:4 has examined the meaning of "legs" and proposed that there is an intentional ambiguity about just how much of Boaz was uncovered. Another avenue of approach is offered by comparing Deut 22:30[Hebrew, 23:1] and 27:20. These verses contain negative commandments using the verb "to reveal, uncover" with the noun "wing," to assert that a man is not to have intercourse with his father's wife. It is simply incomprehensible to me that a Hebrew story-teller could use the words "uncover," "wing" (3:9), and a noun for "legs" which is cognate with a standard euphemism for the sexual organs, all in the same context, and not suggest to his audience that a provocative set of circumstances confronts them.

Nor is that all. Hertzberg has pointed out, in his comment on 3:7–8, that the episode at the threshing floor contains repetition of several common words which have potential double meanings. The verb *škb*, "to lie down," occurs eight times in verses 4–14, most often with the simple meaning to lie down to sleep. With Ruth as subject, in verses 4, 7, and 8, this verb may connote to lie prostrate at the feet of a superior, in a supplicating position, to request a favor (Dommershausen). But surely the audience also recognizes that *škb* in Hebrew (combined with the preposition "with") means to have sexual intercourse, an idiom which has become common parlance in English.

Furthermore there is much too frequent use made of the verb "to know" and its related nouns not to be noticed. The first NOTE on 3:2 has discussed a term translated "covenant circle" and related it to the similar term in 2:1; both are derivatives of the Hebrew *yd'*, "to know." In verse 3, Ruth is to avoid making herself known until the appropriate time; in 4, she is to note—literally to know—the place where Boaz lies down. In verse 10, Boaz observes that Ruth's worthiness is known among the assembly of the people; in 14, it is not to be known that Ruth has been at the threshing floor that night; in 18, Naomi counsels Ruth to wait until she knows how things will turn out. Here is almost the full range of nuances of the Hebrew term "to know," but the audience will doubtless have supplied in their own minds one additional frequent meaning, "to have sexual intercourse with."

Finally, it may be that there is intentional double meaning in the use of the word *b'*, "to come (toward), to go into," which occurs in 3:4, 7, and 14, and will reappear with a clear sexual meaning in the crucial verse 4:13 (so Hertz-berg).

Does this roster of *double entendres* mean that the story-teller is simply seeking to titillate his audience? Emphatically not. His intent is much more serious than that. Having led his audience to participate in the mystery and ambiguity of the scene, he obviously means to say that it is of extreme impor-tance whether or not here at the threshing floor things will go forward ac-cording to what Israelite custom and Israelite *ḥesed*-living calls for. Here is where the modern western audience must beware; Ruth is not to be read as though the sexually provocative scenes are "throw-ins" without any impor-tance to the story's direction. What now happens at the threshing floor is as essential to the story-teller's purpose as what happened on the Moabite high-way between Ruth and Naomi, or what happened in the harvest scene when Boaz praised an impoverished widow who was gleaning, or what will happen in the solemn civil hearing at the city gate. At each of these points in the story, a moment of choice is presented to both actors and audience, and at each of these points the choice is made in favor of what righteous living calls for. To comprehend the outcome of the threshing floor scene, we must be as clear as we can on what Israelite custom and law would call for, and we must observe the developing portrayal of these three remarkable people who are living it.

At 3:9, it is the Moabitess Ruth who presumes a connection between what is clearly some form of levirate marriage responsibility and the responsibilities of a redeemer: "Now spread your 'wing' over your maid-servant, for you are a redeemer." That amounts to saying—see the last NOTE on 3:9—"Your re-deemer responsibility calls for you to marry me." Ruth's presupposition that the responsibilities of redemption and marriage belong together is accepted by all as the story progresses. Boaz never questions the combination; his words in verses 10–13 show clearly that he takes it for granted. It then becomes the basis for the drama in the civil hearing in 4:1–12; when Boaz announces the interrelationship of the two at 4:5, the nearer kinsman raises no objection, but simply takes the available way out. Just as the story-teller had Ruth take the initiative in supporting Naomi and herself at 2:2–7, he has her take the ini-tiative in a matter of applying civil custom.

From the story's point of view, the combination of redemption and levirate marriage is a *presupposition*, and furthermore it is one which this remarkable Moabitess introduces.

Here a difficulty arises. If we judge from attested Israelite law as it is pre-served in the casuistic law materials, those formulations of law which open with a statement of circumstances in an "if such-and-such a thing happens" clause and conclude with a "then . . ." clause of consequence, we have no-where else a connection drawn between marriage and redemption. If we trace redemption custom through the law codes, through narratives, and through the use of redemption language in speaking about God's care for his people, we appear to be in one circumscribed realm; if we do the same for the levirate custom, we are apparently in another. Only the Ruth story combines them. What does this indicate?

Many have concluded that the Ruth story-teller wove his tale at a time after the codification of the Deuteronomic Code, which gives a discrete levirate marriage law in Deut 25:5–10, and of the Holiness Code, which gives a discrete redemption law in Lev 25:25 and 27:9–33. According to such a theory, the Ruth story-teller for the first time brings together what the law codes had as separate, perhaps even having this as his primary purpose in composing. Another, more familiar, line of reasoning is based on Genesis 38, a story in which the younger brothers of a dead man are expected to sire a son from his childless widow; when one younger brother cheats on this responsibility, and the other is held back from doing it by his father's timidity and deceitfulness, the widow Tamar entices her father-in-law himself into fulfilling the responsibility. Her success, and her father-in-law's statement about righteousness in 38:26, suggest that the purposes of levirate marriage were even in this manner properly carried out. In Ruth also, it is not a brother of the widow's husband who is to sire a son, but a more distant relative. Clauses in both the Hittite and the Middle Assyrian law collections suggest the same spreading out of responsibility in this matter. The Deut 25:5–10 law on the subject, however, confines the responsibility to "brothers who live together," and even gives them the right of refusal. One possible conclusion: Genesis 38 and Ruth come from a time prior to the formulation of the Deuteronomic law, which limits the application of the law to a smaller and more intimate family circle and relaxes its stringency.

This way of approaching the legal circumstances in Ruth must yield now to increasingly clear insights into the nature of Israelite casuistic law, and for that matter of all ancient Near Eastern law of this type. The most penetrating recent studies of this subject have been made by George E. Mendenhall, who first attacked it in "Ancient Oriental and Biblical Law," published in BA 17 (1954), 26–46, reprinted in BAR³, pp. 3–24, and has dealt further with it in *The Tenth Generation,* chapter 7. What follows is heavily indebted to him.

We must first make a distinction between "policy," the kind of normative general guideline embodied primarily in the biblical Ten Commandments, and "technique" or specific formulations, which occur in the Bible mostly in the casuistic style we have mentioned. Concerning the latter, it is important not to be misled by such terms as "law code," "codification," "promulgation," and "legislation" into thinking of ancient case law as comparable to the two-thousand-odd-page municipal code of the City of Chicago or to the Napoleonic Code. What we have in case law is a collection of precedents which have arisen from specific experiences preserved as references for settling similar cases, especially the difficult ones. In the codes, a selection from a large pool of available legal lore is "codified." The pool from which the selection was made contained inconsistencies, due in largest measure to the fact that customary precedents arose within local contexts and over a period of time.

Early in Israel's life as a people, in the period we know as the time of the judges, and continuing down into the monarchic period, the place where most civil cases were settled was in the local city gate, and the ones to render such decisions were the town elders, very much as we see them functioning in

Ruth 4. Except in thorny cases, they made their decisions on the basis of a combination of overarching principle, common sense, and a well-preserved if perhaps spotty, probably orally transmitted, legal tradition. While communication between towns and cities across the land on matters of civil custom would take place, especially when issues pertained to the affairs of more than one town or population segment, we are not to think of one common legal code covering the whole land. What was decided in a civil case in Bethlehem could differ from what was decided in nearby Hebron, and all the more readily could differ from what was decided in Shechem or Dan. As for the law codes in Exodus, Leviticus, and Deuteronomy, they constitute political attempts under specific historical circumstances to normalize practice, probably mostly at the capital cities of Samaria and Jerusalem, but they can hardly be thought of as simply overpowering and setting aside the age-old traditional practices in a given outlying town.

Also, we must remember that the law codes as we have them are anything but complete and comprehensive. For example, the Book of the Covenant in Exod 20:22 – 23:19 contains almost no family law, the very kind of law that would include marriage and inheritance regulations—see only 21:7–11 and 22:16–17[Hebrew, 15–16], and the other codes are all significantly deficient in one way or another. Their purpose was probably not to be comprehensive, but rather to be illustrative and didactic. Lack of a comprehensive law code together with localism and the sheer number of local sources for legal lore explains why frequently stories in the Bible portray a set of customary practices at odds with the formulations in the codes. We cannot expect absolute consistency between Deut 25:5–10 and the stories in Genesis 38 and Ruth, and the inconsistency may just as easily arise from differing local practice as from a difference in the time period represented. "Laws are then mutual understandings among human beings, culturally determined and relative— as well as changeable" (Mendenhall, *The Tenth Generation,* p. 195).

I have emphasized this point in order to approach the circumstances in the Ruth story not from the perspective of comparative law but from that of the underlying principles, the policy, at work in ancient Israel. The Ten Commandments, direct and pithy stipulations about the very foundation of living in community, constitute one excellent guide to the basic principles on which the people of Israel built their common life. There are other principles. One is that both persons and property are viewed as God's possession, and therefore a special sense of stewardship surrounds not only the land but also the relationships which human beings have with one another. Another is that social and economic distinctions among people are dissolved (except in a few cases involving slaves) in both civil and criminal justice; all receive equal treatment "before the law." Furthermore, punishment is appropriate to the kind and degree of injury done—an eye for an eye and a tooth for a tooth. There is also a special injunction to look after those members of society who are most likely to be passed by in the handling of justice; if anything, there is a bias in favor of such folk, especially obvious in the Deuteronomic Code (see the second NOTE on 3:11), so that the sojourner, the poor, the slave, the widow, and the orphan are the subjects of particular concern. More such principles could be asserted, and I shall not pause to document the ones here stated; a sensitive presentation of a number of them can be found in Shalom Paul's *Studies in the Book of the Covenant in the Light of Cuneiform and Biblical Law* (Leiden: Brill, 1970), pp. 37–40.

What can be said about legal practices and customs covered by the term "redemption" and performed by someone called a "redeemer"? If the Hebrew word *g'l* is our guide, redeeming in attested law pertains to the responsibility for recovering or retaining family property (Lev 25:25, 27:9–33); buying release of a kinsman from voluntary servitude entered into because of poverty (Lev 25:47–55); receiving restitution (in a curious act of penitence described in Num 5:8); and acting the part of "the redeemer of the blood," the kinsman who avenges a murder—this usage being primarily attested in the passages which establish the Cities of Refuge to which a killer is to flee until the circumstances of the killing have been ascertained (Num 35:9–28; Deut 19:6–13; Josh 20:2–9).

There are two narratives which give some idea of these redemption practices at work. The most directly comparable is the story of Jeremiah's redemption of the field belonging to his first cousin Hanamel, in Jer 32:6–25. The elaborate process of the weighing out of the precise payment, the signing and sealing of the deed before witnesses, and the deposit of both a sealed and an open copy of the deed in a jar, is spelled out in detail. Since this is an action having an important symbolic meaning, one senses, special attention is given to legal propriety. The passage accords fully with the redemption responsibility for recovering or retaining family property, with the exception that Lev 25:25 seems to refer to buying back a field already sold, while Jeremiah 32 pertains to the intention to sell (and thus may compare more precisely to Ruth 4:3). Here the relation of land redemption to principle is also effectively elucidated: Jeremiah's holding title to a piece of the land about to be lost to the people of Judah represents the hope that the future holds a new chance for proper stewardship under God's covenant, in contrast to the failure now being judged.

The second narrative about redemption in action pertains to the "redeemer of the blood." It occurs in the tale, woven by the wise woman of Tekoah at Joab's behest, designed to impel David to receive back his self-exiled son Absalom (II Samuel 14). As the woman tells it, she is a widow who had just two sons, one of whom has killed the other in a quarrel, apparently without witnesses. The rest of the family, that is the sub-tribe or phratry (cf. Ruth 2:1), demands that the widow turn over the killer, her sole remaining support, ". . . 'so that we may kill him for the life of his brother whom he has killed, and (thus) destroy the inheritor as well'" (so the Hebrew, against the RSV). The effect of course would be to leave the widow bereft and her husband without "name or remnant"—a situation not unlike the position Naomi saw herself to be in. The sad tale has its effect, and David promises to take care of the matter. The woman even gets him to give a solemn vow, "as Yahweh lives," that the "redeemer of the blood" would be kept from acting.

There is no great discrepancy between this story and the implication of the passages about the avenging role of the redeemer, although there does not seem to have been any inquiry into the circumstances of the death. There is, however, the clear implication that the members of the larger family are using the excuse of customary procedure to remove the heir and thus gain the inheritance that might have gone to him; their own words betray their motives. Redemption practice, then, is seen with a specific set of mitigating circumstances, and principle must come to bear. The widow cannot claim that her surviving son is innocent, but only that he is necessary for her own welfare and for the continuance of her husband's name. In effect, customary law is interfered with because it clashes with principle, a not infrequent circumstance in the Bible. The principle is that those whose needs can be easily ignored must be given special consideration in practice.

It is not only legal formulations and narratives that show us what redemption meant in Israel. Israel could readily picture her God as redeemer, especially as the one who gains release for his people from servitude, but he was also seen in a role perhaps best described as advocate (Job 19:25; cf. Marvin Pope, AB, vol. 15, NOTE on Job 19:25a). It was Deutero-Isaiah who explored this depiction most fully, but it was used much earlier, as early as Exod 15:13, a twelfth-century triumph song; note also the probably quite ancient blessing in Gen 48:16, where God's angel is praised by Jacob as the one who "redeems me from all evil." This language is old enough to have been used about God very early in Israel's history with the full implication it bears in later legal formulations; God shows familial concern and protects both people and property (Israel is both to him!). It is with such an understanding that we can best speculate about the role of the officials who are designated "redeemers" in the royal retinue of Baasha (I Kings 16:11) and Ahab (II Kings 10:11 according to the Lucianic LXX tradition; see second NOTE on 2:1), and begin to get an idea of what Naomi meant by calling Boaz "one of our circle of redeemers" in 2:20. Redeemers are to function on behalf of persons and their property within the circle of the larger family; they are to take responsibility for the unfortunate and stand as their supporters and advocates. They are to embody the basic principle of caring responsibility for those who may not have justice done for them by the unscrupulous, or even by the person who lives by the letter of the law.

We can be far briefer about the institution of levirate marriage. In a generally perceptive discussion which in many regards runs on parallel lines to the ones we have followed here, Thomas and Dorothy Thompson, in VT 18 (1968), 79–99, have shown that levirate practice in the three places where it is attested in the Bible—Genesis 38; Ruth; and Deut 25:5–10—operates on the basis of two fundamental principles. The first is that the wife of a dead man is to be supported and protected, and the second is that family property is to remain within the family (p. 96). The practice is not simply concerned with producing a male child, nor even with producing an heir to the dead man's property; it is concerned every bit as much with the care of the widow. Indeed, the care of widows is the main motive of Naomi's speculations in chapter 1 about the prospects of levirate marriage for herself—compare 1:11–13 with 1:9.

The basic principles underlying the Israelite use of the levirate practice are very much the same principles pertaining to redemption practice, and are in turn among the basic ones undergirding all Israelite law and custom.

Therefore, the juxtaposition of redemption and levirate practices in Ruth is a natural one, on the basis of principle. The fact that we can find no legal code which put the two together is probably irrelevant and as much due to the paucity of our sources as to any other cause. It is perfectly plausible to speculate that the connection between the two was typical in Bethlehemite, or even generally in Judean village, practice; it can be expected to have ratified itself easily in the mind of the ancient audience. We have suggested, in the COMMENT on Section III, that the complex societal framework in which this practice was to function probably included both blood and covenant ties, the latter reaching out beyond family interests to a circle in which ties were entered upon even more voluntarily and graciously than might be the case in a family. Even should this speculation prove wrong, there is a wide circle of responsibility pertinent, as we shall see explicitly in the scene at the gate which follows.

Ruth, then, has placed before Boaz her recognition of what Israelite custom makes possible for her, and has asked him to see to it. She has done so, the story-teller wants us to see, on her own initiative. It was Naomi who devised the plan to get Boaz' attention, but her instructions to Ruth extended only as far as "go and uncover his legs and lie down. Then he will tell you what you are to do." In fact, it was not so. It is Ruth who tells Boaz what to do, and she is justified in what she asks, according to the basic principles underlying righteous Israelite living. Once more, Ruth has acted as the very embodiment of what constitutes living according to ḥesed, and Boaz praises her precisely for that; the latter ḥesed he mentions in 3:10 is her determination to play her part in keeping Elimelek's inheritance in the family and in making provision for two widows, not only for herself but for Naomi also.

The audience is persuaded, then, of Ruth's valor, and the story-teller hammers it home with his favorite device of ratification, having one character give an affirmative evaluation of another (recall 1:8, 2:11–12, 2:19–20, and 3:18, with more examples to come in chapter 4).

Can we trust Boaz in corresponding fashion? That becomes the point of what follows. Boaz assures Ruth that he will do for her all that she has asked. He will do it as everything else in this story is done—properly and responsibly. Propriety means that he must deal with a factor Ruth apparently did not know of, that there is a member of the circle of redeemers who stands closer to her and must have the first opportunity to take up the responsibility. From a story-telling point of view, this has the marvelous effect of creating one more suspenseful moment, in which Boaz is given his opportunity to show his worthiness; for it is one feature of Boaz' valor that he will not even usurp another man's right to act responsibly!

With the matter of the nearer redeemer still to be resolved, there can be no dangerous implication to what Boaz next says: Spend the rest of the night here, and I will get at the question of your future as soon as morning comes.

Once again, the story-teller signals us: the verb he uses is not "lie down," that ambiguous term, but Hebrew *lwn/lyn,* "to lodge," the same term Ruth had used in her avowal to Naomi in 1:16. No ambivalence here! This term is never used in the Hebrew Bible with any sexual undertone. The dark ambiguity gives way to the clarity of the kinds of human commitments which characterize this story. Now it becomes clear that both of these people are worthy, and will do things in righteous fashion. It is not prudery which compels the conclusion that there was no sexual intercourse at the threshing floor; it is the utter irrelevance of such a speculation. What the scene must end with is something far more fitting, the clear evidence of Boaz' determination to care for these two widows as custom and generosity dictate. He ceremoniously measures out a significant, and sufficient, portion of the threshing floor's produce, and sends it home so that Ruth's mother-in-law, who returned "empty" —so she thought—from Moab, is now in no sense empty any longer (verse 17). How perceptive Naomi is to say to Ruth: Sit tight! This sort of man will not rest until he has seen the matter through—today.

And what about God? Had he in fact averted his eyes at the threshing floor? Was he not in charge here? Of course he was. Naomi signals this with her words "how the matter will fall out" in 3:18, running parallel with her confidence in Boaz' trustworthiness. Once again, God is present in this story where responsible human beings act as God to one another. Nowhere more effectively has the story-teller made this clear than in Ruth's request of Boaz in 3:9: spread your "wing" over me, thereby fulfilling yourself the wish you expressed for me in 2:12, that my payment be full from Yahweh, under whose wings I have come to dwell.

V. THE RESOLUTION AT THE CITY GATE

(4:1–12)

4 ¹ As for Boaz, he had gone up to the gate*ᵃ* and taken a seat there, and just then the redeemer about whom Boaz had spoken passed by. Then he said, "Turn aside, sit down here, so-and-so," and he turned aside and sat. ² He then took ten of the elders of the city and said, "Sit here," and they sat. ³ Now he spoke to the redeemer: "The part of the field which belonged to our brother Elimelek, Naomi, who has returned from the Moab plateau, hereby offers for sale*ᵇ*. ⁴ Then I, for my part, said I would inform you, to this effect: 'Buy, in the presence of those sitting here and in the presence of the elders of my people. If*ᶜ* you are willing to redeem, redeem; if you*ᵈ* are not willing to redeem, make it known to me and then I will know; because there is no one else (called upon) to redeem except you, and I after you.' " And he said, "I will redeem." ⁵ Then Boaz said, "On the day you buy the field from the hand of Naomi, you 'buy' Ruth the Moabitess, wife of the dead man, to establish the name of the dead upon his inheritance." ⁶ Then the redeemer said, "I cannot redeem, lest I imperil my inheritance; *you* take on my redemption-responsibility, because I cannot redeem." ⁷ Now this was (the mode) formerly in Israel with reference to redemption and exchange transactions, to confirm any such matter: a man would draw off his shoe and give it to his counterpart. This

---

ᵃ Syro-Hexapla adds, with asterisk, "of the city"; while asterisked passages are supposed to be additions to the LXX tradition based on the attested reading in the Hebrew, here the addition comes apparently from the native Syriac tradition (see Rahlfs, p. 65; Thornhill, VT 3 [1953], 240).

ᵇ Syriac adds, "to me." Throughout this section the Syriac is more than usually conflate, paraphrastic, and interpretative.

ᶜ LXXᴸ' add "therefore," one of six additions the Syro-Hexapla marks with an asterisk, additions it took not from the proto-Masoretic Hebrew tradition but from the Lucianic. See Thornhill, VT 3 (1953), 236–38.

ᵈ MT: *yig'al* (third person) read second person with a number of Hebrew manuscripts collated by Kennicott and de Rossi and with the versions.

was the process of ratification in Israel. 8 So the redeemer said to Boaz, "You buy[e]." And he drew off his shoe.

9 Then Boaz said to the elders and to all the people, "You are witnesses today, that I hereby buy [f]all that belonged to Elimelek and all that belonged to Kilyon and Mahlon[f] from the hand of Naomi. 10 And, more important, [g]Ruth the Moabitess, wife of Mahlon, I 'buy' as my wife,

> To establish the name of the dead on his inheritance,
>   So that the name of the dead not be cut off
>   From among his brethren
>   Or from the assembly of his town.
> You are witnesses—today!"

11 Then all the people who were in the gate and the elders said, "(We are) witnesses![h] May Yahweh make [i]the wife[i] who now enters your house like Rachel and like Leah, who between them built the house of Israel.

> And may you show fertility in Ephrathah
>   And (then) bestow a name in Bethlehem.

12 And may your house become like the house of Perez, whom Tamar bore to Judah, stemming from [j]the seed which[j] Yahweh will give you from this girl."

[e] LXX adds, "my redemption-responsibility," probably an incorrect explanatory addition; in verse 6 this is the object of the verb g'l, "redeem," not of qnh, "buy."

[f-f] Syriac omits, probably by haplography, "all that belonged to Elimelek." The OL, on the other hand, omits "all that belonged to Kilyon and Mahlon."

[g] Syriac reads Hebrew 't (sign of the direct object) as 'att, "you (fem.)" and has the verse addressed to Ruth.

[h] Syriac adds, "And they blessed him and said to him."

[i-i] Almost the entire LXX tradition: "your wife."

[j-j] LXX[L'] and Theodoret plus a few others wrongly read sou, "your," instead of ou, "which"; two minuscules then conflate and have both.

NOTES

4:1. As for Boaz, he had gone up. The Hebrew word order here is conjunction w[e] plus Boaz plus verb in the perfect. In Hebrew placing the subject before the verb frequently signals a change of actors and scene from what has immediately preceded. At the same time, the verb in the perfect brings to an end a succession of sentences using narrative imperfects with waw-consecutive, which have been keeping the story moving forward since 1:22. The effect of disrupting this succession is to stop the chronological flow; Boaz' "going up" is not simply the next step in the chronological sequence after the women's conversation in 3:16–18. In fact, his going to the gate can be prior to, contemporary with, or later than the scene at the women's home (Joüon, *Commentaire*, pp. 79–80, and *Grammaire*, § 118d–f; Gerleman, p. 35). In view of the portrayal of Boaz which the story-teller has been constructing, as a man of character, trustworthiness, and determination, we are almost certainly to understand that Boaz proceeded directly to the gate from the threshing floor. This produces a nice balance between *yrd* "to go down" in 3:3, 6, and *'lh,* "to go up," here. Furthermore, if the final words of 3:15 are correct in the MT ("then *he* went into the city"—see the NOTE there), the story-teller has created a fine "envelope" effect: Boaz starts out on his responsibility, the focus switches quickly to Ruth and Naomi, and then returns to Boaz.

and just then. The Hebrew construction here is comparable to that in 2:4, a *wᵉhinnēh* clause with a participle—see the first NOTE on 2:4. Here, as there, the scene is set (Boaz taking his place at the gate), whereupon at just the right moment along comes just the right person. Commentators who point out that virtually every male in town was bound to go out through the gate at some time during the morning on the way to work in the field are missing the impact of the Hebrew construction, which at least in Gen 24:15 and in Ruth conveys a hint of God's working behind the scenes. Note also the only other *wᵉhinnēh* clause in Ruth besides 2:4 and 4:1, namely 3:8.

Turn aside, sit down here. The two imperatives have cohortative *ā,* adding emphasis. Throughout the scene now unfolding Boaz acts with authority and at a determined pace.

so-and-so. The Hebrew is *pᵉlōnī 'almōnī,* two rhyming nouns of similar but not identical formation without intervening conjunction (asyndetic), to be found only in I Sam 21:3[Hebrew, 2]; II Kings 6:8, and here, along with the contracted form *palmōnī* in Dan 8:13. The meaning has been determined partly from the contexts of these biblical passages, but more from the way certain versions translated (some LXX manuscripts: *ho deina,* "such a one," —cf. Matt 26:18; the supplementing hand of the OL [see further below]: *quicumque es,* "whoever-you-are"); from the persistence in the Talmud of the first element, meaning, "someone, a certain one"; and from the Syriac and Arabic cognates (Arabic *fulān,* yielding Spanish *fulano,* "John Doe"). The effect is to indicate one who (for whatever reason) will not or cannot be named.

Why did the story-teller use an anonymous expression? (1) Does he mean that Boaz didn't know the name? Hardly, in a small town within a related circle. (2) Did the story-teller not know the near redeemer's name? That would rest on the assumption that the names in Ruth are genuine historically (see Rudolph, p. 29), an acceptable theory, but still a weak explanation. Why advertise ignorance of the names, particularly when the sentence structure does not require using a name? Of course if the story-teller invented the names in his story, this explanation is irrelevant. (3) Did the story-teller avoid the name for fear of offending descendants of the near redeemer (one alternative for Hertzberg, p. 277)? That would assume that what the redeemer did was deplorable (or at least unfortunate if he was really Boaz' brother—see below— because he lost the chance to be David's ancestor!). But there is no particular criticism of him for his decision (see on 4:7–8), and this explanation has a rather modern ring. (4) Is the use of *pᵉlōnī 'almōnī* a way, then, of dismissing an unimportant character? Surely that would be done more easily by using no designation at all here, and by sending the near redeemer off the stage as quickly as possible; compare the brief appearance on the scene of Boaz' foreman in 2:5–7. In the overall structure of the story, the near redeemer plays at least as prominent a role as does his counterpart Orpah (see the COMMENT). None of these explanations will answer the question of why the anonymity.

Nor do proposed etymologies seem to help. The root *ply/pl'*, attested only in the *Niphal* (passive-reflexive) and *Hiphil* (causative) conjugations, is regularly proposed for *pelōnī*; its basic meaning is assumed to be "to be other, different." The noun could then mean "stranger, one about whom one need not concern himself" (so L. Köhler, *Theologische Zeitschrift* 1 [1945], 303–4). The second term may come from the root *'lm*, "to be dumb," the idea being that one who cannot speak is strange and unknown (Gerleman, Rudolph). But neither of these proposals is compelling; in fact both are strained. It is conceivable instead that the idiom developed from two old proper names or gentilics, by a process lost to us (cf. English "Philistine," since the mid-nineteenth century a pejorative term). A gentilic "the Pelonite" is found in I Chron 11:27, 36, 27:10. Ugaritic administrative texts provide the names *pln, pl, plwn*, and in syllabic writing *a-li-mu-nu;* for none of these is the linguistic background certain, but such names were current in fourteenth- and thirteenth-century Canaan (consult the indexes of F. Gröndahl, *Die Personennamen der Texte aus Ugarit*, Rome: Pontifical Biblical Institute, 1967). They serve, at the present state of our knowledge, to warn us that etymological conclusions about *pelōnī 'almōnī* are not safe guides to elucidating the meaning of the idiom.

There is another curious set of data which may afford a hint. An interesting combination of variants in the versions at Ruth 4:1 points toward a connotation of secrecy, hiddenness, or reticence. The LXX[B] manuscript, together with the Lucianic manuscripts and a number of other non-hexaplaric minuscules (see Introduction), reads *kruphie*, a vocative "O Secret one, hidden one," as the translation of our idiom, and LXX[A] and two other minuscules read *kruphē*, "secretly." The OL reads, "and he said, 'Turn aside, sit here.' And he (the near redeemer) said 'What separate/secret?'" The final question (*quid secreti*) is odd Latin, but it conveys once again the element of secrecy. The Targum has "O man whose paths are humble/reserved/hidden"—the final word is a form of the only partially understood root *ṣn'*, found in the Bible only in Micah 6:8. Finally, I Sam 21:3 and II Kings 6:8, which employ our idiom, also have a nuance of secrecy. These passages are in stories in which secret military maneuvers involve "the place of *pelōnī 'almōnī*." Keeping the place secret is a part of the drama, in the former as part of the deception David uses on Ahimelek, in the latter as the piece of secret military intelligence which Elisha's clairvoyance can penetrate.

All of this suggests that a connotation of secrecy was bound up with *pelōnī 'almōnī* in an early interpretive stream, or even in its original meaning. This connotation would have contrasted with the understanding of the expression reflected by Greek *ho deina*, "such a one," by the usage in the Talmud, and by the Syriac and Arabic cognates—and preserved in our lexicons. It is worth observing that several LXX manuscripts have both *ho deina* and *kruphie*, conflating the two connotations; similarly, a supplementary hand to the OL wrote the *quicumque es* which we have already noted, again producing a conflation.

What would a connotation of secrecy imply in our passage? I can only speculate: (1) Perhaps the point is that Boaz spoke in an undertone to the near redeemer, in order to get him seated, before convening the more formal assembly. If so, some of the LXX^L along with the OL and the Syriac may reflect a genuine textual variant with the questions they record: in Greek, "Who are you?"; in Latin, the perplexing *quid secreti;* and in Syriac, "What?" (2) Barely conceivable would be that Boaz expressed a quiet criticism in using *pᵉlōnī 'almōnī,* amounting to "Why have you been hiding, you who should have been looking after your obligations to the two widows?"

In sum: *pᵉlōnī 'almōnī* is an expression with an obscure background and an imprecisely known connotation; apparently it had two different nuances by the time of the LXX recensional developments between 100 B.C.E. and 100 C.E., each of which was remembered in some of the versions. One nuance was simply anonymity, the other was bound up with secrecy, hiddenness, reticence. Quite clearly, an early Hebrew text tradition retained a response from the nearer redeemer, a question probably similar to the one of Naomi to Ruth in 3:16; it meant "What's up? What is this all about? What do you want of me?"

The reader should take this note as speculative, but one thing seems certain: the ancient audience heard something meaningful to the story when the storyteller used *pᵉlōnī 'almōnī.*

3. *The part of the field.* Recall 2:3. The field is the entire area under cultivation, within which the various villagers own plots.

our brother. Rabbinic tradition includes the view that Boaz, Salmon, *pᵉlōnī 'almōnī* (used like a name but hardly thought to be one) and Naomi's father were all blood brothers, sons of Nahshon (*Baba Bathra* 91a, in *The Babylonian Talmud,* tr., ed. I Epstein [London: Soncino, 1935], p. 376). "Brother" is frequently used, however, for other than blood kinship. It designates more distant relatives and even close friends, especially those in covenant relationship to one another. This covenant usage can be extensively documented, but as examples see David's reference to Jonathan as "brother" in II Sam 1:26, the pregnant expression "covenant of brothers" in Amos 1:9 (J. Priest, JBL 84 [1965], 400–6), and the frequent use in the Holiness Code, especially in Leviticus 25, the code being a definition of reciprocal responsibility under covenant (on "brother," see E. Jenni, article *'Aḥ,* in *Theologisches Handwörterbuch zum Alten Testament,* I [Munich: Kaiser, 1971], cols. 98–104, esp. 99–100; Jenni never uses the word "covenant" or "treaty," but he might well have). The term can easily be made consistent, then, with the proposals made in the second NOTE on 2:1 and the first on 3:2.

who has returned. Compare 1:22 and 2:6, the first probably and the second certainly with Ruth as antecedent. See the first NOTE on 1:22. The Syriac omits this entire clause.

hereby offers for sale. MT has the vowels of the perfect, *mākᵉrāh,* and this form of the verb should probably be retained, against the proposal of Rudolph and many recent commentaries to read the participle *mōkᵉrāh* (in fact the only OT attestation of a feminine singular participle of this root takes the alternate form *mōkeret*—Nahum 3:4). The perfect is to be translated here with the sense it can take in formal, legal acts (so Gerleman, and especially M. Sekine, ZAW 58 [1940–41], 137); compare "I hereby buy" in 4:9 and "I hereby give" in Gen 23:11, the story of the formal legal transaction by which Abraham purchases the cave at Machpelah. For the terminology "sell" and "buy," see the NOTE on 4:4, "Buy," and the COMMENT.

4. *I, for my part, said.* The independent pronoun precedes the verb in the Hebrew, signaling as in 4:1 the shift of subject (see the first NOTE on 4:1). The effect is to establish a connection to the end of verse 3 along these lines: "Naomi has decided to offer for sale the plot of land, while my function, I decided, was to let you know. . . ."

We are probably to understand "said" as "said to myself, resolved." This is Joüon's view (*Commentaire*, p. 81) based on comparison to I Sam 30:6 (literally, "the people said to stone him"), I Kings 22:23 (literally, "Yahweh has spoken [*dibber*] against you evil"), and II Kings 14:27 (literally, "Yahweh has not spoken [*dibber*] to blot out the name of Israel"). In fact the syntax in Ruth 4:4 is unique, using a verb in the imperfect following "I said" where these passages use the infinitive or a noun. It is as though Boaz were quoting a promise actually made earlier, so that we cannot entirely dismiss the possibility of a conversation between Boaz and Naomi, presumably falling between the events at the end of chapter 3 and those at the beginning of chapter 4. To my mind, such a proposal would over-rationalize the story. The effect at the beginning of the chapter, as the first NOTE on 4:1 argues, is one of immediate progression from the threshing floor to the gate. The audience of the story is simply left without an explanation of how Boaz knew of Naomi's intention and is at liberty even to conclude that Boaz invented the whole thing as a gambit (see the COMMENT).

inform you. Literally, "reveal/unstop your ears" (*'egleh 'oznᵉkā*), an idiom which accounts for thirteen of twenty-two *Qal* occurrences of the verb *glh*. Of the thirteen, six have God as subject, seven have men. The seven are distributed in two episodes of the conflict between Saul and David (I Sam 20:2, 12, 13, 22:8, 17) and here in Ruth. The two Samuel narratives contain an element of secrecy, even deception, and a flavor of secrecy occurs in I Sam 9:15 with God as subject. One is tempted to link this with the secrecy connotation of *pᵉlōnī 'almōnī* discussed in the last NOTE on 4:1 (cf. C. Lattey, *The Book of Ruth*, on 4:4), and to speculate that Boaz is speaking privately to the near redeemer or at least is recapitulating an earlier private conversation between them (cf. W. Caspari, *Neue Kirchliche Zeitschrift* 19 [1908], 124 f.). It is possible that one early recension of the Ruth story saw the action here in some such way—see the Lucianic variations cited in the last NOTE on 4:1. Nevertheless, the entire episode in 4:1–12 is presented by the story-teller as a public, formal, and legal action; we do better to assume that for the sake of the story all of Boaz' words were spoken in the public forum.

to this effect. Hebrew *lēmōr*, literally, "to say," is expected to introduce the *content* of what the speaker has revealed, as it does, for example, in

I Sam 9:15 and II Sam 7:27. Here, curiously, what follows is the *consequence* of what has been revealed.

Buy. The verb *qnh* here, and the verb *mkr*, "to sell," in 4:3 are according to their primary connotations terms belonging to commercial transactions involving money or goods, almost always in relation to land or to persons (slaves). In all other places where the two terms appear in conjunction with one another, it is just such commercial transactions which are under discussion —see Gen 47:19–23; Exod 21:2–8; Lev 25:14–51, 27:20–28; Deut 28:68; Ezek 7:12–13; Zech 11:5; Prov 23:23; and Neh 5:8. It seems inescapable that the story-teller sets out upon his portrayal of the highly complex transaction in verses 3–10 by intentionally using commercial words. By the time we reach verse 10, this terminology will have led us into certain difficulties, but that is no excuse for supplying a circumlocution for the terms here at the start. For a translator to use "proposes to alienate" instead of "offers for sale" or "acquire" instead of "buy" is to evade the strong likelihood that the audience of the story heard commercial language first. See the COMMENT.

in the presence of those sitting here and in the presence of the elders of my people. The Hebrew is as explicit as it can be that there are two groups alluded to, by reusing the preposition *neged* before each group. The versions support this unanimously. Rudolph proposes, therefore, that the ones "sitting" here are the crowd of people who have gathered about to observe and will function again as witnesses in verses 9 and 11, while the elders are the ten Boaz has selected (verse 2). There is a problem with this explanation, however. From 3:18 through 4:2, it would seem that the story-teller has been using the verb *yšb*, "to sit," to get all of the principals properly located where they should be for the legal transaction. Ruth, first of all, is sitting tight at home. Boaz himself is seated at the gate. The near redeemer has been told to sit at one spot, and he has done so (4:1); ten of the elders of the city have been asked to sit in their place, and they have done so. It is difficult indeed to avoid the conclusion that the "sitters" here in verse 4 are then the ten selected elders. Taking a cue from 3:11 ("all the gate=assembly of my people"), we do better to take the designation "the elders of my people" to refer to the larger group of which the ten "sitters" are the representatives. Instead of introducing at this point the gathering crowd (there doubtless was one), Boaz is underscoring the legal reality; in responding to the obligation to buy, the near redeemer is to act before the duly constituted ten and therefore by extension before the whole legal assembly. (There were certainly more than ten elders at Bethlehem; notice the seventy-seven of them at Sukkoth in Judg 8:14.) If we identify the two groups in this way, we also give a better explanation of the order of the terms; were Rudolph's proposal correct, surely one would expect the ten elders to be mentioned first, followed by the crowd of onlookers.

except you, and I after you. The expression is odd, because the Hebrew *zūlat*, "apart from, except" is always used elsewhere to designate the *only* exception. In the absence of any clear explanation of why Boaz uses this way of speaking when there is indeed another besides the near redeemer who can function, it is fruitless to speculate about whether there were "ranks" or concentric circles of relatives (blood or covenant), with the near redeemer the only one left of one rank and Boaz the first of the next rank. We cannot even tell whether the words mean Boaz was the last available candidate, although it would heighten the drama of the story if he were to be so seen. Most commentators, by not even raising the question, seem to imply that this is simply a picturesque way of saying "you are the one, and if you default I come next."

5. *You 'buy' Ruth the Moabitess.* The clause opens with Hebrew *umē'ēt rūt,* according to the Masoretic voweling, which would mean "and from Ruth." It happens that the compound preposition *mē'ēt* is the normal one after *qnh,* "to buy"; conceivably, then, one can link this to the preceding phrase: "from the hand of Naomi and from Ruth." Entirely apart from the thorny social and legal questions such a translation would raise, it plays havoc with the syntax of what follows, and one would prefer for such a rendering a repetition of prepositions ("from the hand of Naomi and from the hand of Ruth"). In any case, comparison to 4:1 makes it certain that Ruth is the direct object of the verb which follows, and that her name was marked with the direct object particle *'et* here as there. This leaves an unaccounted for *m* in the Hebrew sequence *wm't.* This may be an enclitic *mem* after the conjunction, an explanation requiring no alteration of the consonantal text; the use of enclitic *mem* on *w,* "and," in Hebrew has yet to be fully established, but see provisionally F. I. Andersen, *The Hebrew Verbless Clause in the Pentateuch* (Nashville: Abingdon, 1970), pp. 48 and 124, n. 13. Alternatively, one may posit an original *wᵉgam 'et* as in 4:10 (see NOTE on "And, more important . . .")— notice, against Rudolph, that the syntax here requires the presence of *wᵉ* (after the temporal expression "in the day of your buying"), so that we would have to do with the loss of a *g,* not with the possible confusion of a *g* and a *w.* The latter emendation is favored by most commentators, but I am attracted to the explanation of enclitic *mem;* see the first NOTE on 4:10 on the special significance there of the word *gam.*

As for the verb, "buy," the consonants of the Hebrew, *qnyty,* call for the first person while the Masoretic voweling reads the second person. An attempt by T. C. Vriezen, *Oudtestamentische Studiën* 5 (1948), 80–88, to retain the consonantal text and find a meaning along the lines of "I (zealously) maintain with regard to Ruth the rights to raise up . . ." results in separating the redeeming of the field and the responsibility for Ruth. This fails completely to accord with the language of 3:12–13 and is out of place with the whole thrust of the threshing floor and gate episodes, as H. H. Rowley, *The Servant of the Lord and Other Essays,* p. 185, n. 1, has pointed out (see also Rudolph, p. 59). An attempt by D. R. G. Beattie, VT 21 (1971), 490–94, reasserted in VT 24 (1974), 262–64, to retain the first person reading, states the case for separating redemption and remarriage as effectively as it can be stated, and ends by denying any levirate aspect to the marriage of Ruth and Boaz. What Beattie must do is to violate the internal consistency of the Ruth story, and that is fatal to his thesis. However, his observations are helpful for one who seeks to grasp the complicated problems involved.

What does the verb "to buy" come to mean when applied to Ruth? Is there portrayed here a concept of marriage by purchase? If so, to whom would be paid a bride-price? To Ruth's parents? Hardly! To Elimelek's estate or to Naomi? If so, only by some custom entirely unknown to us. A better explanation can be derived from observations made by D. H. Weiss, *Harvard Theological Review* 57 (1964), 244–48, concerning the way in which qnh is used in the Mishnah with reference to marriage. Weiss claims that qnh for marriage occurs "only in contexts embracing other transactions in which qnh in its proper sense of 'purchase' (acquire property) is applicable" (p. 246). For regular marriages in the Mishnah, the standard words are qdš and 'rs; qnh is used only when an action of purchasing of slaves or property, or of transferring of property, controls the context. In other words, stylistic uniformity leads to using qnh about marriage to a woman when that marriage in some manner relates to a larger commercial transaction in the general context. Qnh literally means "purchase" in the commercial transaction, but it has a more figurative meaning for what affects the woman. In 4:4, 5a, 8, and 9, then, this insight allows qnh to be translated literally "to buy." In 4:5b and 10, where the transfer of Ruth is designated by the same term, the meaning is not strictly "purchase" or "gain by payment"; rather it can be paraphrased "marry as part of a legally valid commercial transaction." Neither the near redeemer nor Boaz is literally to purchase Ruth; cf. M. Burrows, *The Basis of Israelite Marriage* (New Haven: American Oriental Society, 1938), esp. pp. 28–29.

6. *I cannot redeem . . . you take on.* Literally, "I cannot redeem for me . . . redeem for you, you, my redemption-responsibility." Compare "You buy" (literally, "buy for you") in 4:8 and in Jer 32:7–8. The various instances here of leкā, "for you," are examples of what is often called an "ethical dative," frequent after imperatives; very unusual is the parallel lī, "for me," in the first clause. The overall effect can hardly be reflected in translation, but is more a matter of emphasis: "I can't, *you* do it"; still more emphasis is supplied by the independent pronoun "you." Here at the dramatic climax of the scene, the story-teller makes the near redeemer's renunciation as precise and emphatic as he can, even to the point of double redundancy. Correct procedure is followed to the hilt.

7. *Now this was (the mode).* The LXX and the Latin versions all translate with terms that suggest the verse began wezeh hammišpāṭ, "now this is the regulation"; just this term mišpāṭ occurs in the very similar passage Jer 32:7–8. Note, however, that the MT preserves not the masculine demonstrative pronoun zeh but the feminine zōt. Rudolph is probably right (against Joüon, *Commentaire*, p. 85) that the versions, including the Targum ("and according to this manner") are simply giving a correct paraphrase of the Hebrew.

formerly in Israel. These words underscore the similarity of 4:7 to I Sam 9:9, where two former and outmoded features are explained—the procedure for consulting deity and the term "seer" now supplanted by "prophet." The Hebrew lepānīm, "formerly," can indicate a previous time of close proximity or of hoary, even mythic, antiquity. The time span is a generation or less in Job 42:11; Judg 3:2; Neh 13:5; and possibly Josh 11:10, and it is lengthy (seven hundred years!) in I Chron 9:20 and mythic (in effect, back to the beginning of time) in Ps 102:26. In other instances (see Deut 2:10, 12, 20;

1 Chron 4:40; Judg 1:10, 11, 23; Josh 14:15, 15:15) the time separation is difficult to judge. Much more to the point is to note that the passages cited tend to pertain to before and after a radical change in circumstances, whether of land possession, of city name (and perhaps therefore of population), or of social order, matters resulting from invasions, change of government, and the like. Altered circumstances require some altered modes—together with explanation and instruction (see the Introduction, pp. 8–9). The time need not be long.

to confirm. The MT has *lᵉqayyēm*, quite possibly an Aramaism for expected Hebrew *lᵉqōmēm*. Conclusions as to the date of the Ruth story should not depend on the presence of this form, for several reasons: (1) The Hebrew form *qōmēm* has the meaning "raise up, lift" in Isa 44:26, 58:12, and 61:4, all of exilic date (an occurrence in Micah 2:8 is dubious), quite a different meaning from the one assigned to *qayyēm*. (2) Forms of hollow verbs with doubled medial *waw* or *yodh* may not in fact be totally absent from relatively early biblical texts—see the *Hithpael* of *ṣyd* in Judg 9:12 (so Rudolph). (3) There is a large number of examples of *Piel* forms of *qwm* in the OT (Ezek 13:6; Ps 119:28, 106; Esther 9:21–32) with a variety of nuances, which at least suggests a rather early adoption of the Aramaism, if Aramaism it be. (4) Finally, as has been noted, there are strikingly few Aramaisms in Ruth (see the Introduction, p. 24, and the first and second NOTES on 1:13), even if this be counted as one. In the final analysis, the possibility that this is a form from an old Hebrew dialect should be kept open.

a man . . . to his counterpart. The Hebrew combination *'îš . . . rēʿēhû* has two possible meanings. In a number of passages, especially in narratives, it expresses reciprocal activity between or among people, such as "they said one to another"; see, for example, Gen 11:3, 7, 43:33; Judg 6:29, 10:18; I Sam 10:11, 20:41; II Sam 2:16; Jonah 1:7; and notably Ruth 3:14. On the other hand, in a number of passages mostly in legal and customary materials, it is used to express what one person has or has not done, may or may not do, to another; see, among others, Exod 21:14, 18, 35, 22:6, 9, 13; Deut 4:42, 19:4, 5, 22:24, 26; Ezek 18:6, 11, 15. Our passage, while in a narrative context, is a statement of customary practice, and more probably falls into the second category; however, it is not clear at all whether the action is reciprocal or unilateral—we cannot tell from the Hebrew whether both parties gave and received shoes, or only one gave a shoe to the other. The LXX offers a reading which settles the question, by adding "to the one taking up the redemption-responsibility" in apposition to "counterpart," thus making the action one way. This, however, only heightens the uncertainty, because it suggests that the original story was ambiguous on the point and needed explication (see further in the second NOTE on 4:8). Our translation implies that the one-way option is the stronger possibility, but the alternative should be kept in mind; the principle may have been one of transfer of roles symbolized by each party's stepping into the other's shoes.

would draw off. MT: *šālap*, voweled as a perfect tense presumably to be construed as iterative (habitual)—very unusual for a perfect. Instead we can revowel to *šālōp*, the infinitive absolute, a surrogate verb without time reference (a proposal favored by Rudolph, p. 60). A third option is one which quite probably existed in one early Hebrew variation of our story; posit an original *wᵉ* on the front of *šālap* (supported by LXX^BL′, and the OL), which would "convert" the perfect to an imperfective meaning much more amenable to expressing habitual action.

shoe. Or "sandal." Presumably, it is whatever foot covering was being worn. There is pictorial evidence for sandals with straps, for low "desert boots," and for shoes with upturned, pointed toes. See the excellent survey by J. M. Myers, "Sandals and Shoes," *The Interpreter's Dictionary of the Bible,* vol. R–Z, pp. 213–14.

process of ratification. Hebrew *tᵉ'ūdāh* is etymologically related to the Hebrew word for "witness"; here it probably has a quite different meaning from that of its only other OT attestations, Isa 8:16 and 20, where it refers to the prophet's already given "testimony," namely the combination of prophetic credentials and indictments in 6:1 – 9:7. In Ruth, the term must comprehend the "redemption cases and exchange transactions" mentioned at the beginning of the verse.

Two literary devices are worth noting. Verses 6 and 7 each have a fine inclusio, enveloping the content: "I cannot redeem . . . I cannot redeem" and "this was (the mode) in Israel . . . this was the ratification process in Israel." Furthermore, in verse 7 the technical words all have vowel assonance: *gᵉ'ūl(l)āh, tᵉmūrāh, te'ūdāh* (incidentally, the great Leningrad Masoretic codex, B 19^A, which serves as the base text for BH³, has *gu'ūlah* here, but assonance makes that first *u* suspicious and calls for the decision made by the BH³ editor to place the *shewa* there instead—as normal in the book).

8. *So the redeemer said to Boaz, "You buy."* The narrative is resumed with a succinct recapitulation of verse 6, a clear indication that the explanatory parenthesis in verse 7 is an original part of the story. There is a delicious touch of irony that the near redeemer is still designated the *gō'ēl* after having resigned his responsibility. His final words return to using the more comprehensive verb *qnh,* "to buy," the verb with which the transaction began at verse 4 (see the NOTE on 4:5).

And he drew off his shoe. The LXX and OL have an attractive addition: "and gave it to him." If this were in the original text, its loss can be accounted for by haplography, the scribe's eye jumping from one syllable *lō* to the next: *wayyišlōp na'ᵃlō<wayyittēn lō>* (Joüon, *Commentaire,* and Rudolph). Or this longer reading may be an early variant, in a text which was more explicit about the way the near redeemer's words and actions conform to the custom described in verse 7. The shorter text recommends itself, however, because it parallels the brevity of the recapitulation which opens the verse. (Note that LXX, but not OL, attests an expanded reading in the first part as well: "Buy for yourself my redemption-responsibility.")

What is the precise form the custom takes here? The answer is by no means as obvious as it seems. Did the redeemer take off his own shoe and give it to Boaz? This is what a variant in the minor Lucianic witnesses of the LXX states explicitly: "and gave it to Boaz." The Vulgate points in the same direction: "Therefore the kinsman said to Boaz, 'Take up the shoe!' which he had just loosened from his foot" (so in the critical Benedictine *Sacra Biblia* [Ruth published in 1939]; compare Douay-Rheims: "So Boaz said to his kinsman: 'Put off thy shoe.' And immediately he took it off from his foot."). The Targum is just as explicit that Boaz took off the near redeemer's shoe. In all these, there seems no question that it is the redeemer's shoe that is being removed. Midrash Rabbah to Ruth, however, debates just this point, and decides otherwise: "Whose shoe? Rab and Lev disagreed. One said the shoe of Boaz, while the other said the shoe of the kinsman. It is more probable that he who says the shoe of Boaz is correct, for it is usual for the purchaser to give the pledge" (*Ruth Rabbah VII.* 11). E. A. Speiser, BASOR 77 (February 1940), 15–20, adopts without question the position that the shoe was the "price" by which Boaz purchased the right to Ruth, meaning obviously that the shoe had been Boaz'.

We have then, a variety of interpretations, all of which are at least theoretically possible, given the terseness of the Hebrew expression. The near redeemer could have given his shoe to Boaz. Boaz could have removed the near redeemer's shoe, or Boaz could have removed his own shoe and given it to the near redeemer. It is even barely conceivable that each man took off a shoe and gave it to the other (recall the NOTE on verse 7, "a man . . . to his counterpart"), implying that in effect they exchange places. Attempts to unravel the custom and decide the direction of movement all require some speculation (see, among others, E. R. Lacheman, JBL 56 [1937], 53–56; the Speiser article mentioned above; G. M. Tucker, *Catholic Biblical Quarterly* 28 [1966], 42–45; T. and D. Thompson, VT 18 [1968], 79–99, esp. 90–93), and none dispels all the problems. To compound the difficulty, a passage frequently invoked to prove that putting one's shoe on a place means to take possession, namely Ps 60:10 with its parallel Ps 108:10, probably has quite a different meaning—see M. Dahood, *Psalms II*, AB, vol. 17, NOTE on 60:10, "will I plant." In Deut 25:9, where a widow faced with a brother-in-law who refuses to do his levirate duty is to remove his shoe and spit in his face, the circumstances are sufficiently different to make attempts to conform the two practices doubtful.

All this having been said, the most probable conclusion is that the near redeemer gave Boaz his shoe, symbolizing the transfer of the right. The variety of interpretations in the versions probably arose from attempts to understand verse 7 and see its application to verse 8. To my mind, verse 7 is best understood as an overly terse way of describing shoe symbolism in two different kinds of transaction; in an exchange transaction, the parties exchanged shoes, while in the matter of giving up the right of redemption, the one ceding the right gave his shoe to the one taking over the right. Until we have more clearly pertinent evidence concerning this interesting custom, we cannot go farther. Meanwhile we must fault our story-teller for not giving sufficient explanation to allow his distant audience—namely us—to see clearly what was happening!

9. *to the elders and to all the people.* Here, and on the name Mahlon later in the verse, the preposition governing a compound object is not repeated—the only times in the entire book that this happens (cf. the double employment of *neged*, "in the presence of," in verse 4; see NOTE). Either we must supply *l*ᵉ

before the second object here (so Joüon), or let the first *lᵉ* do double duty; the latter course is preferable.

The fifth NOTE on 4:4 proposed identifications for the two groups, the "sitters" and "the elders of my people." Here again we have two designations, the elders and all the people. By this time in the portrayal of the legal scene, we are probably justified in considering the "people" as those who have gathered about the original ten elders and the two litigants; more than mere spectators, they are called upon to play a legal role with the elders, as witnesses.

I hereby buy. As in 4:3, "Naomi . . . hereby offers for sale," the perfect verb has the formal sense of an action now concluded. See the last NOTE on 4:3.

Kilyon and Mahlon. In reverse order from that in 1:2, 5! A few Hebrew manuscripts, the Syriac, and part of the LXX tradition place Mahlon first here, as in chapter 1. Note that the order of the sons' names in 1:2 and the wives' names in 1:4 suggests that Ruth was Kilyon's wife, Orpah Mahlon's. In 4:10 we will learn for the first time that Ruth is Mahlon's widow. After all, then, it is 1:2 which seems to have the sons' names in the wrong order. Rudolph's ingenious suggestion that the order in 4:9 is due to some juristic principle requiring alphabetic order is baseless, and it fails to solve the more interesting problem just mentioned. The story-teller's use of chiasm (see Introduction, p. 14) may be the appropriate explanation instead.

10. *And, more important, Ruth the Moabitess, wife of Mahlon, I 'buy' as my wife.* The Hebrew begins the verse with *wᵉgam,* which here clearly has an emphasizing force. The progression from verse 9 to verse 10 is from one perfect tense to another (here of the same verb) through the conjunction *wᵉgam,* precisely the syntax which C. J. Labuschagne, in the Vriezen celebration volume, eds. W. C. van Unnik and A. S. van der Woude, *Studia Biblica et Semitica* (Wageningen: Veenman, 1966), pp. 193–203, has identified as requiring an emphasizing force for *wᵉgam.* Among his examples given on p. 197, note especially Gen 37:7, 38:22, 24 as occurring in stories comparable to Ruth. It is because of the special value of *gam* here that we should *not* expect it in 4:5; see the NOTE there.

A further indication of emphasis upon Ruth here lies in the way the verb *qnh* is construed syntactically in verses 9 and 10. In verse 10, Boaz uses the emphatic combination *qānītī lī,* as had the near redeemer in 4:6 and 8 (see NOTE on 4:6). In 4:9, concerning the property, Boaz uses only *qānītī.* For the connotation of "buy" here in verse 10, see NOTE on 4:5.

or from the assembly of his town. "Assembly," here as at 3:11, is the appropriate translation of Hebrew *ša'ar,* "gate" (see the second NOTE on 3:11). LXXᴮ and a few other Greek manuscripts have "of his people" instead of "of his town," doubtless in conformity with 3:11, "of my people." The word here translated "town" is *māqōm,* not unusual as a term for "town" or "city," as such passages as Gen 18:24, 26 (*J*), and 20:11, among many others, attest. Perhaps we can account for the use of *māqōm* here by its assonance with *lᵉhāqīm* earlier in the verse, and even with *lᵉqayyēm* in verse 7. The LXX tradition gives a mixed signal, with the major Lucianic witnesses plus a few others including Theodoret reading simply "assembly," LXXᴮ and a few others reading "the assembly of his people," LXXᴬ and a few others reading "the assembly of the people," and LXX^{MN} and a few others reading with the MT. Compare Syriac: "from his people." If the reason of assonance for *māqōm* explains its presence in one old text, possibly another old text, or more than one other, did not have it.

The connotation of "from the assembly of his town" is more than simply membership in the legal body. Consistent with "his inheritance" in the first clause of the long purpose expression in this verse, it connotes his legal rights as protected by the assembly, of which he would have been a member.

today. The word underscores the legal nature of the witness—this applies now and henceforth. And there is another fine rhetorical effect, for, if the audience has listened carefully, they hear an echo of Naomi's "today" at the end of 3:18.

11. *Then all the people who were in the gate and the elders said.* Note the nice stylistic touch of reversing the order of the two groups from that in 4:9 (chiasm). The witnessing function would seem to be connected with Boaz' decision to proceed with the purchase of the property and the acquisition of Ruth (see the COMMENT). The LXX senses that "in the gate" here is to be taken as referring to the location, as in 4:1, rather than to the legal body; the Greek is *pulē* again, not *fulē* as in 3:11 and 4:10. The Hebrew, however, permits the audience at least to enjoy a bit of a *double entendre*.

The LXX tradition unanimously offers an alternate reading on the functions of the two groups. It has all the people who were in the gate agree to be witnesses, then has the elders pronounce the blessing. The result is an attractive balance which has been accepted by a number of commentators (e.g., BH³, Ehrlich, Joüon, Vincent and Tamisier in the Jerusalem Bible). The Syriac reverses the two groups and gives each a verb: the elders answer and the people say "We are witnesses." Nevertheless, in the Syriac and the OL, usually close to the LXX, the two groups act together in pronouncing the blessing that follows. With Rudolph and Gerleman, I retain the MT. In all three places where two components of the legal community appear (verses 4, 9, and 11), they act in concert.

(*We are*) *witnesses.* I have used parentheses to emphasize that Hebrew legal style uses simply the word *'ēdīm*, "Witnesses"; cf. Josh 24:22.

like Rachel and like Leah. The order is interesting. Rudolph is especially struck by it and wonders: "Does this happen because she [Rachel] was Jacob's favorite wife? Or does the false tradition of a grave of Rachel at Bethlehem already exist (Gen 35:19)? Or is there an even more refined subtlety here, since Rachel experienced a lengthy barrenness at first just as Ruth had in her earlier marriage?" One might add to this catalogue the observation that Ruth is second-named in 1:4 and was apparently married to the younger of the two sons (see the last NOTE on 4:9); the subtle touch of the story-teller may involve reminding us that it is Ruth, the least in rank of the story's characters, who is now to receive the reward of her faithfulness.

between them. Literally, "the two of them,'" again with the ending we have proposed as a feminine dual; see the third NOTE on 1:8.

built the house. Compare Deut 25:9, "who does not build the house of his brother"—one of the rather few verbal correspondences between the levirate passage in Deuteronomy and the Ruth story (see the COMMENT). In preexilic narrative, compare Gen 16:2 and 30:3 (both *J*), and such passages where God builds a dynasty as I Sam 2:35; II Sam 7:27; and I Kings 11:38.

And may you show fertility in Ephrathah / And (then) bestow a name in Bethlehem. This succinct poetic couplet is the middle element in the three-part blessing in verses 11-12 which flows to Ruth to Boaz to his offspring; Boaz is central to them all, for the blessing on Ruth is at the same time a blessing pertinent to his "house," and offspring would be an extension of his person. The blessing has a syntactic unity, starting with a jussive ("may Yahweh make . . ."), followed by the two imperatives, each with the conjunction *w-* in this couplet, followed by another jussive with the conjunction ("and may your house become"). This alone favors the retention of the two imperatives here, although the LXX[B] with some other Greek witnesses and OL read the first as a plural indicative, in continuation of the reference to Rachel and Leah: "the two of whom built up the house of Israel and performed power in Ephrathah." The LXX[L'] group, with other LXX witnesses including the hexaplaric ones, have the imperative, and the Syriac also probably attests it.

The translation proposed here builds upon a cogent study of the verse by C. J. Labuschagne in ZAW 79 (1967), 364–67. Without repeating his entire argument, let me emphasize these points:

1) One expects this couplet to be consistent in meaning with the other elements of the blessing which surround it, and therefore to relate to fertility and offspring. Labuschagne proposes a meaning "procreative power" for Hebrew *ḥayl* here, a nuance he finds in Job 21:7–8 and Joel 2:22 (note also the possible double meaning in Prov 31:3; cf. R. B. Y. Scott, *Proverbs, Ecclesiastes*, AB, vol. 18, on this verse, where he translates "virility"). Such a meaning runs counter to expectations; the idiom *'śh ḥyl*, "to do *ḥayl*," is attested at Num 24:18; I Sam 14:48; Pss 60:14 and 118:16, all in war contexts calling for "to achieve victory, to do valiantly." If we guide ourselves by the other occurrences of the noun *ḥayl* in Ruth, at 2:1 and 3:11, we get a different connotation, of substance and worthiness, and most modern English translations follow this lead. If we look to Deut 8:17–18, we have the clear indication that "to do *ḥayl*" can mean "to acquire wealth." It is the very variety of possible meanings which suggests that our story-teller has here an opportunity to indulge his enjoyment of word-play and expansion of meaning. He has already linked two different nuances with his use of *ḥayl* in 2:1 and 3:11 (see the pertinent NOTES); here he expands the term in another direction, pertaining to the prospects for the outcome of the marriage of "substantial" Boaz and "worthy" Ruth.

2) The poetic couplets in Ruth are usually characterized by synonymous parallelism; we expect the second element, then, to relate to, and virtually to repeat, the meaning of the first. Labuschagne proposes, therefore, "become a name-giver," a picturesque way of saying "beget and see born a child." However the idiom for naming is *qr' šm l-X*, "call a name to (someone)," and the idiom without the object of the naming is unattested elsewhere in biblical Hebrew, so the proposal is a bit tenuous. But it does have the distinct advantage

of keeping the meaning close to that of the entire blessing here: fertility and offspring. Furthermore, it obviates some ingenious alternative proposals made by commentators. Thus, some would impose a passive meaning and have the name be Boaz', e.g. Rudolph's "May *your* name be celebrated," comparing verse 14b. Joüon, *Commentaire*, pp. 90–91, takes a different tack and emends *qᵉrā'* to *qᵉnēh*, "acquire," noting that the root *qnh* has been prominent in verses 4–10. Both proposals require emendation from a more difficult reading to a reading which, if original, should have been protected by the context.

3) Labuschagne adds another perceptive dimension: Why is a blessing for fertility expressed for Boaz? Doubtless because he is rather a senior citizen. Like Judah in Genesis 38, to which the rest of the blessing, in verse 12, refers, Boaz is a generation older than his bride and there can be some doubt as to his ability still to sire children. See the next NOTE.

12. *this girl.* As a further reminder of the discrepancy of age between Boaz and Ruth, the story-teller has the blessing return to designating her "this *naʿᵃrāh*," the term used in 2:5 and 6 for her. In chapter 2, it will be recalled, *naʿar* and *naʿᵃrāh*, and their plurals, emphasize the generation gap between Boaz and his workers. Recall also 3:10 and the second NOTE there.

COMMENT

If the third episode of the Ruth story was private and mysterious, the episode at the city gate is quite the opposite. Here the action takes place at the most public spot in town, before elders and a large body of onlookers. Everything is open and aboveboard. The interpreter should probably begin from that perspective, and hence approach the scene with the expectation that things should make sense, in spite of the ocean of ink which has been spilled over a number of unanswered questions raised by the scene. By and large, commentators have had the good sense to conclude that if the answers are not clear the reason lies with our lack of knowledge rather than with the story-teller's carelessness or stupidity. After all, the scene does emerge as a luminous, instructive, and indeed quite enjoyable glimpse into what must have been a common facet of everyday life in ancient Israel.

Each new archaeological discovery of a city gate brings greater clarity about the physical setting of this section. Among the considerable number of city gates of the Israelite period now known, the structures at Gezer and Dan are of special interest for our purposes. See the photographs and plan in illustrations 5–9 for their particular features.

The Gezer gate came into being in the Solomonic period, around the middle of the tenth century B.C.E., and was built from the same architectural "blueprint" as the ones at Megiddo and Hazor, other cities which Solomon refortified, according to I Kings 9:15. The gate building proper was a multiple-storied structure with a ground plan having four stone piers topped with brick on each side of the central roadway. The recesses between the piers formed rectangular chambers about seven by fourteen feet in size. Careful excavation by American teams from the Hebrew Union College Biblical and Archaeological School, during the summers of 1967 through 1971, traced low stone bench foundations overlaid with plaster around the three walls of each of the six bays (see illustration 6). Here people could sit as they carried out commercial transactions or conducted judicial proceedings, but the small size of these chambers, roofed and enclosed as they were, does not recommend them as the site for such an occasion as the hearing in Ruth 4:1–12. Better would be the open plaza just inside the city against the back wall of the gate. The Gezer excavators found benches along the faces of the gate-tower walls, and then along walls at right angles to the back of the gate running on into town. See illustration 5, and for a fuller description of the entire gate complex, W. G. Dever, et al., BA 34 (1971), 112–20.

In this open plaza, quite probably, public business of a more complex kind, to which spectators would be attracted, could be carried on. It happens that the benches around the Gezer plaza went out of use before the end of the tenth century—they were repeatedly renewed within the gate chambers, and changes in that structure produced larger rooms during the ninth and eighth centuries—but the plaza itself persisted throughout the Israelite period. It is in such a site as this that the civil hearing in Ruth would have taken place, a location with benches where everyone involved could follow out Boaz' explicit instruction: sit down here.

At Dan, the plan is quite different but the features are similar. See illustrations 7, 8, and 9, and for fuller detail, A. Biran, BA 37 (1974), 43–50. This gate came into being probably under Jeroboam I in the late tenth century, and persisted until the mid-ninth century, if not, indeed, until the Assyrian conquest in the late eighth century. One approached the outer entrance of the gate from the east along the city wall, crossed the twelve-foot-wide threshold of the outer entrance, and entered a paved, roughly rectangular plaza about sixty-seven by thirty-one feet in size. The main gate entrance opened off this plaza and contained three pairs of piers, forming four interior chambers, two on each side of the central roadway. Inside the city, the paved road continued for a distance and then made a right-angle turn up into the city's interior. It is the plaza which interests us. Against the outer wall of the main gate, a row of stone blocks about fifteen feet long served as a low bench. Between this bench and the main gate entrance is a remarkable structure which appears to be the dais for a ceremonial chair or throne, flanked by four ornamented circular stones each containing a socket suggesting that they supported columns holding up a canopy or other style of roofing over the dais. While some have thought of a shrine or "high place" as the explanation for this structure (invoking II Kings 23:8 for support), the more likely explanation is that it was a ceremonial seat for judgment (see the second NOTE on 3:2). In any event, the open plaza in front of the gate at Dan would also be a natural setting for the kind of civil proceeding in Ruth 4.

Allowing ourselves to assume some such setting, we picture Boaz arriving from the threshing floor in the early light of day, where he at once encounters —hardly by chance, judging from the story's "just then"—the near redeemer.

Boaz instructs him to take a seat on one of the benches. Boaz next gathers, as they come through the gate, ten of the town's elders, and ceremoniously places them in their proper seats. He then addresses the near redeemer as one connected, in a way similar to his own connection, to "our brother Elimelek." "Our brother" here may designate a near or distant relative, or it may belong to the covenant terminology we have suggested (see the second NOTE on 4:3).

The opening issue is the redemption of a piece of agricultural land which belongs to Elimelek and his family; Boaz informs the near redeemer that it should be bought, and verse 5 makes it clear that the purchase would be from Naomi. The need for purchase of the field comes as news to the near redeemer, and he is called upon to decide at once, in front of the ten selected elders who represent the "civil establishment" of Bethlehem, whether or not to take up his opportunity and obligation. He agrees readily. But Boaz, then, in the same ceremonial fashion, goes on to point out that with the purchase goes another factor, the responsibility to take Ruth, widow of Elimelek's heir, and raise through her a son who will then continue the family of Elimelek and become his heir. This the redeemer recognizes as imperiling to his own inheritance—surely he is already married and has a family of his own—and so he formally adopts the way out which has always been available to him, apparently without opprobrium, and changes his "yes" to "no." In doing so, he acts on the implication of Boaz in verse 4 that he, Boaz, stands ready to take up the opportunity and responsibility if the near redeemer refuses. With verse 7 the story-teller intrudes momentarily to explain what one did in former times to formalize such transactions, whereupon verse 8 returns to a summary of the near redeemer's decision and a description of the shoe-removal act.

To insure the legality of the agreement, Boaz turns to the designated elders acting as representatives of local civil authority, and to the bystanders, and asks for ratification of what he now takes on in the wake of the nearer redeemer's refusal, that is, to buy the land from Naomi and "buy" the young widow so as to establish the continuance of the line. In chorus, the elders and bystanders approve, first by acknowledging their role as witnesses, and second by pronouncing an elaborate blessing. The blessing dwells first on the woman and her potential to give offspring as did Rachel and Leah, then on Boaz and his potential for fertility, and finally upon the house which will thereby be brought into existence, that it will be as significant as that of Perez, whom Tamar bore to Judah.

The blessing effectively knits together several themes. In mentioning Rachel it recalls a person for whom barrenness gave way to motherhood. In recalling Tamar and Judah, it brings up another instance where circumstances included the application of levirate custom. In calling for a blessing of fertility, it reminds us that Ruth has been barren and Boaz is getting on in years—with the effect of suggesting that the drama is still not quite over. One further obvious implication of the blessing is that somehow this offspring is not simply to be reckoned to Elimelek and his line but to Boaz' line as well.

While the flavor of this scene is ceremonial and proper, there is no time wasted in it. The verbiage in the speeches is necessary to the formality of the occasion, but not excessive. There is not the languid pace of the scene in the field in chapter 2, nor are many words needed to establish suspense as they were in the episode at the threshing floor. Boaz moves fast. He arranges things. He states the problem. The near redeemer responds with one Hebrew word (it takes three in English: "I will redeem"). Even the antiquarian note in verse 7 is succinct, so much so that we cannot be sure exactly how it applies (see the second NOTE on 4:8). But the best indication of rapidity is the "just then" in verse 1; in effect, it signals that no time elapses between Boaz' arrival and that of the near redeemer. A lot is packed into the eight verses which resolve the potentially tangled web of custom. Yet to the dismay of the modern audience, a number of questions are left unanswered.

*   *   *   *   *   *

There are at least seven questions which have been begged in the synopsis of the scene just given. Some may never be settled, but they are worth looking at nonetheless. Much of what can be said about them is contained in the NOTES, but a brief treatment of each follows.

1. Why is the near redeemer not named, but rather designated "so-and-so" in verse 1? This episode is straightforward; it is difficult to see what the anonymity of one of the protagonists achieves. The NOTE on the subject discards a number of proposed conjectures, and toys with the bare possibility that a connotation of secrecy is somehow involved—an idea suggested by the way some of the versions translated his designation. An indication of the perplexity caused by this anonymity is the strong Jewish tradition that the nearer redeemer was named Tob, taking the Hebrew word in 3:13 which has been translated "well and good," as the subject of the verb instead. All this does, to my mind, is to underscore the expectation that we ought to have been provided a name. But the fact that none is used remains a mystery.

2. Where did the field-plot mentioned in verse 3 come from, and how can it be that Naomi held such property? After all, the two women were thrown back upon the expedient of gleaning at the beginning of chapter 2, and it would seem unnecessary for them to resort to that if there was productive land still in the family and available to them. Those commentators are correct who insist that all productive land would have been under cultivation and that we are not to think of this plot as having been allowed to lie fallow because its owner had been absent for over a decade. The best clue to explain these circumstances is provided by a self-contained episode in II Kings 8:1-6, as a number of commentators, beginning with Gunkel, have suggested. The story concerns a woman, identified in 8:1 as the Shunammite whose dead son was brought back to life by Elisha (II Kings 4:8-37), who left her home and her land at Elisha's urging because a seven-year famine was imminent. When she returned at the end of the famine, she had to appeal to the king for aid in getting her home and land back—and her appeal was successful. From this brief episode, one clearly gathers that a woman could hold land—even if she were not specifically designated a widow—and could get "legal aid" in regaining her property, which clearly would have been occupied and used during the time of her absence. This does not answer everything about Naomi's possession

of a piece of land, but does suggest that she could have held some as a legacy from her dead husband, and could have had a right to appeal for it. Furthermore, it suggests the manner in which Naomi's land has become alienated; when the family left, someone simply moved in on it.

Combined with this, we need to remember the caution in the COMMENT on Section IV; we simply do not know all that we would like about a widow's rights of ownership. No stated law pertains. But the basic principles we have mentioned make it very likely that a widow would at least have the right of disposal (so Hertzberg), if not of inheritance, from her husband. Unless we are inclined to accuse the story-teller of a major lapse in his crafting of the story, or unless we can find some sign of a major textual disruption, we will have to conclude that the civil issues at stake here were not as confusing to the ancient audience as they are to us. As in chapter 3, so here: people provided the explanation out of their knowledge of common practice, and probably gave it barely a second thought.

One thing remains rather strange, however. When did Naomi tell Boaz about the piece of property, which proves so successful as the opening subject in the hearing? The tie between the end of chapter 3 and the beginning of chapter 4 is very much dependent on the rapid march of events, with Ruth off to her home to sit it out, the two women waiting to see what will happen "today," and Boaz going directly to the gate to start everybody "sitting" on this case. The very verb "to sit" signals the close continuity of events. No time here for Naomi to have a talk with Boaz! Had she mentioned the land to him earlier? Possibly. But it is also possible that Naomi did not even know there was land that technically still belonged to Elimelek and could therefore be redeemed. If that were the case, Boaz took the matter into his own hands and presumed upon Naomi's approval. This is speculative, although H. H. Rowley thought of it also, in his "The Marriage of Ruth," p. 175, and others have followed him. It has the advantage, however, of underscoring once again the extraordinary element in Boaz' behavior, his attention to a pivotal circumstance which may not have occurred to anyone else who ought to have been concerned for the welfare of these two women. Either the craftiness of the old woman, or the ingenuity of the old man—in either case the impulse toward caring is the important factor here.

3. What has just been said goes some distance toward explaining another problem. Why is the near redeemer apparently so ill-informed? Why had he not initiated the plan himself, if he was so ready to agree to it when Boaz broached it? And why could he not see coming the "master-stroke"—the term is Rowley's—which Boaz then introduced, that he must take Ruth with the land? The basis for an answer here lies once again with our understanding of the nature of law. If it can be maintained that Israelite law was so well known and well codified that any substantial citizen would have it all at his fingertips, then the near redeemer is to be blamed or else Boaz is to be accused of fabricating law. But we have tried to establish that this is far from the case in Israelite law. To begin with, the near redeemer may very well have had no recollection that there was a piece of land still attached to Elimelek's inheritance; his readiness to accept the responsibility to redeem argues that he was

simply ignorant of it until informed. We cannot tell whether he then figured out, on the spur of the moment, that to buy the land would mean that he had taken responsibility for Naomi. Quite probably he did, and was willing to take that consequence (so Rudolph), because the produce from the land would have offset both his payment (and there may not have been one—see below) and the cost of caring for the old woman. What seems clear is that he did not reckon on having Ruth. And it must be admitted the circumstances requiring judgment here have become so complex by the time Ruth is introduced as a factor that we can understand the near redeemer's failure to have anticipated it. Somehow, however, what Boaz asserts about the levirate responsibility for Ruth must have been valid; once he broaches it, the near redeemer sees the panorama of consequences: a young, probably still fertile woman, whose offspring would ultimately inherit the land, and thus be an appreciable drain on the man's inheritance. He would have to support two women now, Ruth and Naomi, perhaps pay for the field, and accept the likelihood of yet another mouth to feed until the child was grown, whereupon the child would take the field. Income from the produce of the field could not cover all that, and the near redeemer simply could not afford it.

To Rudolph, this decision on the part of the near redeemer makes him a cool and calculating customer. True, there is calculation. But after all, a man's responsibility to his own family must be reckoned with. His relationship to Elimelek might have been at quite a distance. Better is Würthwein's observation that the near redeemer acts the way a normal, solid, responsible citizen would act; but "normal" responsibility is not enough here.

4. What does "buy" really mean when applied to Ruth? The NOTE on using the verb *qnh*, "buy," with Ruth in verse 5 has affirmed Weiss' insight that mishnaic usage of the verb in marriage contexts helps us understand its impact here; it is used for marriage only when there is a related commercial transaction involved. It seems clear that there can be no question of literal purchase of Ruth in this story.

There is one other observation about the verb *qnh* which deserves attention. In studying the impact of the term "redeemer," in the COMMENT on Section IV, we noticed that important nuances attach to the way God acts as redeemer, nuances however which are consistent with the use of the term in the human realm. We also noted that God is said to have redeemed his people in the ancient poem in Exodus 15, at verse 13: ". . . the people whom you have redeemed." At the end of verse 16 of that poem, in closely comparable syntax, there occurs ". . . the people whom you have *qnh*'d." Cross and Freedman once persuasively defended the translation "whom you have created" for this passage (in *Journal of Near Eastern Studies* 14 [1955], 237–50). Their argument was based on Ugaritic mythic language and upon passages like Deut 32:6; Gen 4:1, 14:19, 22. It is worth considering, however, that *qnh* in Exod 15:16 has a double connotation, both "to create" and "to acquire or make one's own," taking the cue from the parallel usage with "redeem" in 15:13. This would seem to fit well with Cross's claim that Exodus 15 shows an intermingling of mythic and historical assertion (see most recently his *Canaanite Myth and Hebrew Epic* [Harvard University Press, 1973], chapter 6 and *passim,* and note that Freedman has returned to translating 15:16 "whom you purchased" in *A Light unto My Path,* eds. Bream et al., pp. 165, 173. If God is confessed as both redeemer and one who does whatever *qnh* means in the "declarative praise" section of this ancient triumph song, a human being who does these actions in Ruth 4:1–10 is thereby praiseworthy as well.

5. Does it mean anything that Ruth is designated "the Moabitess" in 4:5 and 10? The narration had given her this identification in 1:22, 2:1 and 21, and Boaz' foreman had called her "a Moabite girl" in 2:6. At these places, the point seemed to be to emphasize that Ruth was a foreigner (recall 2:10) and yet worthy. Here in chapter 4, the gentilic is in Boaz' mouth.

Jewish tradition pondered the possibility that it was this which turned the redeemer away, for fear he would "contaminate his seed"—this because he was ignorant of the "new law already enacted, 'Ammonite but not Ammonitess, Moabite but not Moabitess'" (*Ruth Rabbah VII.* 7, 10). What the rabbis meant is that the near redeemer did not realize that Deut 23:3, prohibiting Ammonites and Moabites from entering the assembly of Yahweh, was not to be taken to apply to women from these lands.

My own suspicion is that Boaz' use of this gentilic was not designed to turn the near redeemer away, nor does it seem pertinent at all to the near redeemer's decision, so far as the story-teller indicates; perhaps if "Moabitess" had been used only at verse 5, the case would be stronger for this rabbinic understanding. In Boaz' last words in the story, at verse 10, there may after all be an implication of caring for the unfortunate, the theme we have sensed constantly in the story. "Ruth the Moabitess, wife of Mahlon" means Ruth is foreigner and widow both, that is, doubly unfortunate. With these words from Boaz' lips Ruth gains the security and the due recompense for which Boaz had prayed in 2:12.

6. What is the significance of the shoe? Is it a mark of ownership, or transfer of right? Or is it the price of the purchase? And if it is not the price, what price if any did Boaz have to pay for his "purchases"? The NOTE on this subject (on verse 7, "a man . . . to his counterpart") has indicated the ambiguities; it is really not completely clear who takes off whose shoe. The probability is that the one ceding the right removed his own shoe and gave it to the one taking over the right. But then, of course, the shoe is not a payment. And we are left with an unresolved problem. If Boaz paid any price for the property, for example to the one who had moved in and taken over, we are not told about it. Perhaps we can validly assume, as most do, that Boaz would not have had to pay Naomi for the property in addition to supporting her, any more than would the near redeemer. Perhaps, on the other hand, we can take the ceremonial "I hereby buy" in verse 9 as having been accompanied by the payment to whoever held the property—money certainly changes hands in the Jeremiah 32 redemption transaction. By this time in the story, the only thing we can feel confident about is that whatever was called for was properly done!

7. Was the son who would come from this union of Ruth and Boaz going to be reckoned to Mahlon or to Boaz? Apparently to both. The blessing in 4:11–12, if it has been properly understood in our translation, clearly implies that the children of Ruth and Boaz will be Boaz' "seed." Another indicator is

that the Lucianic family of Greek manuscripts attests a reading "she bore *to him* a son" in 4:13, showing that one traditional stream emphasized Boaz' paternity. On the other hand, the implication of the next section, 4:14–17, is that the child is in a legal and customary sense Naomi's, and related to the Elimelek-Mahlon line. Finally, note that the hand which added the genealogy in the final section, 4:18–22, traced the line through Boaz to Obed; we would be unwise to conclude that this later hand misunderstood the implications of custom in the story. It may be the case, in fact, that levirate marriage always resulted in a sort of dual paternity. Something of the same conclusion is to be drawn from Genesis 38, where the twins born to Tamar are implicitly to be reckoned to her first husband Er, but in all the Judah genealogies, from Gen 46:12 to Matt 1:3, Perez and Zerah are reckoned to Judah.

*   *   *   *   *   *

With the blessing of all the assembly, Boaz is ushered from the stage. The audience, ancient and modern, finds their voice in the voice of the chorus: A praiseworthy man indeed is Boaz. The structure of the whole Ruth story leads us to see that Boaz' excellence is especially indicated here, in the same way Ruth's was in chapter 1, by setting him over against a person who went a long way down the road of responsibility but could not go far enough. Mr. So-and-so and Orpah—normal, "law-abiding," relatively responsible—emphasize the extraordinary qualities of Boaz and Ruth.

VI. "A SON IS BORN TO NAOMI!"
(4:13–17)

4 13 And so, Boaz took Ruth *and she became his wife, and he had intercourse with her* and Yahweh made her conceive and she bore *b* a son.

14 Then the women said to Naomi, "Blessed be Yahweh who this day has not let there cease to be a redeemer for you; therefore may his name be celebrated in Israel. 15 For he will become your life-restorer, and one to sustain *your old age*; for your* daughter-in-law, who loves you, has borne him, and she means more to you than seven sons!" 16 Then Naomi took the lad *and held him to her bosom*, and she became his nurse. 17 And the neighborhood women *rejoiced over him*: "A son is born to Naomi!" They gave him the name Obed; he was the father of Jesse, father of David.

ᵃ⁻ᵃ LXXᴮ and one other maverick Greek witness (a₂=509) omit these two clauses, whether out of a sense of decency (Rudolph) or not is hard to say. The major Lucianic witnesses read "And Boaz took Ruth to himself as wife," etc.

ᵇ LXXᴸ' and the Syro-Hexapla with asterisk (one of six places where it marks an addition from the Lucianic tradition; cf. 1:16, 21, 2:2, 4:1, 4) adds "to him." See the COMMENT on Section V.

ᶜ⁻ᶜ Syriac and Armenian read "your city" instead of "your old age," obviously because Greek *polian* was read *polin*.

ᵈ LXXᴮ alone omits "your."

ᵉ⁻ᵉ LXXᴮ inexplicably omits the pronoun object; the rest of the LXX tradition and all the other versions attest it, except that the Syriac lacks the entire clause.

ᶠ⁻ᶠ The Syriac does not have the clause about rejoicing; it reads only, "And the neighborhood women said: 'A son. . . .'"

NOTES

4:13. *took . . . became . . . had intercourse . . . made conceive . . . bore.* The succinctness accords effectively with the rapid progression of verbs in narrative sequence; the translation retains the monotony of the Hebrew syntax to reflect this pace. Cf. II Sam 11:26b–27, where a similarly structured sentence rapidly concludes a story which has been moving at a languid pace.

and he had intercourse with her. The idiom, literally, "he went in to her," is a concise way of saying both that he entered her chamber and that he had sexual intercourse with her (cf. Gen 16:2, 30:3, etc.). Sometimes, as in II Sam 12:24 and Gen 39:14, the idiom is spelled out: "and lay with her," "to lie with me."

14. *may his name be celebrated in Israel.* Whose name—Yahweh's or this new redeemer's? Can *wayyiqqārē' šᵉmō,* literally, "and his name be called," properly connote celebration, especially in the midst of the series running from 4:11 through 14 to 17? And what is meant by "Israel"?

To start from the end, for the Ruth story "Israel" is ideal, the covenanted, socio-religious community. It is that of which Yahweh is the God (2:12); its early customs need explaining (4:7); it is the confederation of the offspring of Rachel and Leah (4:11). This fact alone would suggest that this sentence means "May (Yahweh's) name be celebrated in Israel." In any event, the scope here has been greatly broadened, beyond local realities like Bethlehem and Ephrathah in 4:11, or political units like Judah and Israel as the southern and northern kingdoms.

As for the theme of celebration here, the combination of *qr',* "call," and *šm,* "name," does not usually signify celebration, but in at least one instance it is inescapable: "I will enthusiastically celebrate the name of Yahweh; O ascribe majesty to our God!" (Deut 32:3). Here the verb is active, and the same nuance is probably present in the active participial constructions in Ps 99:6. Jer 44:26 employs the passive in a way similar to Ruth 4:14. Further, the combination "call *upon* the name of Yahweh," using the preposition *bᵉ* before "name," may well bear the sense of celebrating or praising in such passages as Gen 4:26, 12:8; Exod 33:19, and 34:15—the last two in instances of divine self-praise. All of these passages are usually taken to mean that God is being invoked, but it should be realized that invoking and praising or celebrating are much closer in meaning in biblical thought than their English meanings might suggest. Note in this connection Jer 10:25 (=Ps 79:6), where "to call on the name of Yahweh" is parallel to "to know" him, to acknowledge his sovereignty.

All of this supports further the temptation to understand Yahweh as the antecedent of "his," since the nuance of celebration and praise for *qr' (b)šm* is confined to passages about God. But the problem of the antecedent of "his" is very complex. Verse 15 will start off with the new-born son as the subject of the verbs, without any indication of a change of subject from what precedes. The LXX ("may he call your name in Israel") and the OL have "your name" —Naomi's. The Vulgate's rather free translation indicates that its *eius* refers back to a presumed "your family"—hence, "its name." Joüon has tried to make a case (*Commentaire,* p. 93) from 4:5 and 10 that the antecedent is "the dead one," Elimelek, but this proposal is hardly compelling, especially if the nuance of celebration be accepted. Finally, if the "name" in 4:11 be taken to be that of Boaz (see the last NOTE there), Boaz could be the antecedent here.

When all possibilities have been examined, the choice must be between the new-born and Yahweh. In either case, the idiom involving the verb *qr'* and the noun *šm* has a different meaning from what it had in 4:11—and once again our story-teller indulges his enjoyment of meaning expansion. In view of the flow into verse 15, the new-born is the more likely antecedent of "his name," but the alternative of Yahweh as antecedent should not be dismissed (the ambiguity is not at all unlike another one in Ruth, at 2:20—see the first NOTE there).

15. *your life-restorer.* Or possibly, "for you a restorer of your life." The text has no suffix "your" on the word "life," but the parallel expression in the next clause, "your old age," does have it. The "your" on "old age" can be construed as doing double duty—a common feature in Hebrew poetry (so a suggestion from correspondence with F. I. Andersen). The Hebrew reads literally, "one who causes life (*nepeš*) to return"; compare most closely Ps 19:9 [Hebrew, 8], along with Prov 25:13; Lam 1:11, 16, 19, and using a different verb conjugation, the familiar Ps 23:3.

Most noteworthy here is that the story-teller picks up the dominant key word of the first chapter, *šwb*, "to return," especially as it was used in 1:21: "empty Yahweh has brought me back" (or, "caused me to return"). The signal is given: Naomi's complaint, dormant since 1:20–21, is here resolved. See the COMMENT.

one to sustain. The syntax of the two broadly parallel clauses, "life-restorer" and "one to sustain," is unusual: a participle for "life-restorer" followed by an infinitive "to sustain"; Rudolph finds only one good comparable instance, in Jer 44:19: "So we will go right on sacrificing [participle] to the queen of heaven, and pour out [infinitive] to her libations."

means more to you than seven sons. The adjective construction rendered here "means more" involves the Hebrew word *ṭôb*, a term too pregnant in meaning to permit us to use simply "good, better." The function of forms of *ṭb/yṭb* as key words in Ruth is not as obvious as is the case for other key words, but it almost certainly acts as one of these linking terms. Consider the spread: 2:22 (where it is *good* that Ruth go out with Boaz' feminine work corps); 3:1 (where the "rest" Naomi seeks for Ruth is in order that things go *well* for her); 3:7 (Boaz' heart is to be *good*, receptive); 3:10 (Ruth's act of loyal self-giving—*ḥesed*—is even *better* than the act of returning at her mother-in-law's side); 3:13 (if the near redeemer will do his duty, that will be a *satisfactory* outcome of the matter). The story-teller, as he nears the end of his story, gathers something of all of these in his final use of the term, emphasizing not only Ruth's quality of person but also her prime importance to Naomi's well-being (see the COMMENT).

For the entire phrase, compare Elkanah's comforting words to Hannah in I Sam 1:8: "Do I not mean more to you than ten sons?" Seven and ten are both ideal numbers of sons to have—see I Sam 2:5 and recall Job's family in Job 1:2 and 42:13; Elkanah's "ten" is probably no more exalted than the "seven" the women use here.

16. *the lad.* The close of the most poignant and lovely inclusio used by the story-teller, a framing device reaching from 1:5, where Naomi is bereft of her two lads, to this new lad, son of Ruth.

held him to her bosom, and she became his nurse. Obviously, this has nothing to do with wet-nursing. The Hebrew word *ḥēq* is a part of both male and female anatomy—see II Sam 12:3 in the parable of the poor man and his beloved ewe-lamb, and the warm portrayal of God's shepherding his lambs in Isa 40:11. The ḥēq is the location of tender, or possibly angry, feelings, as well as the place for comforting the weak, the unprotected, or the beloved. As for the term "nurse," it is a feminine participle whose masculine counterpart also occurs, as in Mordecai's relation to Esther, or to describe the caretakers of Ahab's sons in II Kings 10:1 and 5. It means guardian rather than wet-nurse.

The question remains whether this action is symbolic only of an affectionate grandmother's care for her new and only grandson or is indicative of a specific, customary act of adoption. Comparable adoption custom can be found only from far distant quarters from which cross-cultural influence can hardly have come. Nevertheless, commentators since Bertholet (1898) and Köhler (especially in ZAW 29 [1909], 312–14) have seen indications of such a custom here, confirmed in the words of the women in the following verse: "A son is born to Naomi!" To Gerleman, among recent commentators, the symbolic act becomes the capstone to a process of "judaizing" this child; he now is given a full Judaic adoptive mother. De Vaux (*Ancient Israel*, p. 51) is more cautious when discussing a series of customs including the one of bearing a child on another's knees (Gen 30:3, cf. 16:2, 48:5, 12, 50:23) and the presumed one here in Ruth: "The legal consequences of such an adoption [all of them within the family line] are therefore not far-reaching." But perhaps this is just the problem.

Legal matters have been scrupulously dealt with throughout the story. If adoption is being introduced here, what has happened to the dictates of levirate custom, whereby if anything the child should have been designated Mahlon's son (or Elimelek's)? Of course we may lack some necessary information about the custom which might make it clear that "A son is born to Naomi" is a way of affirming the completion of the levirate requirement. However, in the present state of knowledge, I seriously doubt (as do Rudolph and many others) that there is any technical or even symbolic act of adoption involved. We have a grandmother delighted in her grandchild, so much so that the women in verse 17 jocularly participate in her delight; and all of this is arched over by the fact that here is the long-awaited male heir, who will in the course of time fulfill the responsibility of caring for his mother and grandmother alike.

17. *And the neighborhood women rejoiced over him.* The story-teller has worked in verses 11 and 14 with interesting nuances of meaning for the combination of the verb qr', "to call," and the noun šm, "name"—see the pertinent NOTES on those verses. If the text of verse 17 is in anything like good order as we have it preserved, his two additional uses of the same combination ought to relate back to those earlier verses. In 17a, we have literally: "And the (feminine) neighbors *called* to him *a name*," and in the latter part of the verse occurs "They *called* his *name* Obed." The second of these conforms to good and common Hebrew grammatical structure and ought to cause no problem. But then what is this first clause all about? If it is a matter of name-bestowing, we expect, "The neighborhood women called him X." The text then goes on to provide us with what sounds for all the world like the *explanation* of a

name: "A son is born to Naomi." Little wonder that many commentators have assumed that a proper name such as Ben-no‘am should appear instead of the word šm in our clause: "And the neighborhood women called him Ben-no‘am, saying 'A son (bēn) is born to Naomi.' " Punning of this sort to explain names is, of course, a frequent feature of the narratives in Genesis—a glance at Gen 29:31 – 30:24 provides one series, enough to see the pattern.

Of course there are problems. The fact is that the word šm is there and no proper name is preserved; indeed the easiest thing to do might be to read "they called him Shem," but then there would be no congruity between the name and the explanation. In addition, there would be two names provided in this verse, and we would probably want to follow the usual expedient of claiming that the second name-bestowal, which introduces Obed, is a later insertion; it displaced the original name, whatever it may have been, with the name needed to get the link to David into the picture, and that displacement explains the grammatical peculiarity at the beginning of the verse.

However, we have another instance here of having to try to explain a more difficult reading: How did the word šm instead of a proper name get into the first clause? If at a later stage of the transmission of the story there was a reason for getting the name Obed prominently into the picture, common sense seems to dictate that a better job of splicing would have been done. Meanwhile, we have noticed how much the story-teller seems to be making of this verbal combination of qr' šm, "call a name." If our reading in 4:14 is correct, that the wish is that the new-born sons's name be celebrated in Israel, then by far the simplest meaning for the beginning of verse 17 is that the celebrating has begun. The neighborhood women, who like a Greek chorus have been the backdrop of both Naomi's struggle in 1:19–21 and the resolution of that struggle here in 4:14–17, have first proposed that Israel celebrate (verse 14) and now get right at doing so.

This understanding of the first clause is, to a degree, ad hoc. It can be supported grammatically only by invoking the same passages for comparison as were used to establish "celebrate" as the meaning for qr' šm in verse 14; see the NOTE there. The main reason for insisting on it is the consistency it offers with the story-teller's delightful style. Here it is especially striking: in 4:11 and 4:17b, the combination has to do with actually naming a baby; in between, at 4:14 and 4:17a, the combination has to do with celebrating this baby. The two acts are linked, of course, and the story-teller artistically uses the various nuances of common words to underscore the linkage.

The Latin versions appear to have sensed the same meaning here as our rendering proposes. Toward the end of chapter 4 the OL manuscript tradition had apparently suffered damage, and a later hand repaired the damage largely by substituting the Vulgate's reading. The Vulgate has "and the neighboring women were offering congratulations (congratulantis)." The OL is identical except for attesting conguadentes, "were rejoicing together." Here is at least one indication, but what indeed may amount to two independent indications, running on the same track. Compare also Ehrlich's rendering: "The neighbor-women spoke of him then in their fashion—'A son is born to Naomi.' "

A son is born to Naomi. With these words, the women confirm the point that the child, celebrated as Ruth's in verse 15, is equally Naomi's (and hence Elimelek's). The verb is a *Qal* internal passive, as are the other apparent *Pual* forms of the verb *yld* in the OT. See the treatment by F. I. Andersen in *Near Eastern Studies in Honor of William Foxwell Albright*, ed. H. Goedicke, (Johns Hopkins University Press, 1971), pp. 8–12, especially the specific note on the unique word order and unique occurrence of a feminine "referential" at the bottom of page 12.

They gave him the name Obed. It is tempting to emend the verb to a singular, either masculine or feminine, making Boaz, Naomi, or Ruth do the naming; that is the standard procedure in name bestowals in OT narrative. A small group of LXX minuscules actually attests a singular verb. Note, however, Luke 1:59, where Elizabeth's neighbors and kin appear to be involved with the proposal to name her child Zechariah, after his father, only to be deterred first by Elizabeth and then by Zechariah himself. The question is of no great consequence, but given the role of the neighborhood women throughout 4:4–17 there is no compelling reason to abandon the reading in the MT.

COMMENT

One staccato sentence, five crisp clauses, and the story resolves the events of 2:1–4:12 in the single verse 4:13. Ruth has a husband, Yahweh gives her conception at once—in striking contrast to those ten barren years in Moab—and the child is a son. No time is wasted here. We must move on to settling the one remaining problem in the Ruth story, Naomi's complaint at the end of the first chapter.

At the end of the threshing floor scene, Boaz had provided a supply of barley which tangibly relieved the emptiness Naomi lamented in her bitter words of 1:20–21. The relief is only partial, however; Naomi had lodged her complaint in legal terms, that Yahweh had brought accusation against her and pronounced sentence inexplicably and unjustly. Complaint in the Bible regularly amounts to bringing a formal case against God. It calls his fairness and faithfulness into question. And, in many instances, the sequel to the complaint fails to exonerate God, fails to explain the apparent injustice. In an earlier remark, I mentioned Jonah, Jeremiah, and Job as comparable to Naomi; we can add others, including Elijah and, in the synoptic gospel portrayals, Jesus on the cross. In the case of all of these, the complaint is not answered with a satisfactory explanation of God's ways; rather the matter is transferred into the future and what resolution there is comes in terms of renewed vocations for the persons involved. The only assurance is that the faithful God is, in spite of all appearances, still about his business, and his people should be about theirs. Elijah complains (I Kings 19:1–14) and gets a new set of tasks (19:15–18); Jeremiah complains (Jer 15:10–18, among several instances in Jeremiah 10–20) and is called anew (15:19–21); Job complains, indeed hammers upon the closed door of Yahweh's (Shadday's!) courtroom, and gets no satisfying response, but only the assurance that God is still in charge of the cosmos and an unexpected vocation—to pray for his unhelpful comforters (Job 42:8; notice 42:10). The same can be said of Jesus' outcry from the cross framed in the words of Ps 22 (Matt 27:45–54; Mark 15:33–39; Luke 23:44–48), especially when one keeps in mind the way in which the gospel writers each think of Jesus' death as "vocational."

I submit that both in terms of genre (complaint-and-resolution) and in terms of theological meaning, the motif of Naomi's complaint and of her taking the new-born lad to her bosom belongs with these others. If that be so, verse 16 contains not a symbol of adoption (see the second NOTE) but the acceptance of a new role. The cause of the disasters in Moab remains unexplained; in effect, Naomi was justified in her complaint. She is answered only with a new vocation, nurse to the child who assures her future well-being, and with a new condition of blessedness. These she accepts, together with the assurance of God's faithfulness made visible in all that has been happening in Bethlehem since he had seen to the needs of his people and set the return journey in motion.

The mood of the vignette which brings the Ruth story to a close is one of joy and happiness. All the words belong to the women, the same chorus which had met Naomi upon her return to Bethlehem from Moab; then they could only hear Naomi out, but here, under new circumstances, they bless. The story-teller conveys the new circumstances first with a single word, "redeemer," applied to the child. There should be no surprise at this. The child is the one now responsible for the well-being of the two widows; he is the one to whom the Elimelek-Mahlon inheritance will go. In every appropriate sense of the word, "redeemer" now properly describes him. He will be the sustainer of Naomi's old age and the one to "cause her life to return." It is no coincidence that the story-teller here uses, in its causative form, the verb "return" which dominated the scene along the road back from Moab in 1:6–22; note that the only other causative of *šûb* is in Naomi's complaint in 1:21. Nor is it unintentional that the child is designated the "lad," the one to replace the "lads" whom Naomi had lost in Moab (1:5).

There is a special deftness to the way the story-teller handles Ruth in the two vignettes focusing on Naomi's complaint, bracketing as they do the three central episodes in which Ruth is prominent. In 1:19b–22 and 4:14–17a, Ruth is all but eclipsed. In the COMMENT on the earlier passage, we noted a certain irony to Naomi's self-centered outcry, while Ruth, the ultimate answer to her predicament, stands virtually unnoticed beside her. Here in the concluding scene once more the focus is on Naomi, the person whose "trial" really holds the whole story together. But in the midst of the blessing and the merry-making, the chorus of neighbor women includes the story's ultimate evaluation of Ruth—the one who loves Naomi, the one who means more to her than seven sons. What more appropriate way to praise Ruth than to say she is worth seven times what the story has made such an absorbing concern—a son! And perhaps we can say that to make Ruth the subject of the sole use of the verb "to love," in a story where words mean so much, belongs also to the ultimate in approbation.

The concluding vignette presents us as well with the final word about Yahweh's trustworthiness. Ostensibly the "enemy" in the dire circumstances in Moab which begin the story—so Naomi implies in her accusation in 1:20–21 —Yahweh saw to his people's needs in 1:6, has been kept before us in a series of greetings, prayers and blessings throughout the scenes in Bethlehem, and has been at work from the shadows in the various "chance" encounters of the key figures (notably at 2:3 and 4:1). Now in verses 13 and 14, first the narrator himself and then the chorus make him directly responsible for the fact that Naomi, and with her Ruth, have their needed redeemer. Valorous people and praiseworthy God—their living is thoroughly intertwined.

If this story has been about such people and such a God, and if the story-teller's primary aim has been to recommend such living, what can we say about the final words of verse 17: ". . . Obed; he was the father of Jesse, father of David"? They take us by surprise. The first NOTE on verse 17 has indicated that the Hebrew syntax here is unusual, leading one to expect a name more pertinent to the context, but it has offered an alternative which makes this not necessarily conclusive. The question seems to come down to this: Did someone take a carefully composed story, magnificent in its inherent quality, and adapt it to fit the great-grandparents of King David? Quite possibly. On the other hand, could a story-teller, aware of the historical fact that David's great-grandmother was a Moabitess, have prepared such a story with the full intent of establishing the quality of the persons and then of concluding his story with the dramatic news that these persons were David's direct ancestors? Indeed he could!

I doubt if we can settle the question. Many a commentator has observed that no tradition could provide David with a Moabitess great-grandmother if he didn't really have one—and in this they are surely correct. Our story-teller did not invent this. He has shown himself so talented that to conclude he could also use that prize of the story-teller's act, the trick ending, is not far-fetched. But he has displayed a panorama of techniques for intertwining the episodes and motifs of his story. Would he not have given us some advance hint of the final trick he was going to play? Or at least would he not have used a word in the final clause which linked it back to something in the story? These are questions to continue pondering.

For myself, I can only invoke the fine inclusio, which was suggested in the COMMENT on Section I, extending from the words "in the days when the judges judged" to the word "David" here. The balance of probability lies with the decision that the story-teller's composition included 4:17b. This son, so much needed in order that caring responsibility be extended to two widows for the rest of their days, this son of a Moabite woman and a worthy man of Bethlehem who lived as persons are meant to live, this son who so easily might not have been, this son was David's ancestor.

VII. A GENEALOGICAL APPENDIX
(4:18–22)

4 ¹⁸Now this is the line of Perez: Perez begot Hezron; ¹⁹and Hezron begot Ram; and Ram begot Amminadab; ²⁰and Amminadab begot Nahshon; and Nahshon begot Salma; ²¹and Salma begot Boaz; and Boaz begot Obed; ²²and Obed begot Jesse; and Jesse begot David[a].

[a] LXX[A] plus one other LXX witness, along with the Syriac, the Armenian, and Matt 1:6, add "the king"; the OL adds "the king; and David begot Solomon."

NOTES

4:18. *Now this is the line.* Literally, "and these are the 'generations'. . . ." This idiom, usually, as here, complete with the opening w^e-, here translated "now," is characteristic of the *P* genealogies in Genesis and at Num 3:1. Since the question of relationship of these final five verses of Ruth to the genealogical material in I Chronicles 2 is important, it is noteworthy that the Chronicler appears to have preferred another, though related, idiom, exemplified at I Chron 1:29. See the COMMENT.

Hezron. Hebrew *Ḥeṣrōn* is transmitted in most of the LXX tradition, the OL, and the Vulgate, with a final -*m* rather than -*n*, and appears as Hesrom in the two New Testament genealogies of Jesus (Matt 1:3; Luke 3:33). Only LXX[B] and a couple of minuscules (one of them Lucianic), along with the Syriac, attest the final -*n*. Names with -*ān*/-*ōn* endings are fairly common in Hebrew (see one group of assumed diminutives listed by Noth, *Personennamen*, p. 38), while those with -*ām*/-*ōm* are rarer. Strikingly, two pairs are attested which suggest that the endings were virtually interchangeable: Gershōm and Gershōn, Zēytān and Zēytām. Once more we may have evidence here of divergent texts of the Ruth book; in any event, Hesrom is not to be considered an "error."

Hezron is the name of a son of Reuben in Gen 36:9; Exod 6:14; Num 26:6; and I Chron 5:3. Our Hezron, son of Perez, appears in Gen 46:12; Num 26:21; and I Chron 2:5, 9, 18, 21, 24, 25. In I Chron 4:1, an alternate tradition of Judahite genealogy may betray a mixture of the two Hezrons; Carmi appears as a brother of Hezron and both as sons of Judah here, while they are brothers and sons of Reuben in Gen 46:9.

19. *Ram.* The transmission of this name shows an even greater complexity than with Hezron. The Hebrew of I Chron 2:9 agrees with that of Ruth, but the versions go in a variety of directions. Thus LXX[B] and the majority of LXX manuscripts at I Chron 2:9 have Irameēl, Ram, Chabel, and Aram in that order. Two LXX minuscules read Aram in place of Ram but then do not repeat it at the end; a few other witnesses keep all four names but read Aran as the final one. As if this were not enough indication of trouble in the transmission of the tradition behind the LXX, LXX[B] then begins 2:10 not with Ram but with Arran, the same name it has at Ruth 4:19 for Ram and at I Chron 2:23 for Hebrew Aram. In I Chron 2:10, the witnesses mentioned above which read Aran persist with it, but all the rest of the LXX witnesses go ahead with Aram, the same spelling with which they ended verse 9. It appears clear from this that in Chronicles the Greek tradition is settling on Aram to the exclusion of Ram; nevertheless, LXX[B] with support from the Syriac indicates that a spelling Ram was tenacious in the tradition.

In Ruth, the versions are unanimous in failing to support Ram. Unanimously they attest a beginning *aleph* plus *a*-vowel, but they differ on the spelling of the rest of the name: LXX[BA] have Arran, the OL has Aran, the Vulgate and Syriac (along with most of the rest of the LXX tradition and Matt 1:3–4) have Aram, and Luke 3:33 apparently had Arni. The Lucan genealogy shows a whole variety of conflations and mixed orthographies in the various manuscripts, and here contains an additional name Admin between Amminadab and whatever reflects Ram/Aram/Aran.

This rehearsal may seem bewildering, but it probably reflects attempts to deal with a firmly fixed tradition of a name "Ram" in the Judah genealogy. The Hebrew of Ruth 4:19 and I Chron 2:9–10, and strikingly the LXX of I Chron 2:9 alone, are the only indicators that this is so. At I Chron 2:25, he or another Ram appears as son of Yerahmeel, Hezron's first-born; perhaps it is to this tradition that we must trace Luke's attestation of another step in the genealogy. As for other Judah genealogies in the OT, none reaches down, or back, to a figure named Ram. If any one factor strongly supports an interdependence of the Ruth and I Chronicles 2 genealogies, this single name is that factor.

Amminadab. One of several Amminadabs (cf. I Chron 6:7, 15:10–11), this is apparently Aaron's father-in-law, who appears in Exod 6:23; Num 1:7, 2:3, 7:12, 17, and 10:14, as father of Nahshon. Among the names in our genealogy, this one alone takes the form of an expression of the patriarchal style of personal religious relationship: "my (divine) Kinsman is generous/noble"; compare Abinadab and Ahinadab, both attested from the time of David and Solomon.

20. *Salma.* The MT poses the problem of this name as baldly as it can be posed, and in such a way as to recall how LXX[B] poses the problem on Ram in I Chron 2:10 (see the first NOTE on 4:19). At the beginning of Ruth 4:21, the Hebrew spelling is *śalmōn*, while here it is *śalmāh*. In the Hebrew of I Chron 2:10 and 11, the spelling is *śalmāʾ*. Once more, the versions show great variety.

In Ruth, the Vulgate has *Salma,* LXX[B] has *Salman* while the rest of the LXX attests *Salmōn* (in Chronicles the situation is very nearly the reverse), the OL has *salam,* the Syriac has *šl',* probably conformed to the name of Judah's third son (see Gen 38:5 ff., etc.), and a dependable grouping of early New Testament manuscripts attests *Sala* at Luke 3:32.

To compound the difficulty, there is no obvious root *šlm* in Semitic from which to derive the name. The usual guess is that it is related to a word for "garment," *śalmāh,* which is itself an oddity, apparently a variant of the more usual *śimlāh* (Ruth 3:3), arising through accidental exchange of the second and third consonants (metathesis). Most commentators accept the evidence from the Hebrew text of I Chron 2:10–11 and the Vulgate, presumably combined with the recognition that the *-ōn* at the ends of the names Nahshon and Hezron in our list could have influenced the rise of Salmon, and decide that Salma is original here. The persistence of both *śalmāh* and *śalmōn* in the Hebrew of Ruth suggests to me instead that variant names were firmly entrenched in the traditions of the Ruth story circulating in the centuries immediately before the Common Era. I suspect we could just as correctly call Salmon "original" in both verse 20 and verse 21. See the COMMENT.

COMMENT

There is all but universal agreement that verses 18–22 form a genealogical appendix to the Ruth story and are not an original part of it. The goal of the story has been reached in verse 17, and it seems most unlikely that the story-teller would backtrack to trace a line from Perez and Judah, whom he had mentioned in 4:12, to Boaz and his offspring. Furthermore, the style of the genealogy is distinctly that of the *P* tradition in Genesis, as the NOTE on the first two words of verse 18 has indicated. These *tol*ᵉ*dot,* "generational," units in Genesis play various roles in the overall redaction of that book. Perhaps most like our Ruth example is the relationship between the *P* list in Gen 5:1–28, 30 and the *J* story in Genesis 4, since the former in some sense recapitulates the chronological material of the latter. But there is really no place in Genesis where a *P* genealogy acts as a colophon to a story. Note that the expression "This is the line of . . ." is a colophon of sorts at Gen 2:4a and 37:2a, but in neither case does a genealogy follow, and in both cases one could translate with "history, story." Speiser, in *Genesis,* AB, vol. 1, NOTE on 2:4 and COMMENT on Section 48, offers perceptive remarks on this question. The point is that the addition of a genealogical appendix to Ruth is unique; we are therefore hard put to assess its precise significance.

Several things can be said, however. First, it is by no means clear that the appendix clashes with the impact of the story. In the COMMENT on Section V, we have seen that custom may well have reckoned a son born of a levirate-style marriage to both his "legal" father and his actual father. Thus, Joüon has over-simplified the matter when he contrasts the appendix and the story as radically as he does in his *Commentaire,* p. 96, and so has Rudolph (pp. 71–72). It should become a standing rule in considering the redaction of two originally unrelated elements, such as the Ruth story and the Ruth appendix, that we give the redactor credit for some sensitivity to the impact his work will have.

There is a connection between this matter of consistency and another question, namely the source of the appendix in the traditions of Israel. The close correspondence between Ruth 4:18–22 and I Chron 2:5, 9–15 has suggested a dependency running one way or the other. Which way? Most commentators are confident that the Ruth genealogy is an extract from the Chronicles one. There are, however, important divergences, among them the possible tradition of a Salmon instead of Salma in Ruth, and the difference in the spelling of Salma (*salmāh* in Ruth 4:20, *salmā'* in I Chron 2:11). It also appears that the Ruth genealogy was fixed in a form characteristic of the *P* tradition (with its phraseology: "These are the generations of . . ."), while Chronicles uses "These are their generations . . ." or "These are the sons of . . ." I prefer, therefore, the conclusion Myers reaches in *I Chronicles*, AB, vol. 12, COMMENT on Section II, that "both lists may go back to an original temple source." We are certainly not compelled to conclude that the later hand which added the Ruth appendix only did so after the era of the Chronicler (around 400 B.C.E.).

One thing seems inescapable, however: the list is schematic and incomplete. Exod 6:3 makes it very likely that Nahshon, son of Amminadab, was of the same generation as Moses and Aaron. This would require the five generations from Salma to David to cover at least 250 years (about 1300 to 1030 B.C.E.). Even with a couple of long generations, for Boaz because he was getting on in years when Obed was born according to our story, and for Jesse because David was his seventh son, this is far too long. As with many of our genealogical sources in the Bible, losses in the transmission of tradition have had their effect; the Lukan genealogy (Luke 3:32–34) suggests a fuller alternative. Nevertheless, the Ruth genealogy did persist, in one stream of tradition, on into Matthew. And here occurs a last and interesting point of commentary. Matthew included three women in his genealogical composition, Rahab the harlot, Bathsheba the not unwilling adulteress, and Ruth the Moabitess. Not particularly happy company for valorous Ruth, but of such as these three, the Bible consistently says, is built up the line of King David, and of one whom a later segment of the people of God would call *the* Son of David.

INDEX OF SCRIPTURAL REFERENCES

INDEX OF SCRIPTURAL REFERENCES

(Ruth citations are included when they occur in the Introduction or in the NOTES and COMMENTS on other passages.)

KEY TO THE TEXT

Chapter	Verses	Section
1	1–5	I
1	6–22	II
2	1–23	III
3	1–18	IV
4	1–12	V
4	13–17	VI
4	18–22	VII